8,54,92

Human values in the poetry of Robert Frost

Human values in the
poetry of Robert Frost

a study of a poet's convictions by George W. Nitchie

Duke University Press
Durham, N. C.   1960

© 1958, 1960, Duke University Press

Cambridge University Press, London, N. W. 1, England
Library of Congress catalogue card number 60-10813
Printed in the United States of America
by the Seeman Printery, Durham, N. C.

For
Laura
Katherine
Rebecca
and
Judith

Preface

No authoritative literary or intellectual biography of Robert Frost has yet appeared, and this study is not designed to fill that particular gap. In view of my title, the disclaimer is an important one; that is, an examination of a writer's convictions inevitably suggests the portrait of a personality, an object of biographical interest that must be tested against biographical facts and reasonable deductions from such facts. That is quite as it should be. Poems, after all, are written by people with personalities, not by clusters of values. At the same time, there is no simple relationship between the writer as personality and the writer as he appears in his writings. The Frost I am concerned with in this study is the second of these two aspects of the writer, the Frost of the published writings. Thus, although I have drawn on available biographical data, I have done so only as a means of throwing light on the poems and the convictions they embody. My primary concern, once more, is not biographical; my primary concern is with the ethical and philosophical convictions implicit in Frost's poems, and I am concerned, not simply with describing those convictions, but with judging them, inevitably in terms of my own convictions. My bias is a moral one, though I should be sorry indeed if it were understood to be directed at a man.

Such an approach is not, of course, obligatory for the critic. Yet among the many kinds of criticism, one is moral, concerned finally with evaluating not degrees of technical excellence, not the aesthetic ordering of parts, not the affective impact of a poem, but the moral and intellectual worth of the ideas it embodies, their coherence, their relevance to the world of human activity, their adequacy as a measure of man's thought and action. Poetry does embody ideas, and those ideas, if only because they are permanently on record, are important—important, that is, not because they are the utterances of an important person but because they are *there*, attracting or repelling us. Hence examination of such ideas is important because it is important to have an understanding of what it is that attracts or repels us, lest we become our own, or another's, victims. Frost's poetry is, I think, a singularly attractive body of writing. Yet the values it embodies are in a number of ways—to be examined in this study— vulnerable, wobbly, incomplete. Such limitations have not prevented Frost from writing excellent poems, but they qualify the worth of that vision of man and the world that Frost's poetry holds up for our inspection and approval.

Thus my principal purpose is negative. The question with which I am chiefly concerned is not whether Frost is a good and important poet. I believe that he is, that he has written some of the finest poems of our time, and in discussing certain of his poems, I have attempted to justify that belief. But I also believe that, good and important though Frost is, his work as a whole cannot finally pass certain tests to which literature may legitimately be submitted and which great literature must pass. In this respect, my study may serve as a corrective in any final estimate of Frost's excellence. Much of the more outspoken critical enthusiasm for his writing is, I believe, excessive; many of his admirers have, I believe, allowed personal admiration of Frost the man to influence their critical evaluations of his thought and writing. But the worth of a conviction does not depend on the worth of the man who propounds it, and this study is concerned with convictions, convictions that reveal among other qualities a degree of incoherence, of incompleteness, even of evasiveness and wrongheadedness. Such characteristics demand attention, though they are not the only characteristics of Frost's writing that demand attention. If I have been principally aware of Frost's limitations, I hope I have not been blind to his excellence.

The extent of my obligation to published writings and writers is indicated by the extent of my quoting and the frequency of my footnotes. Personal indebtedness is more difficult to indicate, and more important. For services of which I am particularly aware, however, I am deeply grateful to Professors Richard Chase and Robert Gorham Davis, of Columbia University, who guided and advised me throughout my research and writing; to Professor Wylie Sypher, of Simmons College, and to Miss Léonie Adams and Professors Albert Hofstadter, Jay B. Hubbell, John Lotz, Dean M. Schmitter, and William Y. Tindall, of Columbia University, who read, praised, and criticized the manuscript; to my wife, who endured what wives do endure while books are being written; and to my students at Simmons College, who have contributed more than they can know or I can say.

Acknowledgments

I am grateful to Henry Holt and Company, Inc., and to Jonathan Cape, Ltd., for permission to quote from *Complete Poems of Robert Frost,* copyright 1930, 1939, 1943, 1947, 1949 by Henry Holt and Company, Inc.; copyright 1936, 1942, 1945, 1948 by Robert Frost.

Contents

1. The world of nature 3
2. Sermons in stones 51
3. An Eden myth 68
4. The world of others 110
5. The human objective 149
6. A momentary stay against confusion 189
   List of works cited 224
   Index 231

Human values in the poetry of Robert Frost

1

The world of nature

That Robert Frost is, in some sense, a poet of nature is hardly a debatable proposition. Birches and wild flowers, woods and stone walls, pasture springs and precarious farms and the snow of northern New England—these things provide, not merely locale, but substance. Remove them from Frost's work and something more than symbol or exemplum is gone, something that is intimately involved with a bent, a way of looking at the world, a set of instinctive, or near-instinctive, affirmations and denials that, from the earliest days of Frost's writing career, have manifested themselves with an almost undeviating persistence.

"Into My Own," the first poem in his first book, envisions stealing away into an unlimited and virgin wilderness in which,

> Fearless of ever finding open land,
> Or highway where the slow wheel pours the sand,[1]

the speaker will cultivate his integrity; and "Directive," the most impressive poem in his most recent collection, sends the reader questing back beyond

> a house that is no more a house
> Upon a farm that is no more a farm
> And in a town that is no more a town

until, finding at last the icy mountain spring that was the farm's source of water and its inheritor, he may

> Drink and be whole again beyond confusion.

That these poems touch on ultimate values seems clear— ultimate, at least, within the framework that Frost allows himself in his poetry. (The qualification is of central importance in evaluating Frost. Integrity and wholeness, self-confirmation and self-renewal, are surely valuable only in terms of what the self is that demonstrates integrity or experiences renewal; they are not self-justifying characteristics. For the present, however, I wish to confine myself largely to describing certain aspects of Frost's work, reserving judgment on them for later chapters.) And that these ultimate values ultimately reveal themselves in a "natural" context seems clear also. The wilderness of "Into My Own" must be trackless; the soberer *mise en scène* of "Directive" is one in which, tracklessness being a fairly unreal condition in New England, nature is at least reasserting its primal dominance—a world of

---

[1] Unless otherwise indicated, all Frost's poems referred to or quoted from will be found in *Complete Poems of Robert Frost* (New York, 1949).

> belilaced cellar hole[s],
> Now slowly closing like a dent in dough.

Briefly, and at the risk of a platitude, one can say that Frost's values and Frost's view of nature are intimately related, a point on which both Frost's defenders and his detractors generally agree.

My purpose in urging the obvious is this: that there are, very broadly speaking, two kinds of poet to whom the label "poet of nature" may reasonably be applied. On the one hand, there is the ingenuous nature lover, for whom trees are green, birds melodious, and rabbits furry, and who reports these observations in verse. Assuming a degree of technical skill, such poets are at worst harmless and at best capable of communicating a degree of genuine, if elementary, wonder, as was W. H. Davies, for example. On the other hand, there is the poet for whom external nature has a philosophically serious significance, either deliberately worked out or revealed by its implicit presence in a substantial body of work. Such poets may be capable of compelling powerful responses in the receptive reader, responses with an ethical or a metaphysical dimension; in their degrees, Lucretius, Wordsworth, Hardy, and perhaps Robinson Jeffers are representative of the class. And while it is true that Frost's poems occasionally suggest the work of a localized New England Davies—"The Pasture," "A Nature Note," or "A Young Birch," for example, particularly if one considers the poems out of the context of Frost's work as a whole—it is also true that, as I have said in speaking of "Into My Own" and "Directive," Frost's view of nature does possess a persistent ethical or metaphysical dimension of very substantial importance in any examination of Frost's work or of the values expressed in that work. To this degree, Frost is of the Lucretian-Wordsworthian kind, as were Emerson and Thoreau and even Bryant before him.

And here one is confronted with difficulties. *De Rerum Natura* expounds a theory of and recommends an attitude toward nature; "Tintern Abbey" and *The Prelude* do the same, if less didactically; Emerson, struck by "the fact that all nature is the rapid efflux of goodness executing and organizing itself,"[2] delighted in "the predominance of the saccharine principle throughout vegetable nature";[3] Thoreau concluded that the depths of ponds and of men could be determined by analogous calculations;[4] in *The Dynasts* Thomas Hardy made it clear that nature is an inscrutable, because mindless, biological process; and in lyric after somber lyric, Robinson Jeffers indicates that nature is the pure matrix out of whose inexplicable sores the human effluvium has risen, like flies from Nile mud. But Frost gives no comparably clear statement of principles, offering instead a mask of skeptical or whimsical equivocation. In "Boeotian" he rejects wisdom that is systematic; in "To a Thinker" he advises his theory-bound subject to "trust my instinct—I'm a bard"; and in the preface to Edwin Arlington Robinson's *King Jasper,* Frost observes that he and Robinson "should hate to be read for any theory upon which we might be supposed to write."[5] "Trust the instinct to the end, though you can render no reason,"[6] said Emerson, and in this respect as in others Frost suggests Emersonian influence.

Such distrust of theory, particularly of other people's theory, is neither surprising nor unreasonable, though it is not inevitable even for a poet. Spenser could say of *The Faerie Queene,* "The generall end therefore of all the booke is to fashion a gentleman or noble person in vertuous and gentle discipline,"[7] a discipline that involved a theory of manners and morals. But Keats, preferring "a life of sensations

[2] *The Complete Works of Ralph Waldo Emerson,* ed. Edward Waldo Emerson (Cambridge, Mass., 1904), II, 310.
[3] *Ibid.,* 317-318.
[4] Henry David Thoreau, *Walden* (Harmondsworth, 1938), p. 243.
[5] Robert Frost, introduction to Edwin Arlington Robinson, *King Jasper* (New York, 1935), p. x.
[6] Emerson, II, 330.
[7] *The Complete Poetical Works of Edmund Spenser,* ed. R. E. Neil Dodge (Boston, 1908), p. 136.

rather than of thoughts,"[8] declared himself satisfied with *"Negative Capability,* that is, when a man is capable of being in uncertainties, mysteries, doubts, without any irritable reaching after fact and reason."[9] It does not follow, however, that Keats had no persistent themes; even a rejection of theory can become theoretical, and the "Ode to a Nightingale" implies a theory of the relationship between man and nature. The two are finally discontinuous orders of being, despite man's desire for meaningful communion; the sense of continuity with nature that was, for Wordsworth, a vital source of values becomes, for Keats, a melancholy "as if." And in this admittedly narrow sense, Frost is more like Keats than he is like Spenser; like Keats, he usually prefers to write without being hampered by restrictions of a preconceived theory, though not without intellectual content.

My immediate point is simply that Frost tends to shy away from explicit statements of a theory of nature, or of man's relationship with nature. And this is interesting because, paradoxically or not, one of the cardinal errors according to Frost's scheme of values is going against nature or natural processes; at least, man does so at his peril. In "A Brook in the City" Frost wonders whether man's unnatural diversion of the brook,

> thrown
> Deep in a sewer dungeon under stone
> In fetid darkness still to live and run,

may not have given rise to the disturbing, vaguely ominous thoughts

> that so keep
> This new-built city from both work and sleep.

[8] *The Selected Letters of John Keats,* ed. Lionel Trilling (Garden City, 1951), p. 99.
[9] *Ibid.,* p. 103.

In "There Are Roughly Zones" the rash attempt to grow peaches in a New England climate too severe for them becomes an exemplum of the "limitless trait in the hearts of men" that leads them to dangerous tinkering with the shifty boundary between right and wrong. In "To a Moth Seen in Winter" the self-destructive moth, desperately pitting itself against nature in order to "seek the love of kind in winter time," exemplifies that limitless trait:

> And what I pity in you is something human,
> The old incurable untimeliness,
> Only begetter of all ills that are.

In less explicit form, this distrust of the unnatural appears in a great many poems. In "Mending Wall" we may not be sure just what it is that doesn't love a wall:

> I could say 'Elves' to him,
> But it's not elves exactly;

but it is clear that, in broad enough terms, it is man who makes walls and nature that knocks them down again. The rabbity professor of "A Hundred Collars" is

> a democrat,
> If not at heart, at least on principle;

but his inability to respond to his drunken roommate's easy good will indicates clearly enough that principle is no adequate substitute for the heart's spontaneous gestures. The farm hand of "The Code" is a natural aristocrat, and his parvenu employer courts death by presuming on his merely economic superiority. In "Range-Finding" a random bullet's interference with natural phenomena—torn cobweb, cut flower, and dispossessed butterfly—epitomizes at least part of the meaning of war. The speaker of "A Star in a Stone-

Boat" "must go measuring stone walls, perch on perch," to
locate the occasional meteorite that has come to so inappropriate a resting place—walls, again—and restore it to something like its natural role. In "The Gift Outright" it was our
failure to give ourselves to the land that kept us weak. And
in "Build Soil," Tityrus, distrusting farm programs, sends
Meliboeus back to his "run-out mountain farm" to co-operate
with nature out of natural love for it, not out of social morality
or economic necessity—in Emerson's phrase, to "do after his
kind, be he asp or angel."[10]

Logical consistency demands that, if tampering with nature
is wrong or dangerous, then successful living should be largely
a matter of getting permanently in tune with nature. But as
indicated above, Frost shies away from merely theoretical
consistency; there are few poems in which such adjustments
appear, and those few are not very conclusive. Loren, of
"Blueberries,"

> Just taking what nature is willing to give,

is the clearest example in his refusal to tamper with natural
processes; but the speakers of the poem have for Loren no
more than grudging respect, and even that is qualified by
contempt. The clergyman of "The Black Cottage," wishing
for a land

> I could devote and dedicate forever
> To the truths we keep coming back and back to,

envisions it as almost wholly natural, untouched by man's
devices:

> So desert it would have to be, so walled
> By mountain ranges half in summer snow,
> No one would covet it or think it worth

---

[10] Emerson, I, 341.

> The pains of conquering to force change on.
> Scattered oases where men dwelt, but mostly
> Sand dunes held loosely in tamarisk
> Blown over and over themselves in idleness.

But the desert land remains a fantasy. Brown, of "Brown's Descent,"

> Bowed with grace to natural law

and took the long way home rather than attempt a two-mile climb over glare ice, but Brown is an at least half-whimsical case in point. "The Ax-Helve" recommends expressing the native grain in things, whether in tool-making or education, and "In Time of Cloudburst" indicates the speaker's satisfaction with a vaguely Emersonian theory of natural compensation whereby soil erosion will be made up for by a world upheaval, bringing mountains out of the ocean with the lost topsoil intact; but in both poems the points are made with a degree of generality that renders problematic any attempt to apply them in specific cases. And if the impulse-following protagonist of "A Lone Striker" prefers New England's trees and cliffs to her factories, other things being equal, he is aware that other things are not always equal and will go back to the factory quite willingly as soon as he is needed urgently enough for someone to come and get him.

Insofar as such poems provide a moral, it is at best an ambiguous one, and in fact there are poems in which such ambiguity is central. Though the speaker of "Reluctance" accepts summer's passing, he does so under protest:

> Ah, when to the heart of man
>   Was it ever less than a treason
> To go with the drift of things,
>   To yield with a grace to reason,
> And bow and accept the end
>   Of a love or a season?

In "The Exposed Nest" man and child construct an artificial screen to shade a nestful of young birds exposed to the sun during mowing, but neither we nor the speaker know whether the action has been valuable or not, or even whether it may not have made a bad situation worse. And in "The Line-Gang" it is not clear whether the bringing of telephone and telegraph does or does not justify the wanton slashing down of forests, whether it is more "natural" to leave forests stand-ing or to subdue them to man's purposes.

These poems suggest that "nature," to Frost, is a fairly protean term; its meaning changes from poem to poem, and that changeableness may partially account for the absence of a clear prescription to follow nature.[11] In "A Brook in the City" natural behavior appears to be a matter of not inter-fering with the phenomena and processes of the inorganic, non-human world; nature is those processes. Organic phe-nomena—meadow grass and apple trees—can be sacrificed, perhaps with impunity, to the utilitarian demands of urban living. But a brook is an "immortal force"; neither made by man nor sharing in his common, protoplasmic mortality, its energies are radically different from man's, not necessarily hostile but demanding respect for their unkillable and un-manageable "otherness." The nature represented by such forces is not precisely a moral phenomenon, as it was for Wordsworth or for the Duke in *As You Like It;* it affords no prescription for living. But it requires man's respectful aware-ness, constantly reminding him that his capacity for really altering the world is narrowly limited.

The same sense of "nature" is implicit in "A Star in a Stone-Boat," but with additions. Here natural behavior mani-fests itself in the speaker's mission to restore fallen meteorites to an undefined proper place in an undefined total scheme of things; nature is that scheme, and man, once more, is not well-advised if he attempts to adapt it to his own utilitarian purposes. The meteorite, like the brook, is too radically

[11] Cf. below, p. 23.

"other"[12] to be exploited with impunity; nature, the inorganic system of which it is an element, is an unknown if not unknowable order, and like the brook demands respect:

> Yet ask where else it could have gone as well,
> I do not know—I cannot stop to tell:
> He might have left it lying where it fell.

Such prudential, non-utilitarian respect is our safest, most rewarding attitude toward what we cannot understand.

In "To a Moth Seen in Winter" we see the consequence of pitting oneself against nature's "immortal force." The wintry world of inorganic process, utterly indifferent to and other than impulses of human pity or the broadly organic "love of kind," simply extinguishes them. But it is difficult not to suppose that some impulse in the near-human moth's "nature" has led it to break itself against that world; nature is such impulses, informed by a purpose that is indifferent to and sometimes desperately at odds with the inorganic determinism it confronts. Yet occasionally, as in "Two Look at Two" and "Iris by Night," "otherness" breaks down, as it were, allowing men a momentary sense of real kinship with the unknown, a sense that their purely organic impulses have been met halfway. And at least once Frost has treated those impulses as final. In "On a Tree Fallen Across the Road," the inorganic tempest "knows obstruction is in vain";[13] man will fulfil himself precisely by mastering the unknowable "other" and compelling it to serve his purposes:

> We will not be put off the final goal
> We have it hidden in us to attain,
> Not though we have to seize earth by the pole
>
> And, tired of aimless circling in one place,
> Steer straight off after something into space.

[12] As we shall see later in this chapter, "otherness" is the most persistent characteristic of Frost's view of nature; see below, pp. 32-37.
[13] Cf. below, pp. 149-151.

Men, if not moths, will have the last word, and it is not easy
to see how such a position can be made wholly consistent with
that of "A Brook in the City" or "A Star in a Stone-Boat."

It would be possible to discover in these poems still more,
and more complex, meanings for the term "nature" than those
I have indicated, though for now the effort would be of
doubtful value. As we have seen, and as we shall see again,
no single definition of the term will really carry one through
a discussion of Frost's poems; Frost's reader has no choice
but to maintain a constantly altering focus, recognizing that
whatever consistency may emerge will be primarily a matter
not of definition but of attitude. That is, Frost is ultimately
not very much concerned with developing a philosophically
consistent concept of nature; important though nature is to
him, he is not really concerned with it as an object of dis-
interested philosophical speculation, as something to be con-
ceptualized. What really interests him is not definitions but
attitudes, not what nature is in itself but how man responds
to it in a world he never made, whatever the organization of
that world may be. As I have said, Frost's writing does not
lack intellectual content, and toward the end of this chapter
we shall see that the shifting concept of nature is related to a
composite sense of man and his potentialities.[14]

But Frost is concerned less with metaphysics than with
the more tangible matter of behavior and attitude, and it
may be partly for this reason that the "nature" one is most
persistently aware of in his poems is expressed in terms of
mountains and brooks, woodlots and pastures and small
farms. Such phenomena do not require an elaborate philosophical apparatus for their apprehension; they are simply
there, and though we are free to define our relationship with
them in philosophical terms, we are not compelled to. Elimi-
nating the necessity for complex intellectual formulations or
social adjustments, they enable Frost's characters to demonstrate a simplicity, a clarity of attitude, sometimes luminous

[14] See below, p. 50.

and sometimes stark, that for Frost is more difficult of attainment in other surroundings. Frost's countryside is consistent with uncluttered attitudes, and in this sense it seems justifiable to say that Frost's "nature" is important less as a concept than as a kind of withdrawal according to plan, a strategic evasion by means of which things are simplified, rendered graspable. And at least one substantial poem—"New Hampshire," in its concluding lines—offers shifty and equivocal acknowledgment of this evasion. Pressed by a cosmopolitan barbarian to

'Choose you which you will be—a prude, or puke,'

the speaker, not unreasonably, prefers to be neither, devoting a good deal of nimble and ironic footwork to avoiding the dilemma. Prudes—pukes do not detain him long—are those who, afraid of nature, take care never to overstep

The line where man leaves off and nature starts,

preferring to remain

on the safe side of the line talking;
Which is sheer Matthew Arnoldism,
The cult of one who owned himself 'a foiled,
Circuitous wanderer,' and 'took dejectedly
His seat upon the intellectual throne.'

We do not know just where that line is to be drawn, or whether, in fact, its drawing is not a purely ironic gesture, for the sake of those to whom "Nothing not built with hands . . . is sacred." Backed into a corner, however, and deprived of the comfort of either engaging in sophistry or being a good Greek, he chooses not to be a prude, even at the cost of being a moderate puke:

> I choose to be a plain New Hampshire farmer
> With an income in cash of say a thousand
> (From say a publisher in New York City).

And we are sufficiently engaged by witty equivocation not to care too much that the natural world of the plain New Hampshire farmer functions primarily as a means of getting away from certain dilemmas—in this instance, an admittedly silly one—that confront one elsewhere. Matthew Arnold also observed that "Tragedy breasts the pressure of life. Comedy eludes it, half liberates itself from it by irony,"[15] and Frost may have gotten more than straw men from Arnold. (In any case, the "foiled, circuitous wanderer" was not Arnold but the river Oxus.)

If, then, Frost's nature is a strategic evasion, the important question again is less what nature is (though we shall return to this question too) than how it functions, and here too "New Hampshire" provides the clue. My point is that the New Hampshire of the poem *is* primarily a refuge, a means of getting away from things, and for the poem's speaker, it is a good refuge. It enables him to escape the rigged dilemmas of cocktail-party intellectuals. It enables him to escape the outcries of literary reformers:

> How are we to write
> The Russian novel in America
> As long as life goes so unterribly?

It enables him to escape the complexities of the commercial life and the salesman mentality:

> Just specimens is all New Hampshire has,
> One each of everything as in a show-case
> Which naturally she doesn't care to sell.

[15] Quoted by Lionel Trilling, *Matthew Arnold* (New York, 1955), p. 342.

New Hampshire has the virtue of reducing things to scale, making our more problematic problems appropriately absurd. There is social reform:

> Did you but know of him, New Hampshire has
> One real reformer who would change the world
> So it would be accepted by two classes,
> Artists the minute they set up as artists,
> Before, that is, they get themselves accepted,
> And boys the minute they get out of college.

There is politics:

> Easton goes Democratic, Wilson 4
> Hughes 2.

There is intellectual innovation:

> 'The matter with the Mid-Victorians
> Seems to have been a man named John L. Darwin.'

Admitting New Hampshire's ideal imperfections,

> She's still New Hampshire, a most restful state.

And in this respect, New Hampshire is something of a microcosm, fulfilling Thoreau's demand for "Simplicity, simplicity, simplicity!"[16] Like New Hampshire, nature simplifies our problems and our attitudes.

Such simplification, however, is not in itself a simple matter. Frost's natural, or bucolic, New England does not act as an automatic problem solver, as is obvious from such backcountry poems as "Home Burial," "The Fear," "The Witch of Coös," or "West-Running Brook." There is little suggestion that the world of nature is a world of pie in the

---

[16] Thoreau, p. 81.

sky. Rather it is, broadly speaking, a world in which situations involving choice, ethically complicated choice, are reduced to something like ultimate simplicity. Thus in "Storm Fear" there is no problem of reconciling conflicting goods or of adjusting oneself to the desires and interests of others; the problem for the snowed-in speaker and his family is simply

> Whether 'tis in us to arise with day
> And save ourselves unaided—

that is, a simple matter of black or white, of surviving or not surviving. In "The Road Not Taken" the problem of choice is in a way even more elementary, since neither self-interest, moral obligation, nor even curiosity provides a real basis for preferring one road to the other. In lectures and conversation, Frost is fond of stressing that, though the road taken had

> perhaps the better claim,
> Because it was grassy and wanted wear,

the literal truth was that

> the passing there
> Had worn them really about the same;

that is, the choice was wholly arbitrary, whimsical, undetermined. And in that grim monologue "A Servant to Servants," the problem is stripped down to a point at which it is hardly a problem at all. The speaker is going mad, knows she is going mad, and knows that she can do nothing about it but wait for it to happen. Neither rebellious nor resentful, she has no alternatives between which to choose; it is difficult to see how the problem of choice could be reduced to more stark simplicity.

In a way, classifying "A Servant to Servants" as a poem

of nature is a pretty arbitrary proceeding. That is, the woman of the poem does not exist alone in Frost's favored world of natural objects and processes, even to the extent that the characters of "The Hill Wife" or "The Fear" at least seem to. It is a poem of nature only in the sense that it demonstrates the same simplification of issues involving choice, the same elimination of a certain kind of psychic effort, as do "Storm Fear" and "The Road Not Taken." But for two reasons I believe that such arbitrariness is legitimate, if not unavoidable, in dealing with Frost. In the first place, as I have said, Frost's formal statements of theory are few and far between; one is compelled to formulate and apply one's own definitions. (The same thing is, of course, true of poets other than Frost.) And in the second place, there are poems in which Frost deals specifically with contrasts between the worlds of natural and of manmade objects, and in which the essential difference between the two worlds is the relative simplicity of the natural. The most obviously relevant of such poems are probably "The Need of Being Versed in Country Things" and "Directive."[17] In "The Need of Being Versed in Country Things" we are explicitly cautioned against attributing to nature or its creatures emotional complexities of grief or regret for the life that has vanished with the burned farm house; by example, if nothing else, nature encourages emotional simplification, as it did for Thoreau.

"Directive" is less explicit, but at the same time more compelling, largely because it reveals more of that ethical or metaphysical dimension I have spoken of. The poem opens with an emphasis on simplicity:

> Back out of all this now too much for us,
> Back in a time made simple by the loss
> Of detail, burned, dissolved, and broken off
> Like graveyard marble sculpture in the weather,

---

[17] Frost's animal poems, in which the animals are not bothered by problems of choice, are also relevant here; see below, pp. 158-160.

> There is a house that is no more a house
> Upon a farm that is no more a farm
> And in a town that is no more a town.

The simplicity here is a fairly complex phenomenon. In the first place, it is the simplicity wrought upon rural New England by population shifts and the erosions of time. It is also a partly ironic sentimentalization of an idyllic past contrasted with a too-complicated present—ironic by virtue of the speaker's awareness that its simplicity is achieved by the wearing away of detail that really was there when the farm really was a farm, and by his awareness that it is a kind of child's play he recommends to the reader, though even child's play may be complex, particularly when it is an adult who engages in it. "Directive" is also concerned with getting back to primal sources of life and energy, and in this sense its simplicity is also that achieved by sacrament or ritual, which by symbolization renders graspable and orderly phenomena that are otherwise mysterious, unattainable, and incoherent. The sacramental drinking with which "Directive" ends *is* a sacrament, bringing wholeness into what is otherwise confusion.[18]

But the simplicity of "Directive" is also the simplicity achieved when a world of human society reverts to natural wilderness, and in this respect Frost's poem is strongly reminiscent of a passage in Thoreau's chapter "Former Inhabitants; and Winter Visitors," in *Walden*. Remembering Hugh Quoil, "the last inhabitant of these woods before me," Thoreau constructs a meditation on nature's persistent reconquest of man's abandoned outposts, a meditation that may have contributed imagery to "Directive." Hugh Quoil's pipe, "broken on the hearth, instead of a bowl broken at the fountain," suggests Frost's "broken drinking goblet" at the waterside. Thoreau's "dim outline of a garden" suggests, more remotely,

[18] Randall Jarrell has called attention to "Directive's" serious parody of the Grail knight's serial ordeal. "To the Laodiceans," *Poetry and the Age* (New York, 1955), p. 48.

Frost's "farm that is no more a farm."   Thoreau's "dent in the earth [that] marks the site of these dwellings" suggests Frost's

> belilaced cellar hole,
> Now slowly closing like a dent in dough,

and Thoreau devotes a paragraph to the persistent lilac.   Thoreau's "new-rising forests" suggest Frost's upstart woods:

> Where were they all not twenty years ago?

Thoreau's "cellar dents, like deserted fox-burrows, old holes" help to illuminate the obscurity of Frost's

> serial ordeal
> Of being watched from forty cellar holes
> As if by eye pairs out of forty firkins.

Thoreau's melancholy over "the covering up of wells" provides a momentary focus for the meditation that, though different in kind, is in degree not unlike Frost's concern for sources of water.   And in both passages, nature, the great simplifier, is manifestly not disturbed by her ironing out of man's complicating interferences.[19]

In that sense, at least, the simplicity of "Directive" is something that only nature can achieve, or at most that only nature can give.   Nature shares man's melancholy over the vanished town no more than she does in "The Need of Being Versed in Country Things," or in *Walden*.   But by completing his quest beyond man's complicating interference with the natural and by receiving the natural sacrament he is directed to, the reader can achieve a like invulnerability, apparently purging himself of and hence mastering his complicated impulses of fear and pity.   The Aristotelian echo is not wholly

[19] Thoreau, pp. 220-222.

irrelevant; whatever Aristotle meant, the purging of pity and
fear is clearly a kind of psychic simplification. And, though
this may be to abandon Aristotle, the choices that confront
at least Sophocles' tragic heroes are the kind that Frost prefers—clear-cut and demanding no elaborate ethical calculation in making the choice, regardless of its tremendous consequences. Oedipus must choose between saving Thebes and
not saving Thebes, between accepting his destiny and point-
lessly rebelling against it; Antigone must choose between
obeying the unwritten law and not obeying the unwritten law;
Electra must choose between vengeance and pusillanimity.
And for the Sophoclean hero, such choices are hardly problems at all; in Emerson's phrase, they are "the choice[s] of his
constitution."[20]   The same thing is true, again, of "Storm
Fear," "The Road Not Taken," and "A Servant to Servants."
Like tragedy, Frost's nature affords a kind of ideal simplification.   In the world of nature one may physically have to fight
for his life, as does Meserve in "Snow," or as do the nameless
speakers of "Storm Fear," "An Empty Threat," and "A Leaf
Treader"; but psychically, emotionally, even though that
world is no island of the blest, one finds no loaded questions,
rigged dilemmas, or impossible problems there.   To this degree, nature is, like New Hampshire, most restful; it enables
one to come to grips directly with ultimate problems of choice,
and it is this fact that makes Frost's evasion a strategic one.

   The sense of nature's relative simplicity in its impingement
on man informs, or at least is implicit in, poem after poem.
"A Prayer in Spring" formulates an appeal to

> keep us here
> All simply in the springing of the year,

free of the economic and emotional complications involved
in "the uncertain harvest."   In "Reluctance" human complications of responsibility and desire become poignant largely

[20] Emerson, II, 140.

through their contrast with nature's impersonal simplicity, and the same thing is true of "Stopping by Woods on a Snowy Evening." In "Stars" the speaker is stirred by his awareness that the stars do not share man's complex emotional life. In "Putting in the Seed" he achieves something like natural simplicity in his "springtime passion for the earth," forgetting even such elementary human complications as supper (compare the ritual or sacramental element in "Directive"). In " 'Out, Out—' " the natural fact of death simplifies everything, even for the living watchers:

> No more to build on there. And they, since they
> Were not the one dead, turned to their affairs.

There is one less area in which the problem of choice might arise. In one degree or another, the same pattern appears in "A Patch of Old Snow," "An Empty Threat," "The Aim Was Song," "Devotion," "The Last Mowing," "At Woodward's Gardens," and "The Rabbit Hunter."

Frost's nature, then, is primarily an evasion according to plan, a condition of strategic withdrawal, and the reason it is so satisfactory a refuge is that, simpler than man, it reduces the problem of choice to a kind of elemental either-or. As the speaker of "An Empty Threat" puts it, in imagination camped in a wilderness of snow and ice on the shore of Hudson's Bay,

> 'Better defeat almost,
> If seen clear,
> Than life's victories of doubt
> That need endless talk talk
> To make them out.'

The precautionary "almost" renders dogmatism dangerous, but it is clear that the Arctic wilderness offers the speaker, as it offered Henry Hudson, a clear and simple finality as alternative to a life of dubious battle. To the speaker, the wilderness *is*

>the old captain's dark fate
>Who failed to find or force a strait
>In its two-thousand-mile coast;
>And his crew left him where he failed,
>And nothing came of all he sailed.

There are elements of paradox here. The natural wilderness clarifies life for the speaker, but it does so by clarifying Henry Hudson out of existence altogether and by—almost—convincing the speaker that Hudson's clarification is the only really ultimate sort there is. And this position, of course, is consistent. The only condition in which problems of choice are totally simplified is the condition of being dead—or perhaps mad, like the woman in "A Servant to Servants"—and that fact may well explain Frost's reluctance to recommend harmony with nature in really unambiguous terms;[21] at least it goes far toward explaining the "almost" in "An Empty Threat." Frost exhibits little of the wistfulness regarding death common in A. E. Housman, Emily Dickinson, Whitman, or Robinson Jeffers; like Keats, he is never more than half in love with easeful death.

But there is another and, I think, more fundamental way in which this paradox is rooted in Frost's feeling for nature. In "The Census-Taker," the speaker, depressed by scalped forest land and deserted shanty, concludes:

>The melancholy of having to count souls
>Where they grow fewer and fewer every year
>Is extreme where they shrink to none at all.
>It must be I want life to go on living.

And in the last line, it is clear that he speaks not only for him-

[21] Cf. above, p. 11.

self, but for nature—clear not only because it is largely self-evident but also because in a good many other poems nature clearly does want life to go on living. In "Ghost House," "The Last Mowing," "The Birthplace," "Something for Hope," and "Directive," humanity has gone but the weeds and the wilderness come back. In "Pea Brush" and "Putting in the Seed" trilliums and beans keep coming up in spite of the apparent odds against them. If death is persistent in "In Hardwood Groves," life is equally so. If in "The Times Table" deliberately cultivated gloom seems likely to lower the birth rate, still it will "bring back nature in people's place." In " 'Out, Out—' " the living watchers have no choice but to leave the dead and return to the business of living. And "Our Hold on the Planet," picking up a suggestion from "In Time of Cloudburst,"[22] asserts that nature, taken "altogether since time began,"

> must be a little more in favor of man,
> Say a fraction of one per cent at the very least,
> Or our number living wouldn't be steadily more,
> Our hold on the planet wouldn't have so increased.

If Frost's treatment of nature is a strategic evasion, it has, once more, intellectual content in its own right.

But if Frost's nature wants life to go on living, still, like Tennyson's, it shows no marked concern for the single life, and it is this fact, I think, that underlies the paradox in "An Empty Threat." At the risk of stretching a point, it is nature's unconcern for single lives that makes the speaker's threat to go hunting for Henry Hudson an empty one; excessive concern for a single life is a violation of nature. Similarly, the woman's grief for her child in "Home Burial" baffles her simpler, more natural husband; he sees it as excessive, scarcely natural.

[22] See above, p. 10.

'I do think, though, you overdo it a little.
What was it brought you up to think it the thing
To take your mother-loss of a first child
So inconsolably—in the face of love.
You'd think his memory might be satisfied—.'

And the dreadful resignation of the woman in "A Servant to Servants" may have its roots in the same perception.

The one indecency's to make a fuss,

says Keeper, in *A Masque of Mercy,* and the indecent here can be seen as a social equivalent of the unnatural—as it was for Swift's natural Houyhnhnms, who knew no problems of choice, who were unmoved by the thought of individual death, even their own, and whose name signifies, "in its etymology, *the perfection of nature.*"[23]

But Frost is not Swift. Swift's nature at least—and it is an important "at least"—prefers Houyhnhnms to Yahoos; like Emerson's, it is a moral phenomenon, satisfied only with the best. Frost's nature plays no such ethical favorites, even to the extent that it does for the creative evolutionist.[24] At first glance, the nature that wants life to go on living looks very much like Shaw's Life Force, as it is revealed in the third act of *Man and Superman.* But whereas the Frostian nature is content that life should go on living, the Shavian Life Force wants, in Don Juan's words, "not only to maintain itself, but to achieve higher and higher organization and completer self-consciousness. . . ."[25] It wants its creatures to evolve, to become something better; and though "Sitting by a Bush in Broad Sunlight" implies some sort of vital evolution—

[23] Jonathan Swift, *Gulliver's Travels* (New York, 1948), p. 227 (Bk. IV, chap. iii).
[24] Lawrance Thompson has detected Bergson's influence in such poems as "West-Running Brook" and "The Master Speed." Lawrance Thompson, *Fire and Ice: The Art and Thought of Robert Frost* (New York, 1942), p. 197.
[25] George Bernard Shaw, *Man and Superman* (New York, 1912), p. 112.

There was one time and only the one
When dust really took in the sun;
And from that one intake of fire
All creatures still warmly suspire.

And if men have watched a long time
And never seen sun-smitten slime
Again come to life and crawl off,
We must not be too ready to scoff—

there is virtually no other indication that any evolutionary
hypothesis plays a significant role in Frost's thinking. It
provides no motive for action, no basis for understanding
man's proper relationship with nature, and no real assurance
that man *counts,* and these are the important functions of the
Life Force. Though "Our Hold on the Planet" insists that
the odds are in man's favor by at least "a fraction of one per
cent," and though "On a Tree Fallen Across the Road" indicates that we really will achieve the nameless

final goal
We have it hidden in us to attain,

still the nature involved in "The Last Mowing," "Directive,"
"Something for Hope," or "The Need of Being Versed in
Country Things" seems as satisfied with trees, flowers, and
birds as it was with men. "Once by the Pacific" suggests that
the long-term odds may be less than even, and "It Bids
Pretty Fair," "Why Wait for Science," "The Planners," and
"Bursting Rapture"—the last three clearly post-Hiroshima
poems—cast some not wholly unreasonable doubt on the
ultimate perdurability of anything particular. Frost's snow,
like that of E. E. Cummings, "doesn't give a soft white damn
whom it touches";[26] Frost's nature is concerned with neither
ethics nor eugenics.

[26] E. E. Cummings, *Collected Poems* (Harcourt, Brace and Company,
1938), poem 198.

Comparison with Wordsworth is clearly more important, and more plausible, than comparison with either Swift or Shaw, since Wordsworth is in a sense the standard against which any subsequent philosophically serious nature poet writing in English must be measured, whether there is any question of direct influence or not. As John Freeman has observed, "It is not my part to prove that . . . but for Wordsworth [Frost] might have been different. But for Wordsworth we should all have been different."[27] And Basil Willey indicates, in sufficiently broad terms, the nature of that difference in his essay "On Wordsworth and the Locke Tradition." As Wordsworth

is the first, so he remains the type, of the 'modern' poets who, 'left alone' with a vaster material than his, must bear as best they can, unaided by any universally held mythology, the 'weight of all this unintelligible world,'[28]

either making poetry "out of the direct dealings of [their] mind[s] and heart[s] with the visible universe," or fabricating "a genuine new mythology of [their] own. . . . Keats and Shelley often follow the second of these methods; Wordsworth typically follows the first."[29] Shaw, with his Life Force (Shaw is of course a poet only in the ancient sense of the word), Hardy, in *The Dynasts,* and Yeats, as the Rosicrucian, Golden-Dawnite author of *A Vision,* are makers of mythologies; Frost, and the Georgian poets among whom he moved during his English years (1912-1915), have largely followed the Wordsworthian precedent, as did Emerson and Thoreau, Bryant and Whittier before them.

Parenthetically, it can be pointed out here that, except for the late masques, the most obviously mythological of Frost's poems—"In a Vale," "My November Guest," "Pan

[27] John Freeman, "Robert Frost," *London Mercury,* XIII (Dec., 1925), 180.
[28] Basil Willey, *The Seventeenth Century Background* (London, 1949), p. 309.
[29] *Ibid.,* p. 297.

With Us," "The Trial by Existence," "The Demiurge's Laugh," and "The Spoils of the Dead," the last poem omitted from later collections and from *Complete Poems*—are all included in his first book, *A Boy's Will*. Sylvester Baxter[30] and Malcolm Cowley[31] indicate that, while the poems of *A Boy's Will* were written before the English journey, those of *North of Boston* and *Mountain Interval* are products largely of the years in England. Cowley suggests that it was from such Georgians as Lascelles Abercrombie, Rupert Brooke, Wilfrid Wilson Gibson, and Edward Thomas that Frost "learned to abandon the conventional language of the late Victorians and to use his own speech without embarrassment."[32] It seems reasonable to suppose that his abandonment of the rather solemn mythologizing evident in the poems I have cited may be a result of the same Georgian influence.[33] As we shall see in Chapter III, Frost's later work does manifest a distinct mythopoeic element, but that element is largely undeliberate, even unconscious, a quite different thing from the deliberate personification of "My November Guest" or the somewhat adolescent animism of "In a Vale."

But if Frost is like Wordsworth in his unmythologized "aloneness with the world,"[34] other resemblances between the two are on the whole superficial in the light of a very important difference between them. The difference, as I see it, is that Wordsworth quite explicitly does, and Frost does not, perceive an organic relationship, a vital continuity between man and nature. In "Tintern Abbey," Wordsworth reports his having felt

[30] Sylvester Baxter, "New England's New Poet," *American Review of Reviews*, LI (April, 1915), 433.
[31] Malcolm Cowley, "Frost: A Dissenting Opinion," *New Republic*, CXI (Sept. 11, 1944), 313.
[32] *Ibid.*, p. 313.
[33] In "Robert Frost," *Adelphi*, XXVII (Nov., 1950), 48, C. M. Bowra sees Frost as essentially Georgian, adding that "the Georgian poet who has matured and found himself is Frost."
[34] Willey, p. 298.

> A presence that disturbs me with the joy
> Of elevated thoughts; a sense sublime
> Of something far more deeply interfused,
> Whose dwelling is the light of setting suns,
> And the round ocean and the living air,
> And the blue sky, and in the mind of man;
> A motion and a spirit, that impels
> All thinking things, all objects of all thought,
> And rolls through all things.

Such moments are ecstatic, in an almost literal sense:

> the breath of this corporeal frame
> And even the motion of our human blood
> Almost suspended, we are laid asleep
> In body, and become a living soul,
> While with an eye made quiet by the power
> Of harmony, and the deep power of joy,
> We see into the life of things.

These are, of course, familiar lines. I quote them thus extensively both because they indicate very explicitly the Wordsworthian sense of an organic, vital continuity between man and nature ("things" have life; the "something far more deeply interfused" is equally at home in "the living air" and "the mind of man"), and because they are drastically unlike almost anything in Frost. John Freeman, again, speaks of the "steady grey light" of Frost's poetry, and adds that it "is distinguished finally from the light of Wordsworth's verse by its raylessness. . . . Both style and temper forbid rapture, as never with Wordsworth."[35]

I think it is not altogether true that there is no rapture in Frost's poems; there are, for example, "I Will Sing You One-O," "To Earthward," "Two Look at Two," "Iris by Night," and perhaps the cryptic "All Revelation." "All Reve-

[35] Freeman, p. 183.

lation"—and I am not at all sure that I understand the poem—seems the most explicitly Wordsworthian. Its last two stanzas very strongly suggest a variety of Wordsworth's and Coleridge's doctrine of imagination:

> But the impervious geode
> Was entered, and its inner crust
> Of crystals with a ray cathode
> At every point and facet glowed
> In answer to the mental thrust.
>
> Eyes seeking the response of eyes
> Bring out the stars, bring out the flowers,
> Thus concentrating earth and skies
> So none need be afraid of size.
> All revelation has been ours.

The eyes that "bring out the stars" exercise the plastic power that "half creates" ("Tintern Abbey") the world around it.[36] The stanzas suggest, in Professor Willey's words,

the capacity of the mind to co-operate with [the] 'active universe,' to contribute something of its own to it in perceiving it, and not, as sensationalism taught, merely to receive, passively, impressions from without.[37]

And in "All Revelation," the sense of a real continuity between the world of human emotion and the world of stars and flowers is clear.

But the other poems at least imply reservations. In "I Will Sing You One-O," the sense is clearly not of a continuity between man and the majestic cosmos he envisions, but of an unbridgeable difference. "To Earthward" presents, not the Wordsworthian feeling of ecstatic kinship with the world, but an almost nympholeptic hunger for that feeling.

---

[36] The doctrine is also Emersonian: "One after another [man's] victorious thought comes up with and reduces all things, until the world becomes at last only a realized will—the double of the man." Emerson, I, 40.
[37] Willey, pp. 299-300.

The sympathy between man and nature in "Iris by Night" is explicitly labeled a

> miracle
> That never yet to other two befell;

that is, it is a wholly special case, not a constantly and freely available relationship. And although the lovers of "Two Look At Two" experience an almost overwhelming sense of kinship from their nocturnal encounter with doe and buck, nevertheless, the favor is unlooked-for, something of a miracle again:

> Still they stood,
> A great wave from it going over them,
> As if the earth in one unlooked-for favor
> Had made them certain earth returned their love.

It may be significant that the whole experience is presented as an "as if." Wordsworth characteristically avoids the "as if" presentation, and the difference is, I think, instructive. In Frost's poem, the belief, if that is the word for it, is much more lightly held than in Wordsworth. In "The Most of It," clearly a complementary poem to "Two Look at Two," the speaker's cry for "counter-love, original response" from nature rather than simply his "own love back in copy speech" receives no meaningful response; the buck that he sees speaks of natural indifference rather than of natural kinship. There is a world of difference between the connotation of " 'This *must* be all.' It was all," from "Two Look at Two," and "and that was all," from "The Most of It." And if "Never Again Would Birds' Song Be the Same" implies a half-whimsical acceptance of the Wordsworthian plastic power, "A Boundless Moment" is a half-serious parody of it. On the whole, Freeman is correct; Frost seldom permits himself the Wordsworthian rapture. On the whole, Frost's nature is impersonal, indifferent, and *other*.

These characteristics are not, of course, novelties in American thought and writing. New England Puritanism, even after its initial Calvinistic rigor had been modified, regularly saw man in relationship with an impersonal other, a God whose decrees were arbitrary, in no way conditioned by one's personal merit. As Perry Miller observes of "Sinners in the Hand of an Angry God," Jonathan Edwards "brought mankind, as Protestantism must always bring them, without mitigation, protection, or indulgence, face to face with a cosmos fundamentally inhuman."[38] And the tradition died hard, if it ever did die. Even Emerson's happy conviction that everything is implicit in anything left room, at least once, for the intuition that "the fate of the poor shepherd, who, blinded and lost in the snowstorm, perishes in a drift within a few feet of his cottage door, is an emblem of the state of man,"[39] that nature's moral benevolence is not always and equally apparent. And Thoreau, who knew nature more intimately than did Emerson, exhibited a more complex awareness of it. Recognizing in the created world a strain of amoral savagery that, in himself, tempted him to seize a woodchuck and devour it raw[40] and, in nature, led him to rejoice that "tender organizations can be so serenely squashed out of existence like pulp,"[41] he could declare that "the moral aspect of Nature is a jaundice reflected from man."[42] Starting with an Emersonian conviction of nature's amiability, "he tended more and more to discover in nature not confirmation of humanity's moral prejudices but a scheme in which these prejudices seemed to be accorded a sometimes frighteningly scant consideration."[43] "The impression made on a wise man is that

[38] Perry Miller, *Jonathan Edwards* (New York, 1948), p. 147.
[39] Emerson, III, 33.
[40] Thoreau, p. 179.
[41] *Ibid.*, p. 265.
[42] Quoted by Joseph Wood Krutch, *Henry David Thoreau* (New York, 1948), p. 62.
[43] Krutch, p. 180.

of universal innocence,"[44] wrote Thoreau, and innocence here means amorality. As we have seen, Frost has evidently absorbed a good deal of imagery from *Walden,* and in his useful *Fire and Ice,* Lawrance Thompson quotes Frost as saying that " '*Robinson Crusoe* is never quite out of my mind. I never tire of being shown how the limited can make snug in the limitless. *Walden* has something of the same fascination.' "[45] Thoreau's secularized Puritanism seems the closest analogue in the New England tradition to Frost's position, and it may be in some degree a source.

Frost's attitude toward pessimistic naturalism is less enthusiastic than his attitude toward Thoreau, though the world of Stephen Crane, Frank Norris, and Theodore Dreiser is marked by the same discontinuity between man and nature as is Frost's. But Frost's much-quoted remarks on realism and potatoes ("There are two types of realist. There is the one who offers a good deal of dirt with his potato to show that it is a real potato. And there is the one who is satisfied with the potato brushed clean. I am inclined to be the second kind."),[46] his fondness for Longfellow as one who felt no need to "fill his soul with sick and miserable experiences, self-imposed and self-inflicted, and greatly enjoyed, before he can sit down and write a lyric of strange and compelling beauty,"[47] and his whimsy on "the Russian novel in America" in "New Hampshire" suggest that Frost has relatively little sympathy for the tradition of American naturalism. The lines from "New Hampshire" may owe something to William Dean Howells' remarks on Dostoievsky and the American novel in "Criticism and Fiction"—Howells' conviction that "whoever struck a note so profoundly tragic [as that of *Crime and Punishment*] in American fiction would do a false and mis-

[44] Thoreau, p. 265.
[45] Thompson, p. 207.
[46] Quoted this time by Louis Untermeyer in *The Pocket Book of Robert Frost's Poems,* ed. Louis Untermeyer (New York, 1946), p. 31.
[47] Quoted by Gorham Munson, *Robert Frost: A Study in Sensibility and Good Sense* (New York, 1927), p. 85.

taken thing," that in America "the wrong from class to class has been almost inappreciable," that "in this new world of ours it is still mainly from one to another one, and oftener still from one to one's self."[48]   Parenthetically, Howells' insistence in the same passage that "in most American novels, vivid and graphic as the best of them are, the people are segregated if not sequestered, and the scene is sparsely populated," that "we excel in small pieces with three or four figures, or in studies of rustic communities, where there is propinquity if not society,"[49] sounds almost like an anticipatory review of *North of Boston*.   And though Frost has not named names in his comments on realism and the literature of masochism, it seems clear that he shares Howells' distaste for naturalism, at least in its unscrubbed forms.[50]   But the naturalism of Thomas Hardy and the pessimism of Joseph Conrad may well be a different matter.   Stearns Morse reports what Frost "wrote to a friend thirty years ago about Thomas Hardy—'one of the most earthly wise of our time.' "[51]   It is possible that Frost has absorbed imagery from Hardy as he has from Thoreau;[52] and whether it is a question of influence, of temperament, or merely of contemporaneousness, some of Frost's important images and themes bear a real resemblance to images and themes in *The Return of the Native, Chance,* and *Heart of Darkness.*[53]

But the idea is more important than its immediate source, and the idea of a discontinuous universe is an ancient one.

[48] Frost also shares Howells' conviction that, at least in America, problems of broadly social origin have no very compelling reality. See below, chap. iv.   But for Howells, though class injustice was "inappreciable," still "all this [was] changing for the worse."   William Dean Howells, *My Literary Passions: Criticism and Fiction* (New York, 1910), p. 252.

[49] Howells, pp. 252-253.

[50] On Howells' attitude toward naturalism, see Alfred Kazin, *On Native Grounds: An Interpretation of Modern American Prose Literature* (New York, 1942), pp. 3-50, *passim.*

[51] Stearns Morse, "The Wholeness of Robert Frost," *Virginia Quarterly Review,* XIX (Summer, 1943), 413.

[52] See below, pp. 37-38, n. 59.

[53] See below, pp. 97, 99, 100, 105.

In *De Rerum Natura,* Lucretius, acknowledging discipleship to Epicurus, envisioned a world that was also impersonal, indifferent, and other. Like Frost's nature, that of Lucretius is a simplifier, and for a more explicit reason: nature, including man, is wholly a matter of the fortuitous collisions and combinations of material atoms in a void, uncreated and devoid of meaning or motive. Outside that flux, to be sure, the gods exist, but they neither created the universe nor concern themselves with it; they are completely, ontologically other. The wise man, recognizing all this, neither fears the unknown, which does not exist, nor yearns after the unattainable, which is unattainable, but contents himself with enjoying such satisfactions as are available to him and with avoiding such pain as is avoidable.[54]

Now Frost, once more, offers no clear theory of the nature of things (it would, of course, be virtually impossible to accept Lucretius' simple mechanism in a Darwinian, Planckian, Einsteinian world), but both the indifferent nature Frost envisages and his feeling toward it contain Lucretian elements. In the opening lines of his second book, Lucretius celebrates the joys of the philosophic man, enabled to

> look below on other men
> And see them ev'rywhere wand'ring, all dispersed
> In their lone seeking for the road of life;
> Rivals in genius, or emulous in rank,
> Pressing through days and nights with hugest toil
> For summits of power and mastery of the world.[55]

"New Hampshire" indicates quite clearly that residence in the less cosmopolitan areas of northern New England can confer much the same privilege. A poem, says Frost, "begins in

[54] Of Frost's infrequent references in verse to other poets, two are to Lucretius ("Too Anxious for Rivers" and "Lucretius Versus the Lake Poets"), the only classical poet so distinguished.

[55] Titus Lucretius Carus, *Of the Nature of Things,* trans. William Ellery Leonard (London, 1921), p. 45.

delight and ends in wisdom,"[56] and frequently, though by no means always, that wisdom is Lucretian in its skepticism regarding purposes other than those man makes for himself, its satisfaction with detached observation. In "The Vantage Point," the speaker is equally content with contemplating live men, dead men, or ants, and none of the three prompts him to teleological speculation. In "Mowing,"

> The fact is the sweetest dream that labor knows,

not speculative deductions from the fact. "Hyla Brook" makes much the same point:

> We love the things we love for what they are,

not for what they may or may not mean or for purposes that may or may not be implicit in them.[57] "The Oven Bird" raises the question "what to make of a diminished thing"—at the risk of overexplicitness, what does the artist do with a world largely devoid of the purpose and meaning that Wordsworth, Spenser, or Dante knew? And "A Drumlin Woodchuck" offers a practical solution to the problem by

> shrewdly pretend[ing]
> That he and the world are friends,

but at the same time acting on the Arnoldian assumption that nature and man, woodchucks and the world, can never really be fast friends. "I never tire," says Frost, again, "of being

---

[56] Preface to *Complete Poems,* p. vi.

[57] William G. O'Donnell calls attention to this point with respect to *A Boy's Will:* "'A Boy's Will' tends to place a special value on the native detail as an end in itself." "Robert Frost and New England: A Revaluation," *Yale Review,* XXXVII (Summer, 1948), 702. And Robert Penn Warren sees it as characteristic of Frost's nature poetry generally: "Frost's treatment of nature . . . remains as a fidelity to particulars which never become quite coherent." "Hawthorne, Anderson and Frost," *New Republic,* LIV (May 16, 1928), 400.

shown how the limited can make snug in the limitless,"[58] and
if the tone lacks Lucretius' high seriousness, the sentiment is
still Lucretian.

And yet this will not do. The Lucretian position is an
unambiguous one. Nature is the fortuitous configurations
made by colliding atoms, without purpose or meaning, and
there is nothing more. The gods are absolutely remote, un-
concerned, and other; as far as man is concerned, they might
as well not exist. Such a position does not rule out either
humanitarian sympathy for those less fortunate than oneself
or the active exercise of charity, but it emphatically does rule
out wistfulness (it is pointless to yearn for a world that might
be but isn't), ambivalence (to reject the world that is implies
a possible alternative, and there is none), and teleological
uncertainty (there is no teleology to be uncertain about). In
fact, it was Lucretius' main purpose to rule out such feelings,
freeing man from error and groundless fear and pointing out
to him the nature and accessibility of happiness, his ability
to make himself snug in the limitless.

But Frost cannot or will not commit himself with equal
finality. Wistfulness, ambivalence, and teleological uncertainty have been persistent characteristics of Frost's poetry,
from "Reluctance," in *A Boy's Will* (1913), to "Directive,"
in *Steeple Bush* (1947); one feels that Frost would like to
believe in the world Emerson preached, and such wistfulness
is clearly inconsistent with Lucretius' position. Thus "The
Strong Are Saying Nothing," though for fourteen lines it
records a practical acceptance of things as they are that is in
no way inconsistent with Lucretian principles, is ultimately
un-Lucretian in both its tone, which is melancholy, and in its
final refusal either to assert or to deny teleology:

> There may be little or much beyond the grave,
> But the strong are saying nothing until they see.[59]

[58] Thompson, p. 207; see above, p. 33.
[59] The second stanza—
  "There is seldom more than a man to a harrowed piece.

The same refusal reveals itself in "For Once, Then, Something"; neither we nor the poem's speaker can be sure whether
the whiteness at the bottom of the well was "truth" or merely
"a pebble of quartz," nor for that matter whether truth may
not be a pebble of quartz. "Design" both approaches and
recoils from belief in a purposive universe—the ambivalent
note—and is equally disturbed by both attitudes. And the
fine "Acquainted With the Night" achieves something like
perfection in its modulated understatement and careful ambiguity. The poem merits quoting in full.

> I have been one acquainted with the night.
> I have walked out in rain—and back in rain.
> I have outwalked the furthest city light.
>
> I have looked down the saddest city lane.
> I have passed by the watchman on his beat
> And dropped my eyes, unwilling to explain.
>
> I have stood still and stopped the sound of feet
> When far away an interrupted cry
> Came over houses from another street,
>
> But not to call me back or say good-by;
> And further still at an unearthly height,
> One luminary clock against the sky
>
> Proclaimed the time was neither wrong nor right.
> I have been one acquainted with the night.

> Men work alone, their lots plowed far apart,
> One stringing a chain of seed in an open crease,
> And another stumbling after a halting cart—"

may owe something to the first stanza of Hardy's "In Time of 'The Breaking of Nations' ":

> "Only a man harrowing clods
> In a slow silent walk,
> With an old horse that stumbles and nods
> Half asleep as they stalk."

(*Collected Poems of Thomas Hardy* [New York, 1928], p. 511.) Hardy
was another who could not accept a meaningless universe with equanimity,
and as we have seen, Frost admires Hardy.

My immediate point is that the poem records the same kind of teleological uncertainty as does "The Strong Are Saying Nothing," but that it records that uncertainty more effectively, without resort to the other's explicit—and questionably relevant—assertiveness in the concluding lines. The statements made in "Acquainted With the Night" all imply, at first sight, a world of Lucretian indifference, impersonality, and otherness; the poem's theme is that of a quest for some kind of meaningful epiphany in such a world, a quest that is apparently frustrated. Yet the final note is not clearly one of frustration.

> I *have* been one acquainted with the night;

it is something in the past. The problem of placing the accent in that line is not a metrical quibble; the line is meaningful either way, with quite different implications that work back through the poem. For example,

> I have walked out in rain—and back in rain.

If the poem's last line is read,

> *I* have been one acquainted with the night

(and presumably still am), then clearly nothing happened; it is the king's horses and the king's men all over again. But if the accent is shifted to "have," then the caesura after the first "rain" takes on additional depth; something did happen, or at least may have happened. We have no way of knowing whether day did follow night, and if so whether that day was one of Lucretian enlightenment or of the desired epiphany or of some third, and quite indefinable, mode of acceptance. Such a suspended conclusion may help to justify Louise Bogan's remark that "Frost's later poems indicate that he knows more than he ever allows himself to say,"[60] but in "Acquainted With the Night" it is difficult to see any alternative that would not be moralistic, thus limiting and falsifying the poem's legitimately complex ambiguities. Elizabeth Shepley Sergeant says of Frost that "In the heart of his starkest tragedy we find the old New England effort to compromise ideals and facts, escaping either in shy tenderness or in a whimsical humor that often verges on irony."[61] In "Acquainted With the Night" the facts are Lucretian, but the emotional ambiance with which they are invested, and perhaps compromised, is Lucretian only as one possibility among others.[62] Parenthetically, it is worth noting that "Acquainted With the Night" is one of Frost's relatively rare poems that are worked out entirely in urban terms, remote from his preferred world of farm and countryside; it may be that not only the time but the place as well is neither wrong nor right.

Thus Frost does not clearly rule out wistfulness and ambivalence as tenable feelings toward the world, though he rejects Emerson's happy certainties. More important, he does not rule out teleological explanations, as is evident from "The Strong Are Saying Nothing" and "Design." I shall return to the teleological problem in Chapter V; for now, the fact that there is such a problem can be indicated by a comparison of "Reluctance" with "Directive." In "Directive," once more, the completed quest will enable one to

Drink and be whole again beyond confusion,

[60] Louise Bogan, *Achievement in American Poetry, 1900-1950* (Chicago, 1951), p. 51.

[61] Elizabeth Shepley Sergeant, "Robert Frost: A Good Greek Out of New England," *New Republic*, XLIV (Sept. 30, 1925), 145.

[62] Keats's account of negative capability—"when a man is capable of being in uncertainties, mysteries, doubts, without any irritable reaching after fact and reason" (Keats, p. 103)—appropriately describes "Acquainted With the Night." And negative capability is one means of coping with that "aloneness with the world" that Basil Willey attributes to the post-Augustan poet, deprived of mediating mythologies (Willey, p. 298; and see above, pp. 27-28).

and it is difficult to see what wholeness consists of if it is
not a Lucretian acceptance, an invulnerability achieved by
purging one's self of fear and pity, the emotional ambiance of
wanting an intelligible purpose behind or within the natural
processes one must live with.   "Reluctance" offers the other
side of the coin:

> The heart is still aching to seek,
>   But the feet question 'Whither?'

And in the concluding stanza, the heart's impulse is treated,
not merely as nostalgic sentiment, but as a moral imperative
not

> To go with the drift of things,
>   To yield with a grace to reason,
> And bow and accept the end
>   Of a love or a season.

Such a moral imperative clearly implies a purpose to be realized—a purpose that, since it is not implicit in the Lucretian
flux of things and since it has an ethical dimension (going
"with the drift of things" is explicitly labeled a "treason"),
must be either a legitimately self-generated thing or an inti-
mation of some kind of reality that lies beyond the world of
material causation.   Either man's ethical orbit exists as a
thing in itself, contained by but independent of nature, or it
is determined by a gravitational field that may occasionally
reveal its presence through nature, as it does, for example, in
"Two Look at Two," but is ontologically other than nature,
as were Lucretius' gods or Plato's world of being.

Characteristically, Frost prefers not to choose between
these alternatives—among these alternatives, if one includes
the Lucretian attitude as a third possibility—and in "The Trial
by Existence" he manages, in effect, to have it both ways at
once.   The poem constructs a myth, in a fashion vaguely
reminiscent of the early Yeats:

And binding all is the hushed snow
Of the far-distant breaking wave.

Such lines could have come from "The Wanderings of Oisin."[63]
To the souls in paradise, God periodically and for obscure
reasons of his own proclaims

The gathering of the souls for birth,
The trial by existence named.

Only volunteers are accepted for reincarnation,

The obscuration upon earth,

and before his final commitment of himself, each volunteer
receives both a detailed account of what his new life will hold
for him and, as a final test, assurance that he will not have
even the grim satisfaction of remembering that he chose that
life of his own free will. None draw back, however, and
hence

'Tis of the essence of life here,
Though we choose greatly, still to lack
The lasting memory at all clear,
That life has for us on the wrack [sic]
Nothing but what we somehow chose;
Thus are we wholly stripped of pride
In the pain that has but one close,
Bearing it crushed and mystified.

[63] There may even be some question of Yeatsian influence with respect
to Frost. R. S. Newdick reports that, of five plays Frost produced in 1910
at Pinkerton Academy, during his school-teaching days there, two—
Cathleen ni Houlihan and *The Land of Heart's Desire*—were by Yeats,
the only contemporary playwright of the group and the only playwright
represented by more than one play. Robert S. Newdick, "Robert Frost
and the Dramatic," *New England Quarterly,* X (June, 1937), 263; and
cf. below, pp. 203-206.

One thinks again of the woman in "A Servant to Servants." Clearly, it would be an error to read the myth as an object of literal belief; my point is that in "The Trial by Existence" purpose is both self-generated, since we choose our destinies, and determined—but not by nature—since the choice is offered us by a benignly cryptic divinity whose objectives we do not understand, the same divinity who appears thirty years later in *A Masque of Reason,* still benign and still cryptic, to baffle Job all over again.

Both "Reluctance" and "The Trial by Existence" are early poems, first collected in 1913 in *A Boy's Will;* but while it is true that the explicitly Lucretian note becomes more marked in Frost's later work—"The Lesson for Today," from *A Witness Tree* (1942), and "Directive," from *Steeple Bush* (1947), are its finest expressions—still the uneasy alliance of seeming irreconcilables worked out in "The Trial by Existence" persists. "The Ax-Helve," again, recommends expressing the native grain of things, but the fact that the native grain needs expressing implies a degree of purpose that mere nature is unable to realize;[64] and if ax handles serve an exclusively human purpose, the education of children—

> Do you know, what we talked about was knowledge?
> Baptiste on his defense about the children
> He kept from school, or did his best to keep—

raises an epistemological question that may be more than utilitarian. In "The Aim Was Song," man's singing shows the

[64] Like "Directive," "The Ax-Helve" may owe something to *Walden.* In his final chapter, Thoreau tells of "an artist in the city of Kouroo who was disposed to strive after perfection." Having determined to make a staff that would be "perfect in all respects," he devoted millennia to the task, while time stood still for him. "When the finishing stroke was put to his work, it suddenly expanded before the eyes of the astonished artist into the fairest of all the creations of Brahma. He had made a new system in making a staff, a world with full and fair proportions. . . . The material was pure, and his art was pure; how could the result be other than wonderful?" Thoreau, pp. 272-273.

merely natural wind what wind can become when endowed with purpose, and "West-Running Brook" implies clearly that even human purposes are ultimately determined by designs far vaster than their own:

> Our life runs down in sending up the clock.
> The brook runs down in sending up our life.
> The sun runs down in sending up the brook.
> And there is something sending up the sun.

"West-Running Brook" labels this ultimate design natural:

> It is from this in nature we are from.

But it seems clear that nature, in this context, means not Lucretius' world of material causation but rather a total order with some sort of prime mover. "Stopping by Woods on a Snowy Evening" rejects nature's impersonal appeal in favor of purpose, but the carefully vague last stanza refuses to indicate whether such purpose is self-generated or determined:

> The woods are lovely, dark and deep.
> But I have promises to keep,
> And miles to go before I sleep,
> And miles to go before I sleep.

And "Two Tramps in Mud Time" puts the matter at least as explicitly as does "The Trial by Existence," if more didactically:

> Only where love and need are one,
> And the work is play for mortal stakes,
> Is the deed ever really done
> For Heaven and the future's sakes.

Love and need define the world of human purpose; Heaven

and the future, that of the cryptic final—or first—cause with whose objectives, at our best, we co-operate.

I have said that this final cause occasionally reveals itself through nature; in fact, though nature and the final cause seem ontologically distinct, it reveals itself only through nature, though its revelations are never complete and sometimes negative. In "The Most of It," for example, while nature clearly does not satisfy the speaker's desire for "counter-love, original response," the reason for that failure can be seen as something in the speaker rather than in the ultimate nature of things; he wants something too explicit, too personal, too unequivocal, and Frost's final cause, once more, is cryptic. Even in "Two Look at Two," the precautionary "as if" of the next-to-last line suggests the presumptuousness of supposing either that the experience involved defines a permanent relationship with nature or that it provides an explicit and personal answer to the lovers' unasked questions. "You must not try to make love definite," says Sherwood Anderson's Dr. Reefy, in *Winesburg, Ohio*.

It is the divine accident of life. If you try to be definite and sure about it and to live beneath the trees, where soft night winds blow, the long hot day of disappointment comes swiftly and the gritty dust from passing wagons gathers upon lips inflamed and made tender by kisses.[65]

Neither Frost nor his characters would talk quite like this, but Frost's transcendence, like Anderson's love, must not be pinned down for answers. "Too Anxious for Rivers," Frost's most explicit statement about the first cause, suggests that the first cause and love are alike because they are the same thing.

What set us on fire and what set us revolving

was quite simply "the effort, the essay of love."

[65] Sherwood Anderson, *Winesburg, Ohio* (New York, 1946), p. 164.

But Frost is seldom this unequivocal, and those intimations of more-than-human love that the obdurate matter of nature permits to filter through are never entirely realized, never more than unverifiable intuitions. Nature imposes limits, and if those limits result in the simplification of issues I have spoken of,[66] they also tend to deny that "limitless trait in the hearts of men"[67] that, impatient of limits, lays men open to mockery, heartbreak, or revelation in their quest for meaning. In "The Demiurge's Laugh," "The Cow in Apple Time," "The Bear," and "The Secret Sits," it is mockery; in "Reluctance," "My Butterfly," "The Pauper Witch of Grafton," "An Empty Threat," and "To a Moth Seen in Winter," it is heartbreak; and in "I Will Sing You One-O," "To Earthward," "Two Look at Two," "All Revelation," and "Happiness Makes Up in Height for What It Lacks in Length," it is revelation, in varying degrees. And "Neither Out Far Nor In Deep," which can be read as any one, or all, of the three, testifies both to nature's indispensability and to its unsatisfactoriness as a vehicle for intuitions of ultimate meaning.

> The people along the sand
> All turn and look one way.
> They turn their back on the land.
> They look at the sea all day.
>
> As long as it takes to pass
> A ship keeps raising its hull;
> The wetter ground like glass
> Reflects a standing gull.
>
> The land may vary more;
> But wherever the truth may be—
> The water comes ashore,
> And the people look at the sea.

[66] See above, pp. 16-22.
[67] "There Are Roughly Zones"; see above, p. 8.

They cannot look out far.
They cannot look in deep.
But when was that ever a bar
To any watch they keep?

Are we being asked to mock, or to pity, or to join the watch?
The only reasonable answer is, All three. The sea has been
a symbol of the infinite for as long as the idea of spatial or
temporal infinity has been with us, and if Freud was correct
in ascribing birth symbolism to dream images involving
water,[68] then at least some of its symbolic value—the sea as
source, as destiny, as the ultimate identity or loss of identity
we long for—is almost as old as human consciousness. In
fact, the sea, with its vastness and its wateriness, is almost the
only natural symbol for intuitions of an infinite source.[69]

   And yet if the sea is a symbol, it is also a natural fact, with
all the stubborn irreducibility of natural facts. The only thing
it can really, pragmatically communicate is itself, visible only
in part, transparent only up to a point, inexhaustible only in
the sense that you can't take it all in at one look—in the last
analysis, only a large but measurable quantity of impure water
that is much more likely to drown you than to tell you the
meaning of life. And there is nothing that the "limitless trait
in the hearts of men" can do to alter its factuality. The inevitable symbol can never be fully realized in the natural fact,
and from this mutual incompatibility comes, in Randall Jarrell's words, "the tone of the last lines—or, rather, their careful
suspension between several tones, as a piece of iron can be

[68] Sigmund Freud, *A General Introduction to Psychoanalysis,* trans.
Joan Riviere (Garden City, 1943), p. 137; cf. Wordsworth's "immortal
sea/ Which brought us hither" in "Ode on Intimations of Immortality."
[69] Citing "Neither Out Far Nor In Deep," with Whitman, Emerson,
Melville, and Hemingway, Richard Chase suggests that "these sea images
should serve to illustrate how very strong in American writers is the
tendency to find among the objects of nature only an occasion for responding to the hypnotic spell of the unconscious and the infinite."
Richard Chase, *Walt Whitman Reconsidered* (New York, 1955), pp. 171-
172.

held in the air between powerful enough magnets. . . ."[70]   One
can laugh at the frustrated message hunters, or be moved by
their wistful, impossible quest, or perceive in that quest the
intuition of some transcendent meaning that nature's stubborn
materiality has somehow let through.   It is ultimately because
it does let through such imperfect revelations that nature, in
Frost's poetry, possesses that persistent ethical or metaphysical
dimension I have spoken of at the beginning of this chapter.

What, then, do these revelations reveal?   Broadly speaking, they reveal a supernatural—in the literal sense—something not ourselves that makes for a higher degree of unity and
design in the universe than either natural process or human
solipsism can wholly account for, though they very nearly do.
The most fully realized revelation poems are "I Will Sing You
One-O" and "All Revelation"; the one has as its central image
a vision of astronomical order and cosmic process, the other
an almost Emersonian intuition of solipsism as reality:

> Eyes seeking the response of eyes
> Bring out the stars, bring out the flowers.

And yet neither poem rests in its image.   In "I Will Sing You
One-O," God is beyond infinite space; orderly natural process
is not all.   And "All Revelation" ends ambiguously:

> Eyes seeking the response of eyes
> Bring out the stars, bring out the flowers,
> Thus concentrating earth and skies
> So none need be afraid of size.
> All revelation has been ours.

Does the last line mean "We ourselves have created all our
revelations," or "All possible revelation has been bestowed on
us"?   Are our intuitions of order self-generated illusions, valid
only in the pragmatic sense that they enable us to get along
more comfortably in a world we never made, or are they legiti-

[70] Jarrell, p. 39.

mate revelations of unity and design that exist independently of our awareness of them? We cannot be sure; as in "Acquainted With the Night" and "Neither Out Far Nor In Deep," the final statement is equivocal.

In the face of such persistent ambiguity of statement, any attempt to reduce Frost's cosmology to diagrammatic accuracy is dangerous.

> We dance round in a ring and suppose,
> But the Secret sits in the middle and knows,[71]

writes Frost, and undoubtedly the safe course is to let it go at that. Nevertheless, it is possible to construct a more or less consistent and coherent statement out of the cosmological implications of Frost's work. Briefly, such a statement would indicate that the universe includes three orders of being—man, nature, and God; that these three orders are almost, but not quite, discontinuous; and that their common element is a tendency to express themselves in orderly configurations. Man builds walls, nature establishes zones and seasons, God constructs a cosmos. Thus in the broadest sense man has both divine and natural sanction for his characteristic effort to find, or invent, patterns and meanings. But only in the broadest sense; it is not at all clear that either nature or God is concerned with man's designs, that there are any moral imperatives other than those man makes for himself. Hence there are roughly three equally legitimate, equally "natural," lines of conduct open to man—for the sake of labels, the anthropocentric, the prudential, and the contemplative;[72] he may

[71] "The Secret Sits."

[72] These terms are not ideally satisfactory. Though they are useful as a means of distinguishing certain rough classes of conduct and attitude that Frost's people demonstrate, they do not, logically speaking, name the same kinds of categories. Yet such alternatives as "physiocentric" for "prudential" and "theocentric" or "teleocentric" for "contemplative" seem worse, not only because they are pretentious but because they suggest systematically clearer distinctions than are really to be found in Frost's poems. "Anthropocentric," however, seems necessary, as naming most accurately

construct his own designs, he may co-operate with nature, or he may wait for revelation. Each is attended by perils of absurdity, heartbreak, and destruction, but each has its appropriate mode of fulfillment. Anthropocentric man may achieve heroism, as in "In Equal Sacrifice,"[73] "To E. T.," "The Soldier," "Hannibal," "Riders," "To a Moth Seen in Winter," "The Lost Follower," or "The Courage to Be New." Prudential man gets by, with a minimum of pain and unhappiness, as in "Mowing," "Hyla Brook," "The Gum-Gatherer," "A Drumlin Woodchuck," "Build Soil," "Something for Hope," "One Step Backward Taken," or "The Broken Drought." And contemplative man may, though rarely, achieve essentially mystical insight into the divine configuration, as in "I Will Sing You One-O," or a sense of inscrutable correspondences among the different orders of being, as in "Two Look at Two."

Frost cannot clearly be said to favor any one of these three varieties of fulfilment over the other two, and it is this fact, I believe, this triple sense of man and his potentialities, that principally accounts for the ambiguity we have seen[74] in Frost's implied definitions of nature. Quantitatively speaking, it is probably true that he has less to say about contemplative man than about anthropocentric man and prudential man. To lapse briefly into judgment, I think that the solidest part of his output is the fine dramatic poems of *North of Boston* and *New Hampshire,* poems primarily concerned with man's qualified success or moving failure in achieving heroism or in getting by. These are, in fact, the ultimate values I have spoken of at the beginning of this chapter, values generated by man's efforts to work out a *modus vivendi* with the natural or supernatural world he has to live in; and it is because of the persistence with which such values provide the dynamics for his poems that Frost is a nature poet in the second of my two senses—the poet for whom external nature has a philosophically serious significance.

---

the particular quality in question, a quality that is of central importance in discussing Frost.

   [73] *A Boy's Will,* p. 44.   Not reprinted.   [74] See above, pp. 11-13.

2

Sermons in stones

To the medieval transcribers of the *Physiologus,* Cetegrande was not merely a fish; he was also a type of the devil, and by understanding Cetegrande's ways with littler fish, the attentive reader could forearm himself against the deceptions practiced by that diabolical original. Working from the same premise—that the moral and spiritual life of man corresponds with the physical and biological organization of the universe in large—Spenser produced ethically meaningful beasts and landscapes, Donne drew instructive analogies from fleas and the cosmos, and Phineas Fletcher, by attracting the praise of his contemporaries for

The Purple Island,[1] demonstrated that the seventeenth century saw more explicit moral significance in the world than does the twentieth. With such a premise, poets ran little danger of really irrelevant moralizing; they might be dull, but the morals they pointed were *in* the phenomena they described, not merely applied to those phenomena.

But that premise had already lost much of its force by the time of Donne and Fletcher. Donne's argument in "The Flea" does not convince the lady to whom he presents it, and in "The First Anniversary," the old correspondence between heaven and earth has been lost. And though the physical world still had ethical meaning to Wordsworth and Emerson two centuries later, that meaning was less accessible than it had been to the medieval mind.

The enormous success of the scientific abstractions, yielding on the one hand *matter* with its *simple location* in time and space, on the other hand *mind,* perceiving, suffering, reasoning, but not interfering, has foisted onto philosophy the task of accepting them as the most concrete rendering of fact. Thereby, modern philosophy has been ruined,[2]

writes Alfred North Whitehead of the intellectual revolution that deprived Cetegrande of his moral dimension and, for John Donne, called all in doubt. And in wrecking modern philosophy, it also complicated life for poets and moralists. When moral significance ceases to be clearly predicable of the world one experiences, when fish are merely fish—or, even more remotely, psychological events—than at least certain kinds of metaphor lose a degree of reality that we are compelled to believe they once had. It is hard to believe that Spenser's great metaphor—that the experience of working out one's salvation is like a series of chivalric quests—was for Spenser

[1] Douglas Bush, *English Literature in the Earlier Seventeenth Century* (London, 1945), p. 88.
[2] Alfred North Whitehead, *Science and the Modern World* (New York, 1948), p. 57.

merely an ingenious comparison, or that the dazzling images in the concluding cantos of the *Paradiso* were merely analogies. Rather they represent, as does the *Physiologus,* a way of looking at a world that was felt as real. Neither literal statements of things seen nor simple comparisons designed to clarify or ornament a statement, they express the conviction that material things are important chiefly because of the spiritual dynamics they embody, that beatific visions and roses, truth and good girls, occupy corresponding positions in their respective spheres of being, and that the making of metaphors is therefore a legitimate and valuable means of approaching truth, of focusing attention on matters of most importance.

But when nature is reduced to the "soundless, scentless, colourless . . . hurrying of material, endlessly, meaninglessly,"[3] then the only "truth" to which it affords an approach is that of an essentially skeptical materialism, with no clear place for beatific visions, spiritual dynamics, or moral edification; one must not look to such nature for immediately meaningful meaning. Addison's spacious firmament on high speaks of a divine creator, but it speaks of little else. Both quantitatively and qualitatively, Addison's universe is less meaningful than Spenser's or Dante's; it says fewer things, and the things it does say have less bearing on the lives of the people it says them to. It is, of course, true that Spenser and Dante were better poets than Addison. But they were not that much better than Wordsworth, for example, and the distinction here is as much a question of metaphysics as it is of talent. Under such circumstances, metaphor, becoming a matter of clarification or embellishment, something useful or something elegant, tended to lose its older status as something true. The attempt to recapture or to compensate for that sense of metaphor as an expression of reality has been a persistent concern of poets at least since the late eighteenth century. Wordsworth's plastic power

[3] Whitehead, p. 56.

of imagination, Matthew Arnold's unsatisfied hunger for a viable mode of feeling,[4] Emerson's ceaseless but not always consistent affirmations, and Wallace Stevens' quest for a supreme fiction all testify to the desire for a poetically valid world, a world that Dante and Spenser could take for granted.

So, more obliquely, do certain aspects of Frost's poetic practice. As Frost has never particularly concerned himself with an explicit theory of nature,[5] so he has never particularly concerned himself with an explicit theory of metaphor. And though he will occasionally construct a poem by developing a single metaphor—as he does, for example, in "The Silken Tent" and "There Are Roughly Zones," or, less obviously, in "All Revelation" and "A Star in a Stone-Boat"—he seldom commits himself, as it were, to any particular metaphor. As Cleanth Brooks observes of "The Code," "The very minimum of imagery is used," and again, "Frost does not think through his images; he requires statements."[6] Brooks cites "Two Tramps in Mud Time" as example, and one can add "Mending Wall," "The Census-Taker," "Birches," "Mowing," "The Tuft of Flowers," "Hyla Brook," "The Need of Being Versed in Country Things," "Sitting by a Bush in Broad Sunlight," "At Woodward's Gardens," and "The Vindictives" as further evidence of Frost's persistent unwillingness to let metaphor carry the final weight of his poems. Frost describes his own tendency in "Revelation":

> We make ourselves a place apart
>   Behind light words that tease and flout,
> But oh, the agitated heart
>   Till someone find us really out.
>
> 'Tis pity if the case require
>   (Or so we say) that in the end

[4] E.g., "The Buried Life," "Growing Old."
[5] See above, pp. 5-6.
[6] Cleanth Brooks, *Modern Poetry and the Tradition* (Chapel Hill, 1939), p. 111.

> We speak the literal to inspire
> The understanding of a friend.

> But so with all, from babes that play
> At hide-and-seek to God afar,
> So all who hide too well away
> Must speak and tell us where they are.

Even when the fundamental statement is conveyed metaphorically, Frost is likely to qualify it. In "Two Look at Two," the metaphor—man is to nature as these two people are to these two deer—is an "as if";[7] we are not allowed to forget that it is, after all, a metaphor. "A Star in a Stone-Boat" indicates that man's proper relationship to nature is epitomized in the speaker's mission to do better by fallen meteorites than putting them into stone walls. But the poem concludes with a strategic shift to mildly self-deprecatory understatement in the last stanza:

> Such as it is, it promises the prize
> Of the one world complete in any size
> That I am like to compass, fool or wise.

Again, we must not take the merely metaphorical statement too seriously. Brooks, again, remarks that in Frost

the occasional bold metaphor is confined to his very lightest poems: for example, to such a sally of self-ironic whimsy as "Canis Major" . . . . The audacity of his metaphor is thus in inverse proportion to the seriousness of the experience.[8]

I doubt that this apparent mistrust of metaphor is wholly accidental, or that it means merely, as R. P. Blackmur has argued,[9] that Frost characteristically ducks the real labor of making a poem. Rather I suspect that it expresses a funda-

---

[7] Cf. above, p. 31.   [8] Brooks, p. 111.
[9] R. P. Blackmur, "The Instincts of a Bard," *Nation,* CXLII (June 24, 1936), 817-819.

mental skepticism about the universe as a conceptually grasp-able phenomenon, about the real efficacy of the human mind as a means of understanding anything except perhaps itself. Lawrance Thompson tells us that Frost's

first and perhaps his keenest interest in the history of philosophy is a poet's pleasure in metaphors: a detached delight in the various analogies invoked by thinkers who have sought to define spirit in terms of matter.[10]

And he quotes Frost, from an unidentified source:

"Another metaphor that has interested us in our time and has done all our thinking for us is the metaphor of evolution . . . . It is a very brilliant metaphor, I acknowledge, though I myself get too tired of [hearing it said that] everything is evolution. I emanci-pate myself by simply saying that I didn't get up the metaphor and so am not much interested in it."[11]

That Frost is begging questions here seems obvious; *who* says that everything is evolution? My point is that, while reducing the history of philosophy to a series of ingenious or even bril-liant metaphors may be a legitimate effort, it is an effort that is likely to go hand in glove with either fanaticism or obscuran-tism. There is little of the fanatic in Frost, but there is a good deal of mistrust of mere intelligence.[12] Yvor Winters writes, of such poems as "The Road Not Taken," "The Sound of the Trees," "The Hill Wife," and "The Bearer of Evil Tidings":

. . . all have a single theme: the whimsical, accidental, and in-comprehensible nature of the formative decision; and I should like to point out that if one takes this view of the formative decision, one has cut oneself off from understanding most of human expe-rience, for in these terms there is nothing to be understood . . . .[13]

And it is on the whole true that one's sense of Frost's "philos-ophy" is a sense less of a coherent, systematic body of doctrine

[10] Lawrance Thompson, *Fire and Ice: The Art and Thought of Robert Frost* (New York, 1942), p. 191.
[11] *Ibid.*, p. 166.
[12] Cf. below, pp. 84-87.
[13] Yvor Winters, "Robert Frost: or, The Spiritual Drifter as Poet," *Sewanee Review*, LVI (Autumn, 1948), 568.

than of a collection of aphorisms, insights, and bits of pragmatic wisdom, quite miscellaneous and sometimes contradictory. Frost tends to distrust all efforts at understanding
the universe in terms of systematic intellectual formulations.

This is not an attempt at sniping; after all, one of the
commonest alternatives to doctrinal miscellaneousness is doctrinaire fanaticism—and in any case it is not necessary that
a poet should have all the answers. What I am getting at, to
take an appallingly literal-minded view of things, is this: to
visualize a situation (two people in relationship with two deer)
and to make a philosophically serious metaphor of it (this
relationship expresses man's relationship with nature) implies
that the larger relationship, though less obvious than the more
limited one, is also real. In "A Valediction: Forbidding
Mourning," the relationship between Donne's lovers is at least
as real as that between the points of his "stiff twin compasses";
in *The Faerie Queene,* the nameless protagonist's attempt to
realize within himself certain ethical and spiritual values is
not less but more real than the adventures of Spenser's alle-
goric knights and ladies. In however limited a sense, a metaphor implies a degree of correspondence between its terms.

But if my argument in Chapter I—that Frost's universe is
all but discontinuous—is valid, then such philosophically
serious metaphors occupy a distinctly anomalous position. If
the relationship between the world of man and the world of
nature is a purely formal one, a matter of those worlds' expressing themselves in orderly configurations whose only like-
ness is that they *are* orderly, then any intimations of a more
organic relationship are automatically suspect. They can only
be "as ifs"; they must be taken with substantial reservations,
with a considerable grain of irony. In terms of Wordsworth's
useful antithesis, they are the work, not of the shaping and
creative power of Imagination, but of the Fancy, a faculty
which "prides herself upon the curious subtilty and the successful elaboration with which she can detect . . . lurking affini-

ties,"[14] and whose function it is merely "to quicken and to beguile the temporal part of our nature . . . ."[15] Frost's metaphors are seldom more than fanciful, a fact that receives whimsical acknowledgment in "The Door in the Dark":

> In going from room to room in the dark,
> I reached out blindly to save my face,
> But neglected, however lightly, to lace
> My fingers and close my arms in an arc.
> A slim door got in past my guard,
> And hit me a blow in the head so hard
> I had my native simile jarred.
> So people and things don't pair any more
> With what they used to pair with before.

Frost's "native simile" is less durable than were Wordsworth's imaginatively perceived affinities. Fanciful comparisons also appear in "Moon Compasses":

> I stole forth dimly in the dripping pause
> Between two downpours to see what there was.
> And a masked moon had spread down compass rays
> To a cone mountain in the midnight haze,
> As if the final estimate were hers,
> And as it measured in her calipers,
> The mountain stood exalted in its place.
> So love will take between the hands a face. . . .

For all the poem's apparent visual echo of Blake's "Ancient of Days," the concluding image asserts no more than a geometric analogy. And in "Afterflakes," the speaker, seeing his own shadow in spite of the "thick of a teeming snowfall," realizes that it is merely the consequence of unusual weather

[14] "Preface to the Edition of 1815," in *The Poetical Works of William Wordsworth*, ed. Thomas Hutchinson (London, 1906), p. 957.
[15] *Ibid.*, p. 958.

conditions, not of appalling darkness in himself. Natural circumstances have tickled the misleading human tendency to find symbolic meaning in natural phenomena. Comparison with Wordsworth's "huge peak, black and huge" in Book I of *The Prelude* indicates clearly enough the difference between the Wordsworthian-imaginative and the Frostian-fanciful treatment of such natural images. For Frost, people and things don't pair any more. Frost's reluctance really to commit himself to metaphor has the same origin as Wordsworth's doctrine of imagination, the symbolists' yearning for transcendent meaning and experience, or Captain Ahab's ambiguously destructive pursuit of Moby Dick; all express the divided world of the post-Renaissance West, the wreckage of modern philosophy that Whitehead speaks of.

And yet Frost is a moralist, and not necessarily in the cant sense of the word; his analogies are regularly pointed ones, and it would be silly to deny that the point is frequently relevant. "In Hardwood Groves" does say something valid, not only about mortality in general but about the myth of progress. The question in "The Oven Bird"—"what to make of a diminished thing"—has plagued a good many of Frost's contemporaries, from Miniver Cheevy to James Joyce, whose Homeric parallel suggests, among other things, nostalgia for the *Odyssey's* epic largeness. "Brown's Descent" legitimately expresses the impossibility of accomplishing the impossible. "I will Sing You One-O" observes accurately enough that stars get along together better than people do; "Good-by and Keep Cold," that one cannot always think about everything; "On Taking from the Top to Broaden the Base," that Burns was right about mice and men. And the list could be extended indefinitely. In spite of himself, as it were, Frost finds the world meaningful.

Often enough, that meaning is arch, pedantic, and intrusive, redolent of the cracker barrel and the symposium in the country store. In "The Kitchen Chimney," Frost pleads with his house-builder to build the chimney "clear from the ground" rather than from a shelf:

> A shelf's for a clock or vase or picture,
> But I don't see why it should have to bear
> A chimney that only would serve to remind me
> Of castles I used to build in air.

In "Evil Tendencies Cancel," he asks:

> Will the blight end the chestnut?
> The farmers rather guess not.
> It keeps smoldering at the roots
> And sending up new shoots
> Till another parasite
> Shall come to end the blight.

"Everything is *really* all right," murmurs the vindicated shade of Doctor Pangloss. And in "Something for Hope," we are advised that we need only let our abandoned pasture develop a good crop of trees and then timber it off in order to have the pasture again as good as new:

> A cycle we'll say of a hundred years.
> Thus foresight does it and laissez faire,
> A virtue in which we all may share
> Unless a government interferes.

As Louise Bogan caustically remarks of the later poems, Frost "has come to hold so tightly to his 'views' that they at last have very nearly wiped out his vision."[16]

Lawrance Thompson points out that Frost's "Yankee manner," unsuccessfully employed, frequently results in "cold flatness, prosaic lines, extrinsic moralizings, faulty ellipsis, and obscurity," and he adds that "Frost knows himself well enough to live in the fear of these poetic vices."[17] And in spite of the

[16] Louise Bogan, *Achievement in American Poetry, 1900-1950* (Chicago, 1951), p. 51.
[17] Thompson, pp. 57-58.

occasional irritated temptation to dismiss Frost as merely an
arch rustic moralist, it is true that the poems are frequently
redeemed from being merely third-rate wisdom literature.
Frost's own formula for such redemption appears in his preface to Edwin Arlington Robinson's *King Jasper:*

The style is the man. Rather say that the style is the way the man
takes himself; and to be at all charming or even bearable, the way
is almost rigidly prescribed. If it is with outer seriousness, it must
be with inner humor. If it is with outer humor, it must be with
inner seriousness.[18]

And the same point emerges in his commendatory notice of
the colonial arch-rogue, Stephen Burroughs:

Could anything be more teasing to our proper prejudices than the
way Burroughs mixed the ingredients when he ran off on his
travels? He went not like a fool with no thought for the future
and nothing to his name but the horse between his legs. He took
with him a pocketful of sermons stolen from his father, in the one
fell act combining prudence, a respect for religion (as property)
and a respect for his father as a preacher. *He* knew how to put
the reverse on a ball so that when it was going it was also coming.[19]

Thus the clincher stanza of "The Kitchen Chimney" contains
sufficient mildly embarrassed self-deprecation to make it, if
somewhat arch, at least legitimately amusing. "Something
for Hope" becomes two-edged in its closing lines:

> Hope may not nourish a cow or horse,
> But spes alit agricolam 'tis said.

The whimsy may be mossy, but the irony is directed, not only
against worriers, but also against complacently timely plati-
tudes. And if "The Bear" presents man's intellectual history
as an endless and futile pendulum swing that "may be thought,

[18] Robert Frost, introduction to Edwin Arlington Robinson, *King Jasper*
(New York, 1935), p. xiii.
[19] Robert Frost, "Stephen Burroughs," in *Cupid and Lion* (New York,
n.d.), p. 14.

but only so to speak," still the speaker includes himself in his indictment.

> The universe seems cramped to you and me,

not just to you, and the man-bear, if essentially baggy and funny, is still pathetic; he has remote affinity with Willy Loman, in *Death of a Salesman,* or even perhaps with Hamlet. Like Burroughs, Frost has the tactical wisdom to mix his ingredients, especially when moralizing. Deprived of the world in which Cetegrande was a moral fact, and apparently unwilling to risk the development of such compensatory doctrines as Wordsworth's plastic imagination, Frost covers himself by irony and self-mockery.

Thus Frost's moralized metaphors are characteristically marked by a kind of defensively ironic whimsy, the gesture of what I have called in Chapter I prudential man, the man who is primarily concerned with getting by and who co-operates with nature because such co-operation enables him to get by.[20] Insofar as they are whimsical, they warn one off from trying to construct metaphysics from them; insofar as they are moralized, they provide a set of practical hints for getting by with the world one must live in. But man, even Frost's man, cannot live by practical hints alone. The only moderately developed figure in Frost's poems who tries—Loren, in "Blueberries"—is, as I have said,[21] an object of at least partial contempt. Loren has no apparent sense of that "limitless trait in the hearts of men"[22] that blesses, or curses, contemplative man, leaving him chronically dissatisfied with mere getting by, with a world that is not broadly and deeply meaningful. To prudential man, such difficulties are likely to be objects of mockery, as they are in "The Bear," "On Looking Up by Chance at the Constellations," and perhaps "The Star-Split-

[20] See above, pp. 49-50.
[21] See above, p. 9.
[22] "There Are Roughly Zones"; see above, pp. 8, 46.

ter." But Frost also treats that "limitless trait" other than mockingly, and when he does, he tends to break away from merely defensive whimsy and the simpler figurative devices of analogy and exemplum toward serious wit on the one hand and toward either statement or symbol on the other.

That wit may be serious is clear from the poetry of Donne and Marvell, from the bitter irony of Swift's *Modest Proposal,* and from the verbal ingenuities of *Finnegans Wake.* The conceit in "The Flood"—that

Blood has been harder to dam back than water

because, since man walks upright, blood is

Held high at so unnatural a level—

is a case in point. So is the grim jocularity of "A Loose Mountain," with its insistence on an at least potentially malevolent universe. In such poems the speaker is not prudential man, concerned with avoiding unpleasantness and excess and making fun of those who are not so concerned. Rather it is contemplative man, recognizing in himself and others an apparently ineradicable tendency to go beyond merely prudential limits in thought or behavior, and accepting, if grimly, what he sees.

And as contemplative man's wit is different, at least in degree, from prudential man's, so are his images. I have said that, under certain circumstances, the work of analogy in Frost's poems is done by statement or symbol. Statement needs no defining; the conclusion of "Two Tramps in Mud Time," in which the speaker insists on a rapprochement between his prudential values and his more-than-prudential desire for meaning in his world, or of "Good-by and Keep Cold," in which he whimsically accepts, with crossed fingers, the limited efficacy of his own officiousness, exemplifies the procedure. By symbol, I mean, roughly speaking, an image with archetypal overtones,[23] an image whose significance cannot be expressed in any simple, single, wholly coherent statement. Such complexity is, of course, characteristic of all metaphors, or at least of all but the most elementary. Even Joyce Kilmer's tree is like a woman in more ways than one. But for practical purposes, a distinction can be made between, for example, the lady's nectar in Ben Jonson's "Song: To Celia" and the vision of mermaids at the close of "The Love Song of J. Alfred Prufrock," though the distinction is not an invidious one; the latter image touches a whole complex of unconscious or half-conscious dynamics that are relevant to our understanding of Prufrock's mind and world. Frost's image of man as a caged bear in "The Bear" exemplifies the one sort; the penetration of subterranean mysteries in "All Revelation," the other.

It is not always easy to distinguish satisfactorily between statement and symbol in Frost's work, and there may be no very compelling reason for insisting on the distinction. How is one to classify such a poem as "The Gift Outright," for example? At first sight, the poem seems wholly statement, quite bare of imagery except for the conventional anthropomorphizing of the land as "she" and the momentarily arresting pun on "deed" in line thirteen:

(The deed of gift was many deeds of war).

The statement the poem makes is one that I personally, and perhaps irrelevantly, distrust. On the one hand, it incorporates the agrarian premise—as expressed, for example, in *I'll Take My Stand*—[24] that man's most important and valuable relationship is with the land; and that premise seems finally as limited, as abstract, and as doctrinaire as the industrial premises that the contributors to *I'll Take My Stand,* and

[23] See below, pp. 72-75.
[24] Twelve Southerners, *I'll Take My Stand: The South and the Agrarian Tradition* (New York, 1930).

Frost with them, dislike. On the other hand, it seems to me to place too high a value on the American historical experience, almost the Manifest Destiny idea, which has surely been a more persistent source of trouble than of the really valuable story, art, or enhancement that Frost attributes to it. My reaction here may be mere bias; my point is that, despite that bias, I find it impossible to read the poem without what I can only call a sense of its profundity, a sense that I believe has very little to do with the essentially geopolitical statement it makes.

And second thoughts indicate that statement does only part of the poem's work, that the statements themselves are made largely in terms of an implicit and quite possibly unconscious metaphor that equates the transition from colonial to national status with a quite complex psychic experience, the experience of freeing oneself from infantile erotic fixations, thus becoming capable of responsible action and self-evaluation and of mature, mutual love. It is not until one has broken away from early Oedipal fixation ("we were England's, still colonials") that one can emerge from fantasy relationships into mature acceptance of reality ("Such as we were," "Such as she was"), undertake responsible action ("deeds of war"), and really give oneself to another (find "salvation in surrender"), to the mutual benefit of both parties (fulfilment of the land's "vaguely realizing westward," development from her "still unstoried, artless, unenhanced" condition to what "she would become"). The land's gender is not merely a verbal convention, nor is the pun on "deed of gift" (giving oneself, the act of love) and "deeds of war" (the act of violence) mere word play; Freud maintains that dream images of "experiencing some violence" or "being threatened with weapons" symbolize sexual intercourse.[25] It would be an unnecessary piece of foolishness to maintain that "The Gift Outright" must be read in this way, that such a reading gives one the poem's real

[25] Sigmund Freud, *A General Introduction to Psychoanalysis*, trans. Joan Riviere (Garden City, 1943), p. 140.

meaning. But the presence of such implications as these, re-inforcing the statements the poem makes, makes it a more powerful poem than would the statements alone. The "limit-less trait" has found its locus and its justification in the com-mon, profound experience of all men and women everywhere.

Thus certain images—better, perhaps, image-statements—in certain poems serve as vehicles for highly complex states of feeling, avoiding the oversimplification likely to accompany prudential moralizing. "An Empty Threat" deals with the opposing pressures experienced by prudential man, with his desire to get by, and anthropocentric man,[26] with his capacity for heroic sacrifice. "A Line-Storm Song" records a powerful but ambivalently felt love experience, touched with a hint of sentimental romantic sadism:

> Oh, never this whelming east wind swells
> But it seems like the sea's return
> To the ancient lands where it left the shells
> Before the age of the fern;
> And it seems like the time when after doubt
> Our love came back amain.
> Oh, come forth into the storm and rout
> And be my love in the rain.

The experience is powerful partly because it does contain un-resolved but psychologically valid implications of cruelty and self-destruction that form a kind of counterpoint with the apparently ingenuous theme of happy love. The quiet meta-phor of "Devotion," if it expresses the relationship of Penelope and Odysseus, also expresses that of Paolo and Francesca:

> The heart can think of no devotion
> Greater than being shore to the ocean—
> Holding the curve of one position,
> Counting an endless repetition.

[26] See above, pp. 49-50.

The speaker of "Desert Places," confronted by wintry desolation and an infinite and empty universe, is more profoundly moved by the infinite desolation that exists within himself—to stretch a point, the id's ambivalent chaos. And "All Revelation," with its penetration of and withdrawal from enclosed places underground—possibly an oblique echo of Plato's cave, or a manifestation of similar unconscious motifs—expresses a pattern not unlike that of "The Gift Outright," an experience by means of which one is enabled to face his responsibility of accepting the world.

Frost's world is the world of Joyce and Yeats, of Eliot and Pound, of the Politburo and the National Association of Manufacturers; a world that does not, as it were, automatically provide one with a viable set of values and the images for expressing it; a world whose common values tend to be pragmatic or ideological, miscellaneous or doctrinaire, rather than metaphysically validated and hence subject to metaphorical exploitation in the manner of the *Physiologus,* of Dante or Spenser. Confronted with such a situation, poets of at least the past century and a half have more and more tended either to work out their own sources of imagery (Yeats reported that the spirits told him they had come "to give you metaphors for poetry")[27] or to rely, deliberately or not, on *felt* images whose justification, at their best, is that, persisting for centuries in art and myth, they express fundamental, common experiences of the race. Frost has, on the whole, been unwilling to work out a system of images comparable to that in Yeats's *A Vision.*[28] But frequently—more frequently, I think, than is usually recognized—he does draw on that ancient reservoir of image material, to the considerable enrichment of his poetry. There are thus two Frosts (in other senses as well)—the analogy-constructor and the myth-exploiter; and in the following chapter I shall be concerned with the second.

[27] Quoted by Louis MacNeice, *The Poetry of W. B. Yeats* (New York, 1941), p. 124.
[28] See below, pp. 207-212.

3

An Eden myth

Like most enduring myths, that of the loss of Eden is not limited by time, place, or ethnic group. Most familiar to Western readers in the version recorded in Genesis and modified by subsequent Jewish and Christian exegetes, it is nevertheless broadly human rather than specifically Judaeo-Christian. The Hesiodic Golden Age is a Greek Eden, the innocent, painless, unproblematic condition from which mankind has degenerated through successive stages of silver, bronze, and iron—for the Jacobean Donne, rusty iron. Genesis leaves man to eat his bread in sorrow and the sweat of his face all the days of his life; the *Works and Days* declares that he will "rest not by day from labour and trouble, nor from the spoiler in the night season."[1] Egyptian prayers and meditations look back to a time before man had learned evil and deplore the loss of wisdom,[2] and the Mesopotamian Tilmun myth offers a curiously wistful Eden in which all things, but particularly unpleasant things, are merely potential and hence painless.[3] Melanesian myth includes explanations of man's loss of immortality and hints at a subterranean Paradise to which he returns after death.[4] In a word, the Eden myth, like the death-and-resurrection myth, is a myth, an expression of a persistent pattern of experience and emotion, fears and desires that are common both to primitive societies and to at least the less fully accessible levels of all men's minds.

This being the case, it would be surprising indeed if elements of the Eden myth did not appear with some persistence in literature. And, of course, they do. Pointing as it does to a lost but infinitely desirable past, a time of idyllic stability and painless virtue, the myth might safely be expected to be particularly popular as a motif in periods characterized by a more than usually emphatic absence of those qualities, and this expectation too has been fulfilled, at least in English literature. It is by now an accepted truth that the seventeenth century was par excellence the English century of intellectual transition and its attendant difficulties, and *Paradise Lost* is the myth's most ambitious English rendering. It may not be true that more seventeenth-century poets found their themes in the awareness of Paradise, lost or found, than did those of any preceding century, but it is clear that Milton was not, in this respect, alone. In Michael Drayton's "To the Virginian

[1] Hesiod, *Works and Days* 109, tr. F. M. Cornford, in *Greek Religious Thought from Homer to the Age of Alexander,* ed. F. M. Cornford (London, 1923), p. 26.

[2] John A. Wilson, "Egypt," *Before Philosophy* (London, 1949), pp. 117-118 and 129-130.

[3] Thorkild Jacobsen, "Mesopotamia," *Before Philosophy,* p. 173.

[4] Bronislaw Malinowski, "Myth in Primitive Psychology," *Magic, Science and Religion, and Other Essays* (Garden City, 1954), pp. 107, 127, and 135.

Voyage," the New World is "Earth's only paradise," still enjoying its Golden Age.   Andrew Marvell's garden is also Adam's, little T. C. names flowers as Adam named animals, and "To His Coy Mistress" opens with an ironic statement of idyllic and Edenic love by a speaker who is only too aware of the fallen state.   Henry Vaughan invokes sinless childhood, the image of

> that first white age when we
> Lived by the earth's mere charity![5]

Thomas Traherne echoes and sometimes intensifies Vaughan's Eden-vision of childhood.   And though Donne's explicitly religious poetry is mainly characterized by a powerful sense of sin and unworthiness without much specific reference to the Fall or the Garden, "The First Anniversary" dwells on postlapsarian degeneration, and again and again the secular love poems develop the theme of two lovers who constitute an entire world—a situation that, in the Judaeo-Christian version of history, existed but once, and in Paradise.

It is not my purpose here to attempt a detailed examination of the Eden myth as it appears in English and American literature—merely to call attention to its presence and to something of its protean variety.   Thus in the eighteenth century Rasselas had the happy valley, Gulliver the land of the Houyhnhnms, and Robinson Crusoe his island; and of course there was Blake, singing of innocence and experience.   Wordsworth's feeling for childhood and for nature has a distinctly Edenic aura; more remotely, so does Keats's yearning for emotional simplicity in "The Eve of St. Agnes," "Ode to a Nightingale," and "Ode on a Grecian Urn."   Thoreau's Walden Pond was a kind of Eden surrogate—and Lawrance Thompson tells us that, with *Robinson Crusoe, Walden* is one of Frost's favorite books.[6]

---

[5] "Metrum V."

[6] Lawrance Thompson, *Fire and Ice: The Art and Thought of Robert Frost* (New York, 1942), p. 207.

Later in the nineteenth century British decadents, equally fascinated by innocence and the impossibly immoral, celebrated both; in "The Harlot's House" and "Impression du Matin," Oscar Wilde juxtaposed pre- and postlapsarian images, and, in *The Picture of Dorian Gray,* presented an absurd but exotic version of the fall of man. Henry James, less flamboyant but more subtle than Wilde, dealt again and again with the ambiguous impact of evil upon the innocent, with the darker ambiguities of innocence itself, and, as William Troy has pointed out,[7] with crucial decisions and disastrous choices that take place in gardens. And in *The American Adam,* R. W. B. Lewis, discussing such seemingly disparate figures as Hawthorne and the elder Holmes, Whitman and the theologian Horace Bushnell, Melville and F. Scott Fitzgerald, compares the history of nineteenth-century American thought and literature to "the unfolding course of a dialogue: a dialogue more or less philosophic in nature and, like Plato's, containing a number of voices," whose central theme is the image of "the authentic American as a figure of heroic innocence and vast potentialities, poised at the start of a new history"[8]—in a word, the figure of Adam in Paradise. One can add, at random, *Lost Horizon, The Plumed Serpent, Back to Methuselah, The Death of the Heart, The House at Pooh Corner,* and *Li'l Abner.*

These later writings bring one a long way from Milton, and in doing so, they testify both to the persistence of the Eden theme and, since most of them have been divorced from a specifically Judaeo-Christian context, to its mythical quality, a quality not dependent on any particular religious tradition. Like Donne's microcosmic lovers, they are by-products of the human condition generally rather than of a theology—expressions, once more, of experience and emotion, fears and desires that are common to us all. All myths—at least all such persistent myths—are presumably similar expressions, though

[7] William Troy, "The Altar of Henry James," in F. W. Dupee, *The Question of Henry James* (New York, 1945), pp. 268-269.

[8] R. W. B. Lewis, *The American Adam: Innocence, Tragedy and Tradition in the Nineteenth Century* (Chicago, 1955), p. 1.

they may express different sorts of impulse, and though they may develop, by changing circumstances and independent literary exploitation, in different ways. Thus, at its most obvious level, the Eden myth is an attempt to objectify, and thus in a sense to master, the felt difficulty, both moral and physical, that is inherent in the ordinary human condition.[9] There was a time when things were different. But through human imperfection (Genesis and Hesiod), antagonism between natural elements (Tilmun myth), or even trivial misunderstanding (Melanesia), Eden has been lost and we must face the world of mortality, pain, ambivalence, and excruciating moral choice. For my immediate purpose, the nature of the particular explanation is of less significance than the thing explained—the contrast, that is, between the world one knows and the world one can imagine. It is the presence of this element that justifies one in treating as a class the writers and writings specified above.

Maud Bodkin, borrowing from Jung, offers a useful term for discussing such mythic themes:

I shall use the term "archetypal pattern" to refer to that within us which . . . leaps in response to the effective presentation in poetry of an ancient theme. The hypothesis to be examined is that in poetry . . . we may identify themes having a particular form or pattern which persists amid variations from age to age, and which corresponds to a pattern or configuration of emotional tendencies in the minds of those who are stirred by the theme.[10]

It is my contention in this chapter that the Eden theme reflects such an "archetypal pattern," and that a considerable portion of Robert Frost's poetry can profitably be examined in terms of that theme.

[9] I am aware that such contemporary anthropologists as Malinowski reject the etiological explanation of myth. Here, however, I am concerned not with the question of origins, of where such a myth comes from, but with the matter of its survival as a living force, removed from the primitive context that gave it birth yet still operative in the psychic life of men who may know nothing of its original value.

[10] Maud Bodkin, *Archetypal Patterns in Poetry: Psychological Studies of Imagination* (London, 1934), p. 4.

At the same time, I do not maintain that Frost is, in any very real sense, a kind of contemporary Milton, deliberately restating the loss of Paradise and the fall of man. The examples of Edenic literature I have cited indicate the widely varying degrees of explicitness with which such themes can be handled. Though Milton was hardly a scriptural literalist, his Eden *is* Eden, his fall the Fall, and it would be hard to believe that the inventor of Shangri-La did not cast a number of backward glances at Genesis and its subsequent tradition. But Portia Quayne's discovery of evil does not inevitably call to mind either Milton or Genesis; and, if one can accept Donne's lovers or Keats's fantasies as Edenic, it must be on the assumption that they represent, not clearly conscious recollections of the story, but rather independent expressions of the same fundamental impulses, of the same archetypal pattern or some part of it. In a word, it is not necessary to assume a wholly deliberate intention in an artist whose work reflects or embodies the myth. As Miss Bodkin observes of certain images in "The Rime of the Ancient Mariner,"

they are symbolic only in the sense that, by the poet as by some at least of his readers, the images are valued because they give— even though this function remain unrecognized—expression to feelings that were seeking a language to relieve their inner urgency.[11]

And again, of John Livingston Lowes's examination of Coleridge's sources, in *The Road to Xanadu,* she urges that

it is not a complete account of the poem, as an imaginative achievement, to trace the literary sources of its imagery and to refer to the effort of conscious thought and will ordering, in accordance with a logically conceived design, the chaos of "fortuitously blending" elements. The design itself, I urge, is determined by forces that do not lie directly open to thought, nor to the control of the will . . . .[12]

It is with such subliminal forces—or, to speak more accurately,

[11] Bodkin, p. 35.
[12] *Ibid.,* p. 54.

with the manifestations of such forces in Frost's poems—that I shall be primarily concerned.

The distinction just made is an important one. To echo a point already made in the preface, I am not primarily concerned with Frost the man, or even with Frost the author of a body of poems, but with the ideas those poems express, as it were anonymously—ideally, assuming only that they are the product of a person of our time with more or less standard psychic equipment and not of an electronic brain. To quote Miss Bodkin again:

. . . our aim here . . . is not primarily to arrive at a conclusion concerning the poet's individual experience, but to penetrate to forces present within the experience of poet and reader alike—[13]

in brief, to an archetypal pattern. And Jung insists (his italics) that

contents of an archetypal character are manifestations of processes in the collective unconscious. Hence they do not refer to anything that is or has been conscious, but to something *essentially unconscious.* In the last analysis, therefore, *it is impossible to say what they refer to.* Every interpretation necessarily remains an "as-if." The ultimate core of meaning may be circumscribed but not defined.[14]

This proposition contains an important precaution for both reader and writer of this chapter—that examination of partly or wholly unconscious elements in a writer's work is not to be confused with analysis of his *Weltanschauung* or his morality, and that, if it is to be used as material for such analysis, it must be handled with infinite caution, in support of rather than instead of evidence of a less cryptic and inaccessible nature. Otherwise, one runs the risk of indulging in a critical snark hunt, and of bagging a boojum.

To make the same point in another way, there is not much

[13] Bodkin, p. 157.
[14] Carl Gustav Jung and Caroly Kerényi, *Essays on a Science of Mythology: The Myth of the Divine Child and the Mysteries of Eleusis,* Bollingen Series XXII (New York, 1949), p. 104.

about Eden and the fall of man in Robert Frost's poems. But there is a good deal about certain themes and motifs that have particularly tended to occur in conjunction with one another in the work of other writers who *have* been concerned with Eden and the fall of man and for whom an Eden myth has provided a focus. Now, much of Frost's work—much of what I believe to be Frost's best work—does not very clearly have such a focus; on the face of things, it is not easy to fit "Design" and "The Discovery of the Madeiras" into the same context with "The Pasture" and "The Peaceful Shepherd." But for purposes of practical criticism—and these poems were after all written by the same man—the assumption of an Eden myth lurking somewhere in the background is an extremely useful device because, as we shall see, such an assumption enables one to see these disparate poems in relationship with one another, a relationship that is something more than the fact of common authorship. This being the case, it does not matter greatly whether the "archetypal pattern" thus revealed is a genuinely determining element or merely a useful hypothesis; either way, it will have served its purpose—to throw some additional light on Frost's poetry.

The Eden motif is most clearly evident in Frost's earlier work, roughly through *New Hampshire* (1923), though it is at least sporadically, and importantly, in evidence through the later volumes as well. Thus in *A Boy's Will* (1913), perhaps the most Edenic of Frost's books, "A Prayer in Spring," "Flower-Gathering," "Mowing," and "Reluctance" all reflect, in different manners to be touched on shortly, the Eden situation. But the same thing is true of "A Winter Eden," from *West-Running Brook* (1928), and of "In the Long Night" and "Directive," from *Steeple Bush* (1947). In terms of this limited approach, the later work is more post- than prelapsarian, hence less immediately Edenic, and I shall show later in this chapter that the deepening anti-intellectual bias of Frost's later work may be thought of as an extension of certain

Eden implications, an attempt to retain a state of innocence amid circumstances that make such retention extremely difficult at best. The merely quantitative and chronological facts, however, are not particularly important. What Frost derives from the myth is less an explicit subject matter to be treated discursively, as in *Paradise Lost,* than a more or less persistent set of motifs that, without too much wrenching, can be seen as constituting a pattern, probably not clearly intended but nonetheless there. Hence the present treatment will be thematic rather than chronological.

The most obvious sort of Eden material clearly consists of direct, specific references or images derived from the familiar Biblical story, and there are a handful of these in Frost's work. "Nothing Gold Can Stay," "A Winter Eden," and "Never Again Would Birds' Song Be the Same" are constructed on such references. "New Hampshire" contains a reference to

> veritable
> Pre-primitives of the white race, dawn people,
> Like those who furnished Adam's sons with wives.

"Unharvested" speaks of

> an apple fall
> As complete as the apple had given man.

And in "The Ax-Helve," Baptiste stands

> the ax there on its horse's hoof,
> Erect, but not without its waves, as when
> The snake stood up for evil in the Garden.

There are other poems in which it seems likely that memories of the Eden story, or more probably of *Paradise Lost,* have been at work. Thus "Paul's Wife" includes a kind of lumberjack version of the creation and marriage of Eve. "Flower-Gathering" and "A Dream Pang" remotely echo Adam's and Eve's brief separation immediately before the Fall. "A Prayer in Spring" is a prayer for dwellers in Paradise. The moral tag, if that is what it is, in "Mowing"—

The fact is the sweetest dream that labor knows—

may be dubious sociology in an industrial world but is a good reading of the prelapsarian psychology involved with Adam's labor in the Garden. And surely "Reluctance," if it suggests Oscar Wilde's Tired Hedonists' Club, also suggests the departure from Paradise.

But the number of such more or less explicit references in Frost's poems—and the less explicit ones are admittedly pretty dubious—is too small to provide the basis for a responsible thesis. My argument—that an examination of Frost's work in terms of the Eden myth, or archetype, may be serviceable as one means toward an evaluation of that work—depends largely on evidence provided by poems in which there is relatively little question of deliberate intention on Frost's part, poems whose implications, fortuitously or not, reveal elements of an Eden pattern—such elements as a condition of innocence, a fallen condition in which one may remember or desire that lost innocence and an attendant condition of melancholy engendered by such mixing of memory and desire, or a situation in which the relationship between two lovers—Donne's theme again—defines, as it were, the entire operative universe.[15] *A Boy's Will* particularly is dominated by such

[15] Jung, again, seems to provide authority for this consideration of fragments that, pieced together, constitute a myth. He speaks of being "forced to assume that we must be dealing with 'autochthonous' revivals independent of all tradition, and, consequently, that 'myth-forming' structural elements must be present in the unconscious mind.

"These products are never (at least very seldom) myths with a definite form but rather mythological components which, because of their typical value, we can call 'motifs,' 'primordial images,' types or—as I have named them—*archetypes*" (Jung and Kerényi, pp. 99-100). I assume that the

implications; at least, to speak more accurately, the Eden motifs in *A Boy's Will* are more persistently apparent than in much of the later work. And while there would be little point in attempting an exhaustive analysis or classification of all the poems in the book, some detailed analysis is clearly in order.

Most obviously Edenic of these Eden motifs in *A Boy's Will* is that of two lovers who constitute their own world— Adam and Eve in Paradise—and Frost exploits it with considerable variety. Thus "Going for Water," "In Neglect," and "A Line-Storm Song" celebrate the lovers' isolation from others of their kind. "Love and a Question" raises, but does not answer, the question of how to deal with intrusions into that idyllic isolation, the appearance of ethical complexity— possibly the serpent as a third personality in Adam's garden; "Paul's Wife," in *New Hampshire* (1923), touches on the same theme. "Revelation" rejects total solitude in favor of a shared solitude, as did Milton's Adam in debate with God. "Flower-Gathering," "Waiting," and "A Dream Pang" render idyllic togetherness more idyllic by presenting temporary or imagined separation. In "Wind and Window Flower," the irresolute flower rejects the wind's plea and fails in love; and that failure is re-enacted, more harrowingly, by the hysterical girl of "The Subverted Flower," in *A Witness Tree* (1942). "Storm Fear," in a way the most interesting of these "two alone" poems, brings the eternal note of ambivalence in; even shared solitude can be dangerous, as it is, with tragic desperation, in such later poems as "The Fear," "A Servant to Servants," "Home Burial," "The Housekeeper," or "The Hill Wife," from *North of Boston* (1914) and *Mountain Interval* (1916). Once more, if the theme is most clearly apparent in *A Boy's Will*, it nevertheless persists.

But its persistence, I believe, is that of a function, in the mathematical sense, rather than of an independent quantity.

Eden myth *in toto* is a "myth with a definite form" and that the implicit elements I have indicated correspond, at least roughly, with Jung's "mythological components."

That is, Adam's and Eve's idyllic solitude in *Paradise Lost* depends on their maintaining a state of innocence, and that solitude becomes a source of melancholy only after the Fall has rendered it unattainable. Similarly, the idyllic lovers in "Love and a Question" feel, quite accurately, that their innocent Eden is threatened by the arrival of the stranger with his unspoken demand for the exercise of fallen man's knowledge of good and evil; and the potential Eden in "The Discovery of the Madeiras" fails to be Edenic because the woman, obsessed by a conviction of sin, finds herself unworthy of it. The theme of shared solitude has its roots and its meaning in the broader themes of innocence and postlapsarian melancholy; it is with these broader themes that I shall be primarily concerned in this chapter, and innocence clearly has logical priority.

Superficially, at least, innocence in Frost means different things in different poems. Inevitably, there is "The Pasture," which exhibits a simple, receptive happiness in common objects and processes. There is the old lady of "The Black Cottage," who believes quite simply that people are people, created free and equal, and that the Civil War had settled the matter once and for all.

> Strange how such innocence gets its own way,

observes the minister to his companion. And the near-Blakeian shepherd of "The Peaceful Shepherd," manifesting an innocence that is nine-tenths irony, wistfully regrets that the constellations include

> the Crown of Rule,
> The Scales of Trade, the Cross of Faith,

because, ruling in our lives, they have produced wars.

But the innocence that I am particularly concerned with here is something more fundamental than the instances just

cited, though it is implicit in them.   Thus the peaceful shepherd's wish is a fantasy of imposing his will on his environment:

> If heaven were to do again,
> And on the pasture bars
> I leaned to line the figures in
> Between the dotted stars,

he would manage things differently.   The old lady's innocence
get its own way by remaining totally unaware of alternative
points of view; the minister, willing to change the Creed "a
very little" to please younger members of his congregation,
cannot bring himself to do so for thought of what it would do
to the "old tremulous bonnet in the pew."   Her universe shapes
itself to her will, even though that will is unexpressed.   And,
at the risk of forcing an issue or laboring over the obvious,
the environment provided by the common objects and processes of "The Pasture," though perfectly real, is the product of
deliberate selection, of that withdrawal according to plan by
which the speaker of "New Hampshire" simplifies his life;[16]
in this limited sense, that environment is a creation of the will.
To be sure, such deliberate selection is something we all do all
the time; it provides the only way of reducing the universe to
manageable size.   I have no intention of either quarreling with
Frost's selection or claiming that the Frost of "The Pasture" is,
or is not, the real Frost—only that here, as in the other poems
just cited, innocence appears in conjunction with an environment that is, to one degree or another, subject to individual
will.

Such plastic environments appear in a good many of
Frost's poems, sometimes as a kind of basic metaphor, sometimes as no more than a brief whimsy.   Without going beyond
the poems in *A Boy's Will,* one can indicate something of the
idea's persistence.   In "Into My Own," the speaker creates
an imaginary wilderness, wishing

[16] See above p. 16.

>   that those dark trees,
> So old and firm they scarcely show the breeze,
> Were not, as 'twere, the merest mask of gloom,
> But stretched away unto the edge of doom.

In "Ghost House," he dwells

>   in a lonely house I know
> That vanished many a summer ago,

and peoples it with ghosts, who provide

>   As sweet companions as might be had.

Surely part at least of his companions' sweetness lies in the fact that they do not interfere with his wistful fantasies.   In "A Late Walk," he whimsically concludes that a late autumn leaf,

>   Disturbed, I doubt not, by my thought,
>   Comes softly rattling down.

In "Asking for Roses," a poem not reprinted in later collections, the boy and his Mary call upon an abandoned rose garden's long-dead owner, who

>   comes on us mistily shining
> And grants us by silence the boon of her roses.

In "In a Vale," a chorus of spectral flower maidens comes out of a ringing fen every night to tell the boy

>   Why the flower has odor, the bird has song.

In "The Vantage Point," the world of men is or is not there, depending on whether or not he is looking at it.   In "Mowing,"

The fact is the sweetest dream that labor knows,

but only, unless one is willing to generalize dangerously, when "labor" means the imposing of one's will on an environment that offers no complicated resistance.   In "The Trial by Existence," we select our destinies.   And in "Reluctance," it is treason of the heart

> To go with the drift of things,
>   To yield with a grace to reason,
> And bow and accept the end
>   Of a love or a season—

that is, to accept a world that is not necessarily molded to the heart's desire.

This link between innocence and manageable environment is not peculiar to Frost, nor is it, I think, accidental; rather it has been one of the irreducible elements of the Eden myth since the time of Genesis and Hesiod.   In Miss Bodkin's term, it is an archetypal pattern, something within us that "leaps in response to the effective presentation in poetry of an ancient theme."[17]   Whatever the Eden myth—or myths—may have meant in its primitive context, it seems clear that its subsequent survival and exploitation have been persistently associated with implications of a world responsive to the innocent will, a world in which no one would have occasion to cry, with the wife in "Home Burial,"

> 'But the world's evil.   I won't have grief so
> If I can change it.   Oh, I won't, I won't!'

because in such a world the wish would be the fact.

Now, whether or not one accepts Jung's dictum that it is impossible to say what such archetypal elements refer to,[18] it

---

[17] Bodkin, p. 4.
[18] See above, p. 74.

is clear that infancy—ultimately, perhaps prenatal infancy—
is the only condition except that of insanity in which we can
suppose ourselves to be characteristically unaware of the categories of possibility and impossibility; it is the only condition
in which the universe properly exists solely and simply to
minister to our wills, as it does for Auden's infant in "Mundus
et Infans," ready

> to take on the rest
> Of the world at the drop of a hat or the mildest
>   Nudge of the impossible,
> Resolved, cost what it may, to seize supreme
>   power, and
> Sworn to resist tyranny to the death with all
>   Forces at his command.[19]

And as parents know, it would be pointless to quarrel with
Auden's characterization. Childlike innocence frequently appears in conjunction with plastic environment and efficacious
will because these phenomena are the conditions of the un-
subdued infantile psyche. The Eden myth, if only among
other things, expresses an infantile psychic condition through
which we all pass and which remains, as a kind of indigestible
residue, in our unconscious minds, revealing its presence in
some, though not all, of our fantasies, our dreams, our myths,
and our art.

This sort of innocence is a very important element in
Frost's work, revealing itself in many, if not most, of his major
themes and preoccupations. Thus the enjoyment of shared
solitude depends on one's ability to banish the rest of the
world; in fact, as we shall see in Chapter IV, the ideal human
relationship projected in many of Frost's poems would be impossible in a broadly social context, because such a context
would inevitably involve conflicting interests and wills and
hence destroy the state of innocence. Melancholy is fallen

[19] *The Collected Poetry of W. H. Auden* (New York, 1945), p. 73.

man's yearning back to that infantile condition; in "The Most of It," Frost's seeker, not content with echoes, cries out on life

> that what it wants
> Is not its own love back in copy speech,
> But counter-love, original response

from the world that surrounds it. Briefly, he wants the magi-cally co-operative, almost coercive relationship with external nature that the boy of "In a Vale" enjoys with the flowers, and his cry differs from that of Auden's infant chiefly by virtue of being more clearly articulate. And insofar as Frost's nature is a state in which choice is clear and uncomplicated, demand-ing no elaborate psychic effort,[20] it is the state of the unfallen infantile will, which admits no problems because it creates its own world.

The innocent attitude toward the world figures in another, and equally important, aspect of Frost's work—I mean its deepening anti-intellectual tendency. Frost's defenders some-times write as though such a tendency does not exist. Thus Sidney Cox speaks of "the fact that no philosopher or artist is better worth listening to, no writer since I have been alive so well worth reading,"[21] and tells us that Frost "now and always thinks astronomic circles round other writers who have weathered the same wars, panics, booms and unemphatic sea-sons."[22] But in the same article, he praises Frost on the ground "that he does not take for granted what almost all the much trained take for granted," and specifies such curious convictions of the much trained as "That history is or can be like a railroad track to El Dorado," "That reason will even-tually make life resemble logic," and "That science will at last render personal risks superfluous."[23] Frost is, and isn't, anti-

---

[20] See above, pp. 20-21.
[21] Sidney Cox, "Robert Frost and Poetic Fashion," *American Scholar,* XVIII (Winter, 1948/49), 78.
[22] *Ibid.,* p. 80.
[23] *Ibid.,* p. 80; and cf. the same author's *Robert Frost: Original "Ordi-nary" Man* (New York, 1929), pp. 39-40.

intellectual; that is, he is anti-intellectual in an intellectual sense. Surely such commentary shows more concern for the slaughter of straw men than for clarification of Frost's position.

More commonly, however, the anti-intellectual tendency is recognized, without squirming. Percy Boynton, praising Frost, observes that "his convictions have not grown so much from what he has thought as from what he has felt."[24] And Robert P. Tristram Coffin recalls Frost's once having told him

how much he was afraid a boy who had it in him to write poetry might be hurt by college. It might blight his natural knowledge of people's nature, and of nature itself, and substitute knowledge of too many books and too many ideas at second hand.[25]

And the pronouncement fits. In *A Witness Tree,* Frost writes,

> I love to play with the Platonic notion
> That wisdom need not be of Athens Attic,
> But well may be Laconic, even Boeotian.
> At least I will not have it systematic.[26]

With hindsight wisdom, one can say that a shying away from too much systematic thought has been evident from *A Boy's Will* on. In "The Trial by Existence," the admirable souls are those who, though forewarned of all that reincarnation will have in store for them and deprived even of the wry satisfaction of being permitted to remember that they made their own choice, still choose to go through it all again. I do not question their admirable quality; I merely say that rationality has nothing to do with it. "The Demiurge's Laugh," with its vision of an elusive, mocking demon luring the speaker on, is identified, by the gloss Frost provided in his table of contents, as expressing the boy's resolve "to know definitely

[24] Percy H. Boynton, "Robert Frost," *English Journal*, XI (Oct., 1922), 462.
[25] Robert P. Tristram Coffin, *New Poetry of New England: Frost and Robinson* (Baltimore, 1938), p. 91.
[26] "Boeotian."

hinks . . . about science";[27] what he evidently thinks
ence is a snare and a delusion. Of the three clearly
men—in the conventional sense of the phrase—in
..... *of Boston,* one is a mere sounding board ("A Servant to
Servants"), the second a skeptical clergyman who apparently
shares his creator's suspicion of excessive intellection ("The
Black Cottage"), and the third a Milquetoast, a snob, and
something of a phony ("A Hundred Collars"). *Mountain
Interval* opens with that hardy perennial, "The Road Not
Taken," which celebrates a crucial choice made under circumstances that gave no opportunity for intelligent decision.[28]
And "The Bonfire," from the same volume, recommends irresponsible and unintelligent measures as a kind of conditioning
process against the irresponsible and unintelligent circumstances that may develop if war should come.

But it is not until the later books that the anti-intellectual
tendency becomes explicit. *West-Running Brook* has "The
Bear," in which, as Yvor Winters bluntly observes, Frost "is
satirizing the intelligent man from the point of view of the
unintelligent. . . ."[29] And *A Further Range* crystallizes the
matter. In "The White-Tailed Hornet," Frost deplores the
tendency

> to see our images
> Reflected in the mud and even dust—

that is, the effort to place man in a context of physical and
biological categories. In "At Woodward's Gardens," he prefers the common-sense resourcefulness of monkeys to the
theoretical understanding of people. In "Neither Out Far Nor
In Deep," he displays ironic tenderness over man's effort to

[27] *A Boy's Will,* table of contents. The gloss has not been reprinted in
later collections.

[28] Yvor Winters discusses this point extensively in "Robert Frost: or,
The Spiritual Drifter as Poet," *Sewanee Review,* LVI (Autumn, 1948),
564-596.

[29] Winters, p. 573.

see into matters that lie beyond his understanding. Tityrus, of "Build Soil," were he dictator, would

> let things take their course
> And then I'd claim the credit for the outcome.

And the subject of "To a Thinker," whose thought does not follow an undeviating straight line, is advised,

> So if you find you must repent
> From side to side in argument,
> At least don't use your mind too hard,
> But trust my instinct—I'm a bard.

It may not be true that, as R. P. Blackmur says, "a bard is at heart an easygoing versifier of all that comes to hand,"[30] but it is clear that he is not an admirer of mere intelligence.

There are at least two ways in which such an attitude toward systematic thought may be related to the element of innocence in Frost's work. First, and obviously, the sense that environment is something plastic, directly and easily responsive to the operation of the will, cannot bear much systematic analysis. One can respond to such poems as "In a Vale" and "The Telephone" only by suspending one's reasonable awareness of what flowers can and cannot do. "What flowers say?" questions my three-year-old daughter, and my critical awareness of the universe takes a mild licking in the effort to provide an answer. But I believe that there is a more fundamental connection than this, one involved with Frost's sense of man as a free agent. The point is that Frost's freedom is a special, limited sort of thing. Sidney Cox records a suggestive reminiscence in this respect:

One day as we legged it along a Plymouth road, something led to [Frost's] remarking that there are three grades of task. The

[30] R. P. Blackmur, "The Instincts of a Bard," *Nation,* CXLII (June 24, 1936), 818.

most servile and the one that demands least from the worker is the assigned task done under supervision. Freer and more exacting is the task assigned by another but left to be carried out at the discretion and according to the judgment of the worker. The one that takes most character of all is the self-assigned task carried out only at the instant urgency of the worker's own desire.[31]

Now it is not original, but it is true, to observe that there are, broadly speaking, two senses of "freedom"—that of not being subject to external restraints, and that of being enabled to achieve objectives. And I think it is clear that the freedom enjoyed by Frost's third and freest worker is essentially of the first sort. The two sorts are not mutually exclusive, at least not necessarily, but surely the worker's freedom in the first sense limits his freedom in the second to those objectives that a man can achieve unassisted. He might conceivably achieve an automobile or even a refrigerator; but unless he is willing to deny to others the freedom that he enjoys himself, he cannot achieve a corporation or a university or a national state, and it would be merely querulous to insist that these things have no value or that they are incompatible with a meaningful degree of freedom. Frost's worker is subject to no external restraints except those inevitably imposed by the material he is working with and by his own skill. "Mowing" and "Two Tramps in Mud Time," published twenty years apart, suggest the concept's persistence. As we have seen,[32] *Walden* and *Robinson Crusoe* are two of Frost's favorite books, and both are classic statements of this sort of freedom. And in the 1939 essay "The Figure a Poem Makes," Frost appears to make the matter explicit:

We prate of freedom. We call our schools free because we are not free to stay away from them till we are sixteen years of age. I have given up my democratic prejudices and now willingly set the lower classes free to be completely taken care of by the upper classes. Political freedom is nothing to me. I bestow it right and

[31] Sidney Cox, "Robert Frost at Plymouth," *New Hampshire Troubadour*, XVI (Nov., 1946), 20.
[32] See above, pp. 33, 70.

left. All I would keep for myself is the freedom of my material—
the condition of body and mind now and then to summons aptly
from the vast chaos of all I have lived through.[33]

As is often the case with Frost's pronouncements, it is not easy
to separate the serious from the whimsical here. At the risk
of playing it straight, however, one can indicate that, while the
freedom to leave school at any time is freedom, it is still true
that college graduates can wash cars, while those who do not
complete high school usually cannot become professors of
economics, neurosurgeons, or Supreme Court justices. And
surely enjoying the freedom of one's material depends heavily
on selecting such material as one is capable of acting freely
with respect to.

That is my point—that Frost selects his material, as I
have already suggested in speaking of "The Pasture."[34] Recognizing, as the sane man must, that restraint is inevitable, he
deliberately or instinctively tends to deal with areas of experience in which restraint is imposed by oneself or one's material, not by one's external, social relationships.[35] Frost's
world is not necessarily an easy world or an unreal world, but
it is a simplified one.[36] To a degree, such simplification can
be seen as a kind of holding operation in defense of the innocently efficacious will. That is, as we discover that our desire
cannot always and easily subdue our environment, then one
way of saving the sense of free will is to erect something like
taboos, to declare certain areas of experience off limits for the
exercise of will, and hence largely devoid of interest. Obviously, those forbidden areas will be pre-eminently those in
which complications arising from external restraints are most
insistent in their demand for some sort of genuine synthesis,
for a degree of systematic thought. In "To a Thinker," again,

[33] *Complete Poems of Robert Frost 1949* (New York, 1949), p. vii.
The essay first appeared as preface to the 1939 edition of *Collected Poems
of Robert Frost* (New York, 1939).
[34] See above, pp. 79-80.
[35] Cf. chap. iv.
[36] Cf. chap. i.

the subject (F.D.R.?) has placed himself in one of those difficult areas. Frost's advice, as the thinker attempts the tricky
and infinitely revisionistic business of translating social theory
into social fact, is not to be careful in his revising and translating but to act as though the wilful hunch were an adequate
substitute for intelligence—and, by fairly clear implication, to
abandon theory. The innocent sense of environment as something responsive to one's will has been projected into an essentially obscurantist distrust of trying to will one's environment
other than it is, into a rejection of group effort and social
planning. Good fences may not necessarily make good neighbors, but they do make a manageable world, as Frost indicates
in "Triple Bronze":

> The Infinite's being so wide
> Is the reason the Powers provide
> For inner defense my hide.
> For next defense outside
>
> I make myself this time
> Of wood or granite or lime
> A wall too hard for crime
> Either to breach or climb.
>
> Then a number of us agree
> On a national boundary.
> And that defense makes three
> Between too much and me.

And none of the three defenses calls for too much of that
"sway[ing] with reason more or less" that Frost attributes to
his thinker.

I have already said that Frost's Eden is not all sweetness
and light, that innocence may be a source of pain and danger
as well as of idyllic happiness.[37] Such an element is, of

[37] See above, p. 78.

course, an essential part of the Eden myth, particularly if one
sees the myth as a means of understanding the sometimes excruciating difficulty of the common human lot.   The important
thing about the Garden is that it has been irretrievably lost,
thus becoming a source of persistent melancholy.   And as *A
Boy's Will* is, at least superficially, the most innocent of Frost's
books, so it is the most obviously melancholy.

Melancholy is revealed in the frequently mannered, derivative, and nostalgic yearning that characterizes such poems as
"Waiting," "Ghost House," "My Butterfly," and "My November Guest."   As William G. O'Donnell has put it, "The poet
dwells in a vanished abode with a strangely aching heart; his
sorrow talks, and he is fain to list; he walks afield at dusk,
carrying a worn book of old-golden song,"[38] and the catalogue
could be extended.   Such poeticisms can perhaps be seen as
the almost inevitable growing pains of a young poet coming
of age in the post-Swinburnian generation of Dowson, Symons,
and Wilde.   Yeats underwent a comparable ordeal.   Frost
was, to be sure, almost forty when *A Boy's Will* was published,
but many of the poems were written as much as twenty years
earlier; "My Butterfly," for example, was first printed in 1894.[39]
Frost himself seems to have been somewhat disturbed by his
own verbal sentimentality; "Into My Own" was orginally
"Into Mine Own," the "desolate, deserted trees" of "My November Guest" were originally "The fallen, bird-forsaken
breeze,"[40] and there is little of this exhausted verbiage in the
later volumes.

But, like innocence, postlapsarian melancholy in Frost's
work is more a matter of theme than it is of verbal mannerism,
persisting as such in later poems.   If "Into My Own" is a fantasy escape from the world of social considerations and ethical
complexity, the melancholy-engendering world of fallen man,

[38] William G. O'Donnell, "Robert Frost and New England: A Revaluation," *Yale Review*, XXXVII (Summer, 1948), 701.
[39] Wesleyan University Library, *Robert Frost: A Chronological Survey*
(Middletown, Conn., 1936), p. 15.
[40] *Ibid.*, p. 17.

so, more responsibly and ambivalently, is "Stopping by Woods on a Snowy Evening," from *New Hampshire,* ten years later. With still further modification, so is "Come In," from *A Witness Tree,* almost thirty years later. It is true that the latter poems explicitly reject the woods, while "Into My Own" at least yearns to enter them, but we shall see that this fact is less a simple contradiction with a clear chronology than an ambivalence.[41]   In similar fashion, "Stars," with its sense of cosmic nature's utter indifference to man, parallels "The Most of It" (from *A Witness Tree,* again), with its sense of organic nature's indifference, and both owe their poignancy to their speakers' ability to imagine, and yearn after, a quite different sort of nature, one that offers "counter-love, original response"[42]—as it did to Adam in Paradise. And "Acquainted With the Night" (from *West-Running Brook,* 1928) can be seen as a more sharply defined and fully realized version of "A Late Walk," with its sense of man's psychic alienation from the world in which he must live and move and have his being.

Much of Frost's finest work exploits melancholy themes, especially the somber—and surely, in some instances, great—dramatic poems from *North of Boston.* "Mending Wall" deals with man's wilful separation from man, as does "A Hundred Collars," at least by implication. In "The Death of the Hired Man," Mary and Warren achieve understanding of and sympathy for the innocent Silas only at the moment of his solitary death. The condition of shared solitude becomes an ordeal of mutual alienation for the women, especially, of "Home Burial" and "The Fear." In different degrees, "A Servant to Servants" and "After Apple-Picking" present the consequences of man's condemnation to earning his bread in the sweat of his brow—in the one poem, madness; in the other, an almost morbidly acute sense of mortality, of death in life. And in "The Self-Seeker," the innocent collector of orchids is broken by a machine-dominated environment that his will cannot subdue.

---

[41] See below, pp. 94-99.
[42] "The Most of It."

In each instance, at least part of the poem's effectiveness is determined by one's subterranean awareness of the innocent world in which such painful circumstances would not, or should not, occur. Once more, Eden may be a source of pain as well as of happiness. In this sense, it is an object of ambivalent feeling, and that feeling is a central fact in Frost's handling of the Eden theme.

That ambivalence should be characteristic of one's feeling for the infantile Eden hardly seems surprising. Even as we yearn back to the uncomplicated emotional life of the not-yet-born, we are aware, more or less, that such simplicity could be recovered only by rejecting and even destroying the entire fabric of our laboriously achieved humanity. From this clash of not-always-conscious impulses arise at least some of those images of pain and horror that often accompany the literature, fantasy, and ritual of the Eden archetype. Milton's Paradise, at the end, is ringed about with flaming swords; the primitive tribesman, reborn through initiation, must first undergo ordeal; the Grail knight, seeking spiritual rebirth, is confronted with a pilgrimage of privation, terror, and sometimes death; and Conrad's Marlow, journeying into that heart of darkness that is in some sense himself, achieves self-awareness and a consequent revitalization only by understanding and to a degree experiencing the ambivalent, nightmare horror projected in Mr. Kurtz, the man who, giving free rein to his infantile will, has attempted to realize his yearnings for Eden.

Now, there is relatively little of the explicitly nightmarish in Frost, but there is ambivalence. It is revealed, for example, in his handling of such characters as Loren, in "Blueberries," Brad McLaughlin, in "The Star-Splitter," and Brother Meserve, in "Snow." Quite simply, the question is, Are we to admire or to despise these men? and the only possible answer is, Both. All three are innocent types. Loren,

> Just taking what Nature is willing to give,
> Not forcing her hand with harrow and plow,

has achieved something like an ultimate in what I have described as a holding operation in defense of the innocently
efficacious will; he wills only those things that are going to
happen anyway. McLaughlin, who

> burned his house down for the fire insurance
> And spent the proceeds on a telescope
> To satisfy a life-long curiosity
> About our place among the infinities,

not only shares Loren's irresponsibility but, in his unscientific
effort to impose his will on the stars, compelling them to
render up metaphysics, is more ingenuous. And Meserve, who
in spite of the Coles' pleading goes back into the storm because
the storm wants him to, is Auden's infant again in his inability
to yield before the mildest nudge of the impossible. The Eden
dweller in all of us shares Fred Cole's grudging admiration,
while his mature, responsible wife voices our mature, responsible contempt.

But if ambivalence manifests itself in Frost's rendering of
such dramatically conceived Edenic characters, it also appears,
and more significantly, in his treatment of certain essentially
lyric themes, most notably in that of yearning back to Eden, as
I have suggested in speaking of "Into My Own," "Stopping by
Woods on a Snowy Evening," and "Come In."[48] My point
was that in a fairly direct fashion, all three poems are concerned with an imagined withdrawal from the complicated
world we all know into a mysterious loveliness symbolized by
woods or darkness. The earlier poem accepts the call, at
least in fantasy, while the later two, though recognizing its
appeal, reject it. The temptation here may be to consider the
poems in their chronological sequence, as the record of a kind
of development, recognizing in "Into My Own" (1913) adolescent yielding to nostalgia, in "Stopping by Woods on a
Snowy Evening" (1923) an ethically responsible rejection

[48] See above, pp. 91-92.

of the nostalgic appeal, and in "Come In" (1942) a mature and ironic ability to enjoy the appeal without granting it the slightest real validity. And such treatment would necessitate qualifying the proposition that ambivalence is a persistent characteristic of Frost's work.

But for two reasons such treatment would be misleading. In the first place, there are other poems that would be difficult to fit into such a pattern of clear, chronological development. In "An Empty Threat" (1923), the speaker does, to be sure, reject the call of the wilderness, as does the speaker of "Stopping by Woods on a Snowy Evening," but in the former poem it is questionable whether the speaker's quixotic mission to find Henry Hudson is not a more genuine element in his psychic machinery than are the unnamed motives that keep the mission a fantasy. In "Iris by Night" (1936), probably a tribute to the memory of Edward Thomas, an excursion into the dark is rewarded by a kind of meteorological accolade that seals "a relation of elected friends," though the darkness of "Iris by Night" seems less symbolic than that of "Come In." "In the Long Night" (1947) accepts the appeal in precisely the fashion of "Into My Own." And in "Directive" (also 1947), the reader, directed by a guide

Who only has at heart your getting lost

(compare Browning's cripple in "Childe Roland to the Dark Tower Came"), moves back beyond civilization, beyond childhood, almost beyond death itself to achieve his quest and "be whole again beyond confusion." All of which is to say that attraction toward and rejection of the Eden condition are concurrent rather than successive themes.

And in the second place, I am not sure that Frost's rejections of the retreat to Eden are always and unequivocally rejections. Here I have in mind something other than the relatively simple pull of opposing tendencies manifest in "An

Empty Threat" or "Stopping by Woods on a Snowy Evening,"
something that has to do with two peculiarly persistent images
—stars and snow,[44] and particularly the latter. To anticipate
conclusions, my point is that, if dark woods symbolize one
aspect of the Eden condition, stars and snow at least sometimes symbolize other aspects of the same thing, and in one of
the apparently most explicit rejection poems—"Come In"—
the woods are rejected not in favor of the world of responsibility and commitments but in favor of stars.

Now stars appear with some frequency in Frost's work as
images of cosmic nature's indifference to man. I have spoken
of the poem "Stars" in this connection,[45] and in "On Looking
Up by Chance at the Constellations," "Lost in Heaven,"
"Bravado," and "On Making Certain Anything Has Happened," the stars have, in varying degrees, the same symbolic
value. So do they in "I Will Sing You One-O," but, I think,
with a significant difference, in tone if in nothing more explicit. "Stars" is yearning; "I Will Sing You One-O," contemplative. In "Stars" it is a question of what is not there,
the organic response that the speaker cannot get. In "I Will
Sing You One-O" it is a question of what is there, the vision
of a tremendous, majestic, and somehow frightening unity that
man can contemplate though not achieve; the stars, and the
cosmos of which they are a part, are in fact an absolute em-
bodiment of that Edenic freedom from external restraint that
man must shuffle and compromise to achieve even the illusion
of.[46] The stars *are* Eden, as it were rendered safe by its re-
moteness, as perhaps they are for Brad McLaughlin in "The
Star-Splitter." The rejection of woods and darkness in favor
of stars, in "Come In," is as much a hypostasis of Eden as it
is a disavowal.[47]

[44] T. K. Whipple has called attention to Frost's images of stars and
snow in "Robert Frost," *Literary Review* (March 22, 1924), p. 606.

[45] See above, p. 92.

[46] See above, pp. 87-89.

[47] In "Out for Stars: A Meditation on Robert Frost," *Atlantic Monthly*,
CLXXI (May, 1943), 64-67, George Whicher gives a sensitive reading of

The snow image is more persistent. Even the most casual reader of Frost can hardly avoid being aware of the frequency with which winter landscapes appear in his work, and adequate explanation of the fact may lie no further off than the next New England winter; in New Hampshire and Vermont, snow is one of the more obvious facts of life. But Frost's snow is symbolic as well as representational and hence demands more than climate for its elucidation. For my present purpose, there are two points about Frost's exploitation of such images that are particularly relevant—the dual, ambivalent use that he makes of them, and their frequent appearance in conjunction with those other ambivalent images of stars and dark woods.

The second point is perhaps already clear. In "Stopping by Woods on a Snowy Evening," the dark woods are filling up with snow; in "I Will Sing You One-O," the monistic vision of co-ordinated stars occurs during a night of blinding snowfall; and in a poem not yet cited, "Desert Places," falling snow and darkening woods suggest the desolation of lifeless stars and interstellar space. Whether or not one can attach precise significance to these images, it seems clear that they overlap in some fashion and that at least part of their common quality derives from their use as vehicles for ambivalent states of feeling.

And that Frost's snow is a vehicle for ambivalent feelings seems clear also. Sometimes positive in value, sometimes negative, and sometimes both, it suggests Conrad's ocean, Hardy's heath, and the snow in Joyce's "The Dead" and Mann's *The Magic Mountain*. In "Dust of Snow," it provides psychic revitalization; in "Good-by and Keep Cold," it pre-

---

"Come In" that differs substantially from mine. I will suggest only two points in favor of mine: first, that it is consistent with the implications of many other poems; second, that while Professor Whicher is concerned mainly with Frost's deliberate intention in the poem, I am concerned with persistent patterns in Frost's work that are archetypal in their nature and hence less revealing of conscious conviction than of unconscious bent. See above, p. 77.

serves life itself; in "Dust in the Eyes," it restrains *hubris;* and in "The Pauper Witch of Grafton"—a minor instance but perhaps less trivial than it appears; certainly the poem is no trivial accomplishment—Arthur Amy gathered snowberries in dark woods as a lover's tribute to his young and bewitching wife. On the other hand, in "Storm Fear" and "A Leaf Treader," snow is the antagonist against which life must pit itself or be destroyed; in "There Are Roughly Zones," it is the unalterable law of the world that man's will is powerless against; and in "The Onset," in conjunction again with dark woods, it is an ominous reminder of death and mortality.

In other poems these meanings coexist. Meserve's snow, again, is both a threat of death and a calling out of life; in "Wind and Window Flower" the winter wind speaks of both love and death to the reluctant house plant; in "Our Singing Strength" the untimely snow briefly destroys the birds' world but provides an at least quantitatively remarkable vision of potential song; in "An Empty Threat" it is both a refuge from

> 'life's victories of doubt
> That need endless talk talk
> To make them out'

and also a condition of sterility and death:

> 'You and I
> Off here
> With the dead race of the Great Auk!'

And in "A Winter Eden," if it lifts existence closer to heaven, it does so at the price of sterility:

> So near to paradise all pairing ends.

Once more, it seems clear that Frost's rejections of the retreat

to Eden are qualified rejections, that his feeling for the state
of innocence is persistently marked by ambivalence.[48]

I have said that there is little of the nightmarish in Frost's
exploitation of ambivalent feeling. I do not mean that there
is nothing dreadful. To the characters involved in "Home
Burial," "The Self-Seeker," "A Servant to Servants," or "The
Fear," life offers more than enough dreadfulness, but the
reader is more aware of a kind of tragic inevitability in such
poems than of the irrational, seemingly gratuitous horror of
"Heart of Darkness" or a bad dream. Closer, perhaps, are
" 'Out, Out—' " and "The Vanishing Red," with their exhibi-
tions of pointless cruelty, or "Design," with its revelation of
either an insane teleology or a gruesome coincidence. But the
horror in "Heart of Darkness" is different from these, and I
think that the difference is largely a matter of empathy and of
psychic depth, of the degree to which one is invited to project
himself into the character's personality and of the distance one
is carried below the threshold of consciousness. In "Heart of
Darkness" we are made to share Marlow's horrified realization
that he is akin, not only to the jungle savages, but to the un-
speakable Kurtz himself, that the clashing impulses that Kurtz
has allowed to become overt and that have destroyed him
exist in us as well. Thoreau's adventure with the woodchuck
brought him face to face with similar clashing impulses within
himself.[49] One is not tempted or even invited to make such

---

[48] Images of whiteness occasionally have this same ambivalent value.
In "For Once, Then, Something," the whiteness at the bottom of the well
may be either "truth" or merely "a pebble of quartz"; in "The Onset,"
whiteness is snow and death in the first stanza, but buildings, trees, and life
in the second; and in "Design," the collocation of white objects—
> a dimpled spider, fat and white,
> On a white heal-all, holding up a moth
> Like a white piece of rigid satin cloth—

presents, in Randall Jarrell's phrase, "the Argument from Design with a
vengeance" ("To the Laodiceans," *Poetry and the Age* [New York, 1953],
p. 42.)—on the one hand, evidence of a deliberate consciousness manifesting itself in nature in a manner that, on the other hand, appalls one. One
remembers the whale's whiteness in *Moby-Dick*.

[49] Henry David Thoreau, *Walden* (Harmondsworth, 1938), p. 179; and
cf. above, p. 32.

identification of himself with the murderous miller in "The Vanishing Red":

> You can't get back and see it as he saw it.

And in none of the other poems mentioned does one have the sense that fundamental human values have been overtly violated.

But there is at least a handful of poems in which such fundamental violations do take place and in which one is at least not warned away from a degree of self-recognition. The handful includes such poems as "The Discovery of the Madeiras," "The Subverted Flower," "The Thatch," and perhaps "The Pauper Witch of Grafton" and "The Lovely Shall Be Choosers." The common quality I am concerned with in these poems is an erotic relationship that, revealing ambivalence, is transformed sometimes into something rich and strange but more often into something close to nightmare in its destructive equating of love and cruelty. Thus in "The Thatch," some sort of quarrel has sent the speaker out into a night of winter rain,

> Intent on giving and taking pain.

Stamping around in the dark, he accidentally flushes birds out of their nesting places in the low-hanging roof thatch to last out the night as best they can, and the realization of his pointless, unintentional cruelty to the birds enables him (I am being substantially more explicit here than the poem is) to come to grips with and master his mutually destructive impulses of love and hate, as does Marlow's realization of the potential Kurtz within himself. The speaker has descended into his own unconscious and has to a degree mastered the ambivalent chaos that confronts him there; the poem is a kind of night journey in miniature. Something of the same pattern appears in "A Line-Storm Song," "Directive," and perhaps the cryptic "All Revelation."

The other poems I have mentioned, however, do not exhibit the self-mastery of "The Thatch"; ambivalence remains a matter of unresolved pathos or unresolved horror. In "The Pauper Witch of Grafton," it is pathos, largely because the love cruelty of Arthur Amy and his witch has been a matter of mutually affectionate give-and-take. If Amy undermined her early reputation as a witch, still, once married to her,

> He got to saying things
> To undo what he'd done and make it right,
> Like, 'No, she ain't come back from kiting yet.
> Last night was one of her nights out. She's kiting.
> She thinks when the wind makes a night of it
> She might as well herself.'

And if the witch

> made him gather me wet snow berries
> On slippery rocks beside a waterfall.
> I made him do it for me in the dark,

still, she

> showed Arthur Amy signs enough
> Off from the house as far as we could keep
> And from barn smells you can't wash out of plowed
>   ground
> With all the rain and snow of seven years;
> And I don't mean just skulls of Rogers' Rangers
> On Moosilauke, but woman signs to man,
> Only bewitched so I would last him longer.

It is not hard to believe that Arthur Amy "liked everything [she] made him do." But love and cruelty do coexist, and that ambivalence projects itself into the old woman's pathetically guilt-ridden recollection of her early wilfulness:

> All is, if I'd a-known when I was young
> And full of it, that this would be the end,
> It doesn't seem as if I'd had the courage
> To make so free and kick up in folks' faces.
> I might have, but it doesn't seem as if.

It is also pathos, though of a different sort, in "The Lovely Shall Be Choosers," a terrible parody of the Seven Joys of the Virgin. The woman's every impulse to love is held in check by pride, reticence, or external circumstances. As wilful when young as was the witch of Grafton—

> 'She *would* refuse love safe with wealth and honor!
> The lovely shall be choosers, shall they?
> Then let them choose!'

says the Voice—she is more desolate at the end because her love, incapable of expressing itself in the affectionate teasing of the Amys, has been early transformed into a kind of stony isolation from husband, children, friends, and potential lover.

But in "The Subverted Flower" and "The Discovery of the Madeiras," though pathos is in evidence, it is less apparent than the pathological ugliness of the erotic transformations that take place. The runaway lovers of "The Discovery of the Madeiras" understand neither their own motives nor one another's:

> The most he asked her eyes to grant
> Was that in what she does not want
> A woman wants to be overruled.
> Or was the instinct in him fooled?
> He knew not, neither of them knew.

> They could only say like any two,
> 'You tell me and I'll tell you.'

Dependent thus on resources that they do not have, they discover that the transformation of love into cruelty, of willed action into paralyzed guilt, comes easily and brings destructive consequences. Stung by her trivial teasing,

> in a moment of cross unruth
> He thought, "All right if you want the truth!"

and tells her the slave-ship captain's tale of subhuman cruelty to another pair of lovers. Appropriately—and ambivalently—love is death in the captain's story, but a death that is a kind of triumph over the murderous crew; these lovers, like the speaker of "The Thatch," have achieved self-mastery. But the lady

> withdrew back in self-retreat
> Till her heart almost ceased to beat.
> Her spirit faded as far away
> As the living ever go yet stay.
> And her thought was she had had her pay.

She dies of it. Appropriately, again, and with shattering if unintentional irony, her death takes place on a nameless and uninhabited island in an Edenic solitude shared only by the lover she can no longer communicate with. It is not easy to see how Paradise could be more thoroughly lost or postlapsarian melancholy more complete.

Similar transformations take place in "The Subverted Flower," a somewhat anomalous poem in Frost's work by virtue of its explicit concern with sexual pathology; it is more Lawrentian than Frostian in some respects. The poem opens with an image that equates love and cruelty:

> She drew back; he was calm:
> "It is this that had the power,"
> And he lashed his open palm
> With the tender-headed flower.

And although it is not always clear whose point of view is given in a particular line, since the point of view fluctuates among the girl, the man, and an impersonal third-person observer and commentator, it is obvious that, to the girl, the man's love is bestial, dangerous:

> with every word he spoke
> His lips were sucked and blown
> And the effort made him choke
> Like a tiger at a bone.
> She had to lean away.
> She dared not stir a foot,
> Lest movement should provoke
> The demon of pursuit
> That slumbers in a brute.

But the man is not the only one to undergo transformation, as the observer explains:

> A girl could only see
> That a flower had marred a man,
> But what she could not see
> Was that the flower might be
> Other than base and fetid:
> That the flower had done but part,
> And what the flower began
> Her own too meager heart
> Had terribly completed.

In the closing lines it is the girl who appears as beast:

> Her mother wiped the foam
> From her chin, picked up her comb
> And drew her backward home.

In this final image, the poem's wobbling point of view justifies itself in a significant ambiguity; we are not sure whether the final metamorphosis is a function of the observer's view of the girl, in which case she is merely a grimly pathetic object, or whether it represents the girl's sudden vision of herself, transformed by God knows what machinery of guilt and fear, but momentarily *seeing* herself—at the risk of overworking a reference, as Mr. Kurtz saw himself at the moment of whispering, "The horror! The horror!"[50]

These five poems are related to the Eden myth in a more explicit fashion than that provided by their exploitation of ambivalence. In terms of the myth, they deal with the problem of adjustment to the fallen state, in which contradictory impulses may baffle and sometimes cripple the innocent will. One such means of adjustment, of course, is provided by anti-intellectualism and the related narrowing of one's interest to those areas in which one's will can operate more or less freely.[51]   But, as I have already indicated, such adjustment strikes me as one of the shabbier elements in Frost's pattern of values.   In these other poems, adjustment is a sterner business; it attributes to humanity a dignity and a capacity for self-knowledge, for growing up, that are not implicit in the sometimes glib obscurantism of "The Bear," "To a Thinker," or "The White-Tailed Hornet." In "The White-Tailed Hornet,"

> to see our images
> Reflected in the mud or even dust,

to institute "downward comparisons," is to lose oneself "piece-

[50] Joseph Conrad, *Heart of Darkness and The Secret Sharer* (New York, 1950), p. 133.
[51] See above, pp. 84-90.

meal to the animals," in "disillusion upon disillusion." But it is not until the girl of "The Subverted Flower" has seen herself as animal, has recognized the incomplete humanity of her own "too meager heart," that she achieves the kind of self-knowledge that would enable her to accept love and to be fully human. I do not suggest that this further development actually takes place in the poem—merely that it could not take place without the realization of her incompleteness. As it is, the girl seems as irretrievably lost as the lady in "The Discovery of the Madeiras," and for the same reason—an inability to accept her own, or others', share in common mortality. The enslaved lovers, accepting love and death, transform the cruel parody of marriage into something genuinely sacramental and confound their persecutors, giving the captain a story he evidently cannot forget—a situation remotely reminiscent of "The Rime of the Ancient Mariner." The speaker of "The Thatch," recognizing and accepting in himself a cruelty that coexists with his love whether he wants it to or not, is armed as it were against himself, as the wife in "Home Burial," for example, or the lady in "The Discovery of the Madeiras" is not. I think it is this recognition and acceptance that keep the closing lines of "The Thatch" from being sentimental and irrelevant:

> They tell me the cottage where we dwelt,
> Its wind-torn thatch goes now unmended;
> Its life of hundreds of years has ended
> By letting the rain I knew outdoors
> In on to the upper chamber floors.

Like the house, he has let in the rain, vaguely an image of the cold cruelty he has recognized in himself; and, having gained from the experience a degree of immunity to destructively sentimental feelings of guilt and self-pity, he does not have to project such sentimentality onto the house, which after all is not human anyway. "A house isn't sentient," as the speaker of "The Star-Splitter" observes. In their emphasis on justice, which is often cruelty, and mercy, which is a manifestation of love, *A Masque of Reason* and *A Masque of Mercy* indicate the persistence with which Frost has been concerned with this sort of adjustment in his later poems, though I shall reserve discussion of the masques until Chapter V.

These poems indicate Frost's capacity for a kind of power frequently ignored or underemphasized by his admirers. In *Come In* and *The Pocket Book of Robert Frost's Poems,* the latter an expanded version of *Come In,* Louis Untermeyer included none of the five poems in question; and that Untermeyer's Frost is the popular Frost is suggested by the fact that, between February, 1943, and September, 1946, the two selections went through eight printings.[52] The poems also suggest the degree to which that power is rooted in unconscious elements, in those archetypal patterns that help to keep myth alive and art vigorous. Frost's friendlier critics sometimes prefer not to recognize this element either. Robert P. Tristram Coffin, praising Frost, condemns Joyce and Eliot as "pseudo-radicals" on the grounds that

they pursue the novelty of grafting healthy tissue on to dead. They take the healthiest myths the race has yet created—the myths of Telemachus and Odysseus and Arthur, and they graft them upon the dull and ingeniously jaded living by the day in gray Dublin or London houses. And there you have something new in the way of mysticism! Actually, much of the matter and the imagination of the pseudo-radicals, separated from the novelties of parody, word-twisting, and psychopathic abnormality, is jaded and stuffy Victorian material as dated as plush furniture.[53]

It is my argument that Frost has grafted the healthy Eden myth upon the sometimes dull and jaded life of gray New England,

[52] *The Pocket Book of Robert Frost's Poems,* ed. Louis Untermeyer (New York, 1946), copyright page.
[53] Coffin, p. 71.

and that by so doing he has, like Joyce and Eliot though less deliberately, rendered that life more meaningful.

That Frost is less deliberate than Joyce or Eliot in his exploitation of the unconscious and its motifs is clear. *Finnegans Wake* is still a unique book; the tempters in *Murder in the Cathedral* and the Eumenides in *The Family Reunion* more clearly have their origins in the unconscious than do, for example, the voices in "The Lovely Shall Be Choosers." Frost is, of course, aware of Freud; Sidney Cox speaks of "the new psychological theory [Frost] passed on to me, that all men's acts resolve into an effort to regain the warm safety of the womb."[54]   But Frost's work rarely suggests direct Freudian influence.   One need not, however, be particularly concerned with the unconscious as such in order to record its operations; *Finnegans Wake* probably could not have been written if Freud had not written first, but Euripides' ambivalent *Electra* could.   It might be possible to explain the fatal melancholy of the lady in "The Discovery of the Madeiras" as a wholly conscious matter of her remembering the ethical proprieties that her elopement has broken, but it does not seem possible to explain the exact impact that the captain's story has on her—"her thought was she had had her pay"—without reference to a tangle of largely unconscious emotional dynamics: for instance, "If these *honest* lovers died, I have no right to go on living"; or, "These lovers found consummation in death; I can both find consummation and expiate my sin by dying"; or, even more complicated but still consistent, "By dying I can find consummation, expiate my sin, and punish my lover for his cruelty both in abducting me in the first place and in springing this thing on me in the second."   I do not mean to defend any of these statements of hypothetical unconscious motive—only to say that psychoanalysis does reveal the presence of such constructions in the unconscious and that reading the poem with them in mind can be of real value in

[54] Cox, *Robert Frost: Original "Ordinary" Man,* p. 15.

drawing certain motifs into focus, in enabling one to see order instead of miscellaneousness.

And also this: unless one simply rejects psychoanalysis and its findings, such readings testify to what is sometimes a very subtle psychological accuracy in much of Frost's work. Rooted as it is in the ambivalent dynamics of the unconscious—the infantile will to possess the universe on one's own terms, the counterbalancing mechanism of guilt feelings, and the necessary adjusting of both to the exigencies of mature living—that accuracy, together with the Eden myth it expresses, has to do with emotional experiences that in some fashion we have all undergone. And if this is so, then the Eden myth and Frost's exploitation of it touch on the very bedrock of human experience; the myth is a major theme not only quantitatively but qualitatively as well, the stuff from which great and enduring art may be wrought. That is one reason that Frost is such an unescapable phenomenon of modern poetry. It remains to be seen whether he has wrought greatly with that material, and in the remaining chapters I shall be largely concerned with this question.

4

The world of others

$\mathcal{S}$ing me a song of social significance," chanted the chorus of *Pins and Needles*,[1] and to the international generation of Clifford Odets, Elmer Rice, Kenneth Fearing, and the Auden group, the injunction was one to be taken seriously. It is in fact difficult to see how writers of the 1930's could have avoided social significance, even if they had wished to. The stock-market crash and subsequent depression, the Soviet Union's consolidation under Stalin, the growth of European Fascism, the Sino-Japanese

[1] Marc Blitzstein, *Pins and Needles*. Apparently the play was never published.

war to the west and the Spanish Civil War to the east all contributed to an ominous background of social forces that writers might choose to discount, as A. E. Housman chose to discount the First World War ("The Great War cannot have made much change in the opinions of any man of imagination."),[2] but of which they could hardly be unaware. The "low dishonest decade,"[3] as Auden characterized it, compelled the attention of its children and its adults alike, whether they understood it or not. Archibald MacLeish moved from the palpable and mute aestheticism of "Ars Poetica" (1924) to the social themes of *The Fall of the City* (1937) and *America Was Promises* (1939). By the early 1940's, even Edith Sitwell had largely abandoned the "luscious artifice"[4] of *Façade* in favor of an indictment of irresponsible privilege in "The Song of the Cold."

But in 1932, Frost's Tityrus declared, self-approvingly,

> I will go to my run-out social mind
> And be as unsocial with it as I can,

recommending that we

> Keep off each other and keep each other off.[5]

And in 1936 Frost published *A Further Range,* a book that, including such poems as "A Lone Striker," "A Drumlin Woodchuck," "In Time of Cloudburst," "A Roadside Stand," and "Departmental," declares in effect that Frost, at least, has not been taken in by gloom mongers, collectivists, bureaucrats, or "greedy good-doers."[6] Aware of the disastrous 1930's,

[2] From a letter to Maurice Pollet, Feb. 5, 1933; quoted by Grant Richards, *Housman 1897-1936* (New York, 1942), p. 271.

[3] *The Collected Poetry of W. H. Auden* (New York, 1945), p. 57.

[4] William York Tindall, *Forces in Modern British Literature* (New York, 1947), p. 122.

[5] "Build Soil."

[6] "A Roadside Stand."

Frost chose to discount them, at least in his published poems, turning to the world the face of the whimsical, sensitive, sturdy, self-reliant—but sometimes wistful and sometimes cantankerous—New England yeoman. In spite of a few fine poems, *A Further Range* is, on the whole, Frost's first bad book.

This judgment of *A Further Range* is not, I hope, merely doctrinaire, is not based on the dubious proposition that a poet is somehow obligated to deal with certain pre-eminently social issues from a certain set of premises. Rather, to anticipate my argument, it is based on the propositions that, as poet, Frost seldom exhibits any very vital or immediate sense of collective aims, of broadly social values, and that in *A Further Range* he implies that such aims and such values are somehow undesirable in themselves, are absurd or unnecessary, wasteful or destructive. The first proposition involves no more than the altogether necessary limitation of one's subject matter; such limitation may be productive of excellent poetry at the very least, as it is, for example, in such poems of personal relationship as "Home Burial" or "A Servant to Servants," or in much of the Western tradition of love poetry. It is only in the last—and utterly Olympian—analysis that one can criticize a writer for not dealing with matters that are not relevant to his particular purposes. But if the second proposition is true, then certain poems in *A Further Range* imply what is surely a fundamental untruth about human experience. To put the matter another way, no one is required to write about social issues, and no issues are exclusively social; but if one chooses to write about issues that do possess an important social dimension, to write about them in terms of ways and means, of analysis and recommendation, then one must deal convincingly and responsibly with that social dimension or else stand convicted of triviality, vagueness, evasiveness, or a kind of doctrinaire individualism, with the emphasis on "doctrinaire." It is my contention that Frost's broadly social values are, on the whole, less than responsible.

Frost has written a handful of poems that do assert the desirability, even the necessity, of a degree of collective action, but characteristically such assertions are made with a degree of generality that makes it impossible to derive any really prescriptive social ethic from them. In "The Tuft of Flowers,"

> 'Men work together,' I told him from the heart,
> 'Whether they work together or apart,'

and "Haec Fabula Docet" concludes,

> The moral is it hardly need be shown,
> All those who try to go it sole alone,
> Too proud to be beholden for relief,
> Are absolutely sure to come to grief.

These poems represent Frost's most explicit statements of our social nature, and while the concluding generalizations are relevant in their contexts, they *are* generalizations, and qualified generalizations at that. The working together of "The Tuft of Flowers" is really a kind of happy accident, not a deliberate process, and "Haec Fabula Docet" is jocular. Lest we miss the jocularity, the notes to *Steeple Bush* (possibly a delayed parody of "The Waste Land"; the notes are not reprinted in *Complete Poems*) include an alternative moral with a joke about Vermont:

> The Moral is it hardly need be shown
> All those who try to go it sole alone,
> Or with the independence of Vermont
> Are absolutely sure to come to want.

In "The Code," we actually see men working together, but under so touchy and hair-triggerish a compact that it is a little surprising that any work gets done at all. As T. K. Whipple remarks of "The Code" and "The Vanishing Red," "evidently what at most would make a normal man swear makes a Frost character commit murder."[7]   And if "Triple Bronze" recognizes the desirability of nationhood and the need for collective endeavor to create it, still nationhood justifies itself primarily as an extension of one's own protective devices:

> Then a number of us agree
> On a national boundary.
> And that defense makes three
> Between too much and me.

Such poems, however, are relatively rare in Frost's work; so, to be fair, are poems in which collective operations as such are decried or written off.   There is "Build Soil," once more, in which our best course of action is to

> Keep off each other and keep each other off.

There is "A Drumlin Woodchuck," whose coexistence with the world is no more than a shrewd pretense of sociability. There is "A Roadside Stand," in which individual farming, however submarginal, is preferred to any enforced benefits imposed by the community at large.   The protagonist of "A Lone Striker"

> never would assume that he'd
> Be any institution's need;

confronted by a situation involving choice between his individual whim and the collective effort of a factory, he scarcely hesitates before deciding in favor of whim.   "To the Right Person" suggests a preference for closed school houses, as more conducive to meditation than the open ones that educate

----

[7] T. K. Whipple, "Robert Frost," *Literary Review* (March 22, 1924), p. 605.

people in groups.   And "The Egg and the Machine," in
which someone proposes throwing turtle's eggs at locomotives,
does quite a bit to justify Yvor Winters' suggestion that

Frost's real objection to the machine . . . is its social nature; it
requires and facilitates cooperation, and Frost is unwilling to
recognize its respectability mainly for this reason.[8]

It may be no more than an unfortunate coincidence that
most of these poems were published in book form during the
depression years, and of course we are not required to suppose that Frost wrote "Build Soil," "A Lone Striker," or "A
Drumlin Woodchuck" with the prototype of Tom Joad in
mind.   Sidney Cox, who has known Frost since 1911[9]—two
years before *A Boy's Will* was published—writes:

begin to sigh or smile at him for becoming genial and conservative
now that certain of his friends are men of wealth and economic
and political influence, and you will hear a menacing note in his
voice and see stern lines around his mouth as he talks of un-
avenged injustices.[10]

From hearing Frost speak, I have no doubt that the implied
characterization is accurate, though it may be significant that
injustice means something to be avenged rather than remedied.
In "The Vindictives" conquered Incas collectively avenge the
injustice committed against them by their Spanish overlords,
and in the process contribute to the destruction of their own
social existence.   Admittedly, the Incas had little choice.   But
when Frost does deal with what may as well be called social
injustice, injustice that might be remedied rather than avenged,
he is likely to be cutting, derisive, or at most ambiguous.   "A
Roadside Stand" has its "greedy good-doers, beneficent beasts
of prey."   "A Case for Jefferson" has Harrison:

[8] Yvor Winters, "Robert Frost: or, The Spiritual Drifter as Poet,"
Sewanee Review, LVI (Autumn, 1948), 578.
[9] Wesleyan University Library, *Robert Frost: A Chronological Survey*
(Middletown, Conn., 1936), p. 57.
[10] Sidney Cox, *Robert Frost: Original "Ordinary" Man* (New York,
1929). p. 19.

He's Freudian Viennese by night.
By day he's Marxian Muscovite.

Loving his country, Harrison means thereby

Blowing it all to smithereens
And having it all made over new.

And "The Lost Follower" concerns a poet, "passionate and fine," who has given up poetry in favor of political action and living in a slum; the poem's tone is a mixture of mockery, pathos, and reluctant admiration.

Such judgments may, of course, be completely valid in their contexts. Revolutionaries sometimes are both dubiously eclectic and irresponsibly destructive, and it is not clear, for example, that Ezra Pound's political agitation on behalf of Mussolini is of equal value with his "Homage to Sextus Propertius" or his adaptations of the troubadours; one may think of Satan in *A Masque of Reason,* very nearly carried off by a "tendency." But Frost's social reformers are always more or less undesirable types; they never really justify their activities. Frost writes, with malicious irony,

I read in a sort of Sunday-school leaflet from Moscow, that the grievances of Chekhov against the sordidness and dullness of his home-town society have done away with the sordidness and dullness of home-town society all over Russia. They were celebrating the event. The grievances of the great Russians of the last century have given Russia a revolution. The grievances of their great followers in America may well give us, if not a revolution, at least some palliative pensions. We must suffer them to put life at its ugliest and forbid them not, as we value our reputation for liberality.[11]

This too was written in the middle thirties, and it is difficult wholly to avoid the suspicion that Frost resented the depression partly because of the impetus it gave to social and political

[11] Robert Frost, introduction to Edwin Arlington Robinson, *King Jasper* (New York, 1935), p. vii.

readjustments based on the premise that some forms of suffering are social in origin and hence may be ameliorated by manipulating social structures. "Give us immedicable woes— woes that nothing can be done for—woes flat and final,"[12] Frost demands, and by including these two passages in the same essay, he virtually invites us to put them together.

This preference for "immedicable woes" and the complementary stiffness toward those who are convinced that some woes at least are remediable by social action are reflected in Frost's attitude toward New England. That Frost is a New England writer has, of course, been evident from the start, and this fact is something more than a matter of residence and locale. As we have seen, Frost is in the tradition of Emerson and Thoreau; not only that, he is in the tradition of the New England writers of local color, whether by literary descent or by simple, but more compelling, attraction to similar characters and situations. The piecemeal apparition of Jehiel Lommedieu in Harriet Beecher Stowe's "The Ghost in the Mill" has a sort of kissing kinship with the rattletrap skeleton in "The Witch of Coös"; both pieces exploit the oddly cockeyed sense of the macabre that has been an element of the New England imagination perhaps from the time of Cotton Mather's *Magnalia Christi Americana.* Closer resemblances can be detected between Frost's New England writing and that of Sarah Orne Jewett. The case of Elijah Tilley, in Miss Jewett's "Along Shore," has some of the pathos of "An Old Man's Winter Night"; the crippled Thankful Hight, of "A Dunnet Shepherdess," suggests Frost's "The Self-Seeker"; and the deliberate renunciation made by Joanna Todd, of "Poor Joanna" and "The Hermitage," the full commitment to an act of choice and its consequences, sounds a note that Frost strikes again and again—in "The Self-Seeker," "The Housekeeper," "A Servant to Servants," and "The Lovely Shall Be Choosers." And the New England stories of Mary Wilkins Freeman often anticipate characters or situations that Frost has made use of.

[12] *Ibid.,* p. xv.

In "The Revolt of 'Mother,' " Adoniram Penn confronts and finally accepts a situation that John Hall, of "The House-keeper," confronted and was beaten by; Luella Norcross, of "Life-Everlastin'," who accepts Jesus Christ because she can find no other means of rescuing the murderous John Gleason from the hand of a merely just and angry God, exercises an off-center logic not unlike that of the sister in "Place for a Third"; Maria Primrose, of "Up Primrose Hill," might well be the woman of "The Lovely Shall Be Choosers"; and Caroline Munson, of "A Symphony in Lavender," whose love is crippled by an irrational horror of her beloved, demonstrates, if in sentimentalized form, the same human incompleteness as does the girl in "The Subverted Flower." Frost is in the tradition of New England writing.

But my immediate point is that, in spite of the traditionality and reality of Frost's New England, still that New England is a product of deliberate selection on a narrowly limited basis.[13] With what is really very little variation, it is a rural, Protestant, Anglo-Saxon New England that Frost offers us, taking little note of city or mill town, of Irish or Italian Catholicism in the south, or of French-Canadian Catholicism in the north. It is a pre-industrial, almost a pre-urban New England, one whose characteristic social and economic unit is the individually owned and operated family farm. There is less *village* life in Frost's New England than in that of Miss Jewett or Mrs. Freeman. And Frost's characteristic social values are those appropriate to such a society. Gorham Munson writes:

. . . it is important to see that the classicism of Robert Frost has been evolved in a simplified world, the world of the New England farmer. Such a farmer has a settled routine of living dependent upon the regular processions of the seasons. He leads a village life in which most of the human factors at work are tangible and measurable. The intricacies of commerce and industry, the distress wrought by machines, the flow of vast crowds, the diversity of appeals of a great city, do not reach him. Churches are what

[13] Cf. above, pp. 80, 89.

they were, intellectual currents do not disturb, and science, arch-upsetter of former values, finds no opening to intrude.[14]

And again:

. . . out of a settled social framework, an honest necessary struggle for existence, and a fair amount of well-being, something like a representative man can emerge. There are balances and checks to trim down his uniqueness while at the same time there is permitted a reasonable scope for his emotional and reflective life. In such a state the acquisitive impulse gets no favoring head start and instead of haste we find reticence and deliberation characteristic.[15]

In essence, the world Munson describes is the world of *North of Boston, Mountain Interval,* and *New Hampshire.*

But Munson's version is the idyllic one; it does not wholly account for such New England poems as "Home Burial," "A Servant to Servants," "The Hill Wife," or "The Pauper Witch of Grafton"—elegies, in a way, for a social pattern that no longer possesses the vitality to sustain its members. Robert P. Tristram Coffin writes:

. . . a place where much living has been and is no longer there is lonelier than a virgin wilderness. And to the south in the great cities that machinery has built greater, in a Boston larger than Emerson's, there is something very vital gone. . . . But here it is not people so much as a pattern that is wanting. Confidence has gone out of men, confidence in certain designs of the spirit that were once the breath of life to New Englanders, from Transcendentalists to men in the street who basked in their optimism.[16]

And it is of course true that rural, agrarian New England is not what it once was. W. G. O'Donnell cites census statistics indicating that, during the half-century following the outbreak of the Civil War, New England agricultural land shrank from a total of 12,000,000 acres under cultivation to only 7,000,000, while at the same time "the population of the

---

[14] Gorham B. Munson, "Robert Frost," *Saturday Review of Literature,* I (March 28, 1925), 626.

[15] *Ibid.,* p. 626.

[16] Robert P. Tristram Coffin, *New Poetry of New England: Frost and Robinson* (Baltimore, 1938), p. 23.

region doubled. In short, New England became largely urban and industrialized."[17]

Now Frost does not shrink from the fact that agarian New England has in some fashion decayed. The image of the abandoned farm persists in his work to a degree that almost warrants calling it obsessive—a symbol of a kind of vitality that is not to be found save in a largely inaccessible past—an Eden symbol, in fact. The same emphasis appears quite explicitly in Frost's essay on Stephen Burroughs. Pelham, Massachusetts,

is the kind of town I should have wanted to magnify anyway . . . just one high old street along a ridge, not much to begin with and every year beautifully less. The railroads have worked modern magic against it from away off in the valleys and the woods have pressed in upon it till now there is nothing left but the church . . . a few houses . . . and here and there a good mowing field of about the size of a tea-tray in the sky.[18]

"The American," writes George W. Pierson, "moves with a fine abandon, but the abandoning leaves its mark."[19] Out of his awareness of that mark, out of his awareness of social contraction and social loss, Frost has written many passable and some excellent poems—"Directive," for example, or "The Witch of Coös," or "The Generations of Men." But out of that awareness he has also developed two implicit assumptions that are less clearly defensible: first, that the old New England symbolized by abandoned farm and shrinking village *is* New England, the norm from which other forms of social vitality are aberrations; second, that the values appropriate to that norm may be transposed into other contexts for the purpose of rendering judgment.

The first of these assumptions, though questionable, is not

[17] William G. O'Donnell, "Robert Frost and New England: A Revaluation," *Yale Review*, XXXVII (Summer, 1948), 703.

[18] Robert Frost, "Stephen Burroughs," in *Cupid and Lion* (New York, n.d. [*ca.* 1924]), p. 11.

[19] George W. Pierson, "The Moving American," *Yale Review*, XLIV (Sept., 1954), 111.

in itself damaging. That it is questionable is indicated clearly enough by O'Donnell's statistics. On the one hand, commercial and industrial New England is a fact; on the other hand, agricultural New England still exists, as Vermont dairymen and Massachusetts apple growers know. "It is a curious thing," writes Gladys Hasty Carroll,

how often this Northeast corner has been declared dead. We died when ships began to be made of steel instead of wood, when steam came in and sails went out, when kerosene replaced whale oil. . . . we were dead. The West and the South said so and we believed them.[20]

But Frost's relative unconcern with industrial and urban New England, or with the agricultural New England of extension services and the New York and Boston milksheds, is a matter of relatively little importance as long as he is able to produce such poems as "Directive" or "The Gift Outright." In itself, it represents no more than that limitation of subject matter that makes literature possible. Professor Pierson, again, writes that

the geography of New England is all broken to pieces, and the economy ailing. In politics it may be divided, its ancestral and religious allegiances in confusion. *But,* as a region of the heart and mind, New England is still very much alive. . . . the old-time Yankee independence and the unquiet Puritan conscience still walk abroad in this land.[21]

Frost's poems represent a distinguished locus for that walking abroad.

But regions of the heart and mind may be deceptive. There are, I think, valid grounds for saying that that first assumption is not simply a thing in itself, that it carries Frost imperceptibly into the second assumption I have specified. And the second assumption—that values appropriate to a

[20] Gladys Hasty Carroll, "New England Sees It Through," *Saturday Review of Literature,* XIII (Nov. 9, 1935), 3.
[21] George W. Pierson, "The Obstinate Concept of New England: A Study in Denudation," *New England Quarterly,* XXVIII (March, 1955), 17.

society in which subsistence farming is the rule, other things the incidental exception, are equally appropriate to other societies—can be damaging. Louise Bogan puts it thus:

In *North of Boston* Frost briefly possessed himself of a humane realism and insight which he was never quite able to repeat. And even here he deleted facts which would have broken a frame he wished to keep intact, the frame of a folk culture at its dead end when the loneliness of moral isolation is bringing madness, obsession, and a collapse of the will to people whose only weapons are a shrewd humor and calculation. In reality, this dead end had been broken by industrialization; but Frost skirts the problem of the mills and of a new immigrant population. By so doing he is able, at first, to crystallize his drama. By continuing to eliminate these facts he finally leaves the entire situation dangling and incomplete.[22]

To be specific, in "Home Burial" (1914), arduous and narrowly limited living gives Frost the occasion for a moving presentation of emotional entrapment and human loss; in "A Roadside Stand" (1936), for an expression of irritable resentment directed against money, machines, the city and social planning. Or as Merrill Moore says, of "A Lone Striker,"

There is at times a faint, almost pathetic tinge to his lines suggestive of an order of life which is passing away. To some readers, his refusal to become ruffled may smack of complacency, especially when he tells his rather idyllic tale of the lone striker who decides to leave the factory and retreat to the tall trees [one thinks of the Edenic dark woods]. . . . There may be some sufficiently realistic to wonder how many factory hands are in a position to retreat.[23]

In New England mill towns in 1936, such realism frequently had a good deal of relevance. The poem's tacit assumption that one can always quit the mill and go back to the woods or the farm is dubious at best.

Thus, although Frost has written poems in which collec-

[22] Louise Bogan, *Achievement in American Poetry, 1900-1950* (Chicago, 1951), p. 49.

[23] Merrill Moore, "Poetic Agrarianism: Old Style," *Sewanee Review*, XLV (Oct.-Dec., 1937), 508-509.

tive endeavor is seen as desirable, and although his resistance
to social significance, in the *Pins and Needles* sense, becomes
explicit only on occasion, nevertheless that resistance provides
a powerful undercurrent, particularly in his later works. And
while that undercurrent is not clearly or always implicit in the
earlier poems, it is consistent with them. I have said that
Frost seldom exhibits any very immediate sense of collective
aims or of broadly social values,[24] and this negative fact is as
much in evidence in the early volumes as in the later ones.
There are very few poems indeed in his total output in which
individuals are seen as parts of or in relationship with collective units. Even Frost's families tend to be man-and-wife
affairs, without dependent relatives or grown children; and
when a more complex unit does appear, or when a complicating element does thrust itself into the husband-wife relationship, special things happen, as is clear in the eight more
or less "family" poems in *North of Boston*. In "The Death of
the Hired Man," the dependent Silas comes home, but only in
time to die, bringing husband and wife to a fuller understanding of each other and themselves. In "Home Burial" nothing
outside themselves can touch the wretchedly estranged couple.
In "The Black Cottage" the old lady had grown-up sons, but

> valued the considerate neglect
> She had at some cost taught them after years.

In "Blueberries" husband and wife find "Loren, the fatherly,"
and his democrat-load of young Lorens an object of amuse-
ment. In "A Servant to Servants" contact with even village
society only increases the burden on the already intolerably
overburdened wife. In "The Generations of Men" Frost
assembles Starks from all over the country at their ancestral
cellar-hole—decayed New England, again—but principally
in order to bring together two of the younger ones, sufficiently
remote in kinship to marry and revitalize the family farm. In

[24] See above, p. 112.

"The Housekeeper" the common-law wife Estelle's mother functions only as narrator and chorus, while the visiting neighbor only gives her someone to talk to; they cannot really reach John Hall or the absent Estelle. In "The Fear" contact with others is a source of perpetual dread to another common-law wife. And while it is obviously not true that all Frost's married couples are happy, it is very nearly true that his most happily endowed people are those whose social horizon is very nearly defined by relationship with one other person.[25] Frost's real social group is the family, in its minimal form.

I do not mean that the simple expedient of turning one's back on society in order to keep the home fires—farm-house fires—burning is offered as a panacea; Frost's world has no panaceas. If his most happily endowed people have turned from the world of social significance, so have his most moving failures; both nature and shared solitude, once more, are sources of ambivalent feeling. On the one hand, there are such poems as "In the Home Stretch," "Two Look at Two," "West-Running Brook," and "A Drumlin Woodchuck." On the other hand, there are "Home Burial," "A Servant to Servants," "The Lovely Shall Be Choosers," and "The Discovery of the Madeiras." If foregoing broadly social relationships in favor of domestic intimacy in the latter poems is a source of strength, surely it is the strength of desperation.

The implication here, I think, is that for Frost all values, both positive and negative—at least the most important ones— are ultimately defined in terms of relationships of individual to individual (the husband-wife unit) or, to extend the principle, of the individual to himself or to his natural environment, not of the individual to society. Like nature, such relationships make possible a kind of ideal simplification,[26] providing a context for what Frost sees as both the most vital

[25] E.g., "In Neglect," "Going for Water," "A Line-Storm Song," "In the Home Stretch," "Paul's Wife," "Two Look at Two," "West-Running Brook," and "Happiness Makes Up in Height for What It Lacks in Length."

[26] See above, pp. 16-22.

affirmations and the most crippling denials. For example, in
"West-Running Brook," the fine relationship between man
and wife—

> 'It must be the brook
> Can trust itself to go by contraries
> The way I can with you—and you with me—'

which is also a relationship with their natural environment—

> 'We've said we two. Let's change that to we three.
> As you and I are married to each other,
> We'll both be married to the brook.'—

makes possible the eloquent restraint of the husband's insight,
which deserves quoting in full:

> 'Speaking of contraries, see how the brook
> In that white wave runs counter to itself.
> It is from that in water we were from
> Long, long before we were from any creature.
> Here we, in our impatience of the steps,
> Get back to the beginning of beginnings,
> The stream of everything that runs away.
> Some say existence like a Pirouot
> And Pirouette, forever in one place,
> Stands still and dances, but it runs away,
> It seriously, sadly, runs away
> To fill the abyss' void with emptiness.
> It flows beside us in this water brook,
> But it flows over us. It flows between us
> To separate us for a panic moment.
> It flows between us, over us, and *with* us.
> And it is time, strength, tone, light, life, and love—
> And even substance lapsing unsubstantial;
> The universal cataract of death

That spends to nothingness—and unresisted,
Save by some strange resistance in itself,
Not just a swerving, but a throwing back,
As if regret were in it and were sacred.
It has this throwing backward on itself
So that the fall of most of it is always
Raising a little, sending up a little.
Our life runs down in sending up the clock.
The brook runs down in sending up our life.
The sun runs down in sending up the brook.
And there is something sending up the sun.
It is this backward motion toward the source,
Against the stream, that most we see ourselves in,
The tribute of the current to the source.
It is from this in nature we are from.
It is most us.'

My immediate point is that such laying bare of the speaker's heart, with its perception of a truth that is at once heart-breaking and invigorating, is scarcely imaginable in any less intimate situation, save at the risk of seeming a kind of spiritual strip tease. But there is more than that. For one thing, the perception has no very clear social corollary; neither a summons to action, nor an accusation of injustice, nor an invitation to discipleship, it defies translation into social terms. It is, in fact, an awareness of one of those "immedicable woes" that Frost has expressed a preference for.[27] Insofar as it is heart-breaking, there is nothing to be done but to accept it. Insofar as it is invigorating, there is nothing to be done but to go on paying one's own tribute to the source by one's own resistances. (I am not necessarily recommending the speaker's attitude—merely trying to describe it.) And for another thing, even in its context, the speech does not really convince one that it really is speech, the largely unpremeditated observation of a flesh-and-blood person. This is not intended as unfavor-

[27] See above, p. 117.

able criticism. The same sort of unreality is characteristic of the speeches in the interlude in Hell from *Man and Superman,* of the monologues in *The Ring and the Book,* of Shakespeare's soliloquies,[28] and of Greek tragedy. To misquote Aristotle, such speech is not what somebody *did* say but what somebody *would* say if he were capable of it, the ideally definitive utterance of a completely realized, completely articulate character, who can make final pronouncements. What he utters is, of course, a statement of ultimate values; in context, it means that the two people are right in trusting one another to go by contraries, that they are right in imposing the made pattern of their marriage on the "stream of everything that runs away," because such processes, such resistances, *are* life. In the terms I suggested toward the end of Chapter I,[29] the poem is a kind of vindication of anthropocentric man, the man who, aware that he is in some degree subject to inscrutable forces of which he can only be aware, aware further that yielding prudentially to the natural "drift of things" (from "Reluctance"; "West-Running Brook" provides a rationale for the earlier poem) will only negate his own vitality, makes his own patterns as an affirmation of life, a testimony to his own existence. It is the closest man can come to achieving the Edenic plastic environment in the intractable world he inhabits, and it is a considerably more distinguished approximation than that provided by simple anti-intellectualism.

"In the Home Stretch" offers similar affirmation in a similar context, though here the relationship is one of age rather than of youth. The elderly couple, like the younger, can trust one another to go by contraries, as is evident from their semi-serious maneuverings to wangle from the other an admission that retiring to a farm was *his* idea. The women in both poems express a whimsical sense of a relationship with external nature; the one proposes marriage with the brook, the

[28] "Frost's lyrics are soliloquies, as are his drawings of people." Constance Rourke, *American Humor: A Study of the National Character* (Garden City, 1953), p. 217.

[29] See above, pp. 49-50.

other detects friendly sympathy in the moon, and both whim-
sies appear in conjunction with a perception of the speakers'
newness.   And in both poems, accustomed intimacy makes
possible a kind of speech that, in almost any other context,
would have the ring of pedantry or of excessive ingenuousness.
In this respect, there is nothing in "In the Home Stretch" that
is quite comparable in degree with the husband's speech in
"West-Running Brook," but, for example,

> 'The meals we've had no one can take from us.
> I wish that everything on earth were just
> As certain as the meals we've had. I wish
> The meals we haven't had were anyway'

is of the same kind.   So, more significantly, is the wife's

> 'You're searching, Joe,
> For things that don't exist; I mean beginnings.
> Ends and beginnings—there are no such things.
> There are only middles.'

Broadly speaking, she means that the self-created patterns
anthropocentric man imposes on his world are not the last
word, however indispensable they may be if man is to fulfil
himself.   More explicitly, what Joe wants to do is to confirm
his lordship of all he surveys:

> 'Is it too late
> To drag you out for just a good-night call
> On the old peach trees on the knoll . . .
>
>   .   .   .   .
>
> The first thing in the morning, out we go
> To go the round of apple, cherry, peach,
> Pine, alder, pasture, mowing, well, and brook.
> All of a farm it is.'

What she wants is to get him to bed before he's hit by a throm-
bosis or an attack of paranoia. Yet the affirmation is at bottom the same as that of "West-Running Brook." For all the
wife's prudential reservations, they *are* on their farm, " 'fifteen
miles away' " from the

> 'fools in towns who think
> Style upon style in dress and thought at last
> Must get somewhere'—

briefly, who have made a cult and a parody of the anthropocentric perception in "West-Running Brook" that we must
make our own patterns of value. Even for the wife, the risk
was apparently worth taking. Parenthetically, it can be
pointed out that the women in Frost's poems frequently,
though not always, do exercise this prudential restraint on their
men; the wife in "In the Home Stretch," Mrs. Cole, in "Snow,"
and Thyatira, in *A Masque of Reason,* are the most obvious
examples.

But if the individual-to-individual relationship of childless
married people makes possible such affirmations, so does it
make possible the most dreadful forms of failure, negation,
and waste. On this side of the coin Frost gives us nothing as
explicit as the husband's speech in "West-Running Brook,"
but the fact is obvious enough in such poems as "Home
Burial," "A Servant to Servants," "The Fear," "The Lovely
Shall Be Choosers," and "The Discovery of the Madeiras."
The ideal simplification of "Home Burial" is one in which, all
polite reserve stripped away by the habit of intimacy, husband
and wife reveal their absolute failure to achieve a viable
rapprochement, a vital pattern of resistance to the "stream of
everything that runs away." A pattern is there, of course, and
ironically enough it is a pattern of a sort that only people can
produce; more "natural" creatures do not cripple themselves
by hysteria and blunted perception. But there is no affirma-

tion, even of the sort one finds in tragedy; Oedipus accepts his destiny, Theseus and Hippolytus at last see eye to eye, Hamlet perceives a destiny that shapes our ends.   Here there is no resolution.   The closest thing to one is the husband's proposal for

> 'some arrangement
> By which I'd bind myself to keep hands off
> Anything special you're a-mind to name.'

Such an arrangement could provide only the most perilous sort of equilibrium; it is a mode, not of trusting one another to go by contraries as in "West-Running Brook," but of deliberately denying one's human individuality on behalf of a pattern that has no positive meaning:

> 'I don't like such things 'twixt those that love.
> Two that don't love can't live together without them.
> But two that do can't live together with them.'

Such speech is the speech of anthropocentric man, making his own arrangements, as is the wife's passionate refusal to accept the fact of death or the nature of grief, but their struggle to achieve something of value is that of Yeats's fly in marmalade, or of Frank Norris' McTeague, lost in the desert and handcuffed to a corpse.   Again, one is confronted with an immedicable woe.

"The Discovery of the Madeiras" has come up for considerable discussion in Chapter III, but it is relevant here also. The man and his "stolen lady" are married only by—apparently—mutual consent, but the very irregularity of the union, "leav[ing] the English law behind," makes it the more a pattern of their own making, without even the sanction of legality, that codification of relationships that social man prudentially agrees to accept as a means of getting by with nature or of fulfilling divine purposes. (Except for the whimsical "Triple Bronze," Frost gives little emphasis to law as a means whereby anthropocentric man stabilizes those collective designs that only man can produce: see below, pp. 135-138.) Having established their pattern, however, the man and woman are unable to do anything with it:

> she and her lover would sit opposed
> And darkly drink each other's eyes
> With faint head shakings, no more wise.
> The most he asked her eyes to grant
> Was that in what she does not want
> A woman wants to be overruled.
> Or was the instinct in him fooled?
> He knew not, neither of them knew.
> They could only say like any two,
> 'You tell me and I'll tell you.'

Admittedly, the odds are against them; as passengers on a sailing ship in an Atlantic hurricane, they cannot very well devote themselves to managing a farm or even a household. And it is perhaps no more than appallingly bad luck that the captain's story of a supremely meaningful marriage relationship reaches them at a time when they have every opportunity to be bored with one another. Be that as it may, they—at least the woman—cannot rise to the occasion, cannot find sufficient meaning in their relationship to tide them over the crisis. The woman dies of a sort of moral, emotional, and intellectual paralysis:

> The story is she died of thought.

The man lives, but the experience that should have been crucial to him is hollow at the core:

> Then he gouged a clumsy sailing trough
> From a fallen tree and pushing off

Safely made the African shore;
Where he fell a prisoner to the Moor.
But the Moor strangely enough believed
The tale of the voyage he had achieved,
And sent him to the King to admire.
He came at last to his native shire.
The island he found was verified.
And the bay where his stolen lady died
Was named for him instead of her.
But so is history like to err.
And soon it is neither here nor there
Whether time's rewards are fair or unfair.

Discounting the final three lines, which merely dilute the poem, this passage is dreadfully empty, as it is meant to be. The moral impotence of second-rate humanity is translated into a commonplace adventure story and immortalized in an island named for the wrong person and for the wrong reason; the important human failure is vulgarized into an irrelevant triumph of dumb luck—and I trust it is clear that it is not Frost who has vulgarized the experience. Yvor Winters, contrasting "The Discovery of the Madeiras" with the border ballads on the ground that the ballads deal with "an important decision consciously made," concludes that "Frost's poem deals with the accidental impingement of a brutal fact upon a morbid sensibility and the collapse of the sensibility. Frost's poem to this extent is the product of a decadent state of mind."[30] It seems to me that Winters' description of the poem is accurate but his judgment of it thoroughly misleading. Surely the failure consciously to make an important decision may be as ethically meaningful a fact as deliberately energetic decisiveness; and surely it is the ethical waste of the situation that Frost's poem stresses, an element that is very much in evidence in "The Battle of Otterburn" or "The Hunting of the Cheviot."

Thus the marriage relationship provides the characteristic

[30] Winters, p. 593.

setting within which the people of Frost's poems develop, or fail to develop, sustaining values. There are other relationships that have a similar function—those of the individual to himself, to his environment, to his own active interests. Such relationships exclude, even more markedly than does that of marriage, any very broadly social element. Thus "The Gum-Gatherer" has achieved frictionless adjustment to a world that, for all practical or social purposes, includes no one but himself. "A Drumlin Woodchuck" apparently has a wife, but his real achievement is a matter of the slickness with which he has fitted himself into the chinks and crannies of a generally inimical environment; the "rankly warm insider" of "In the Long Night" has done much the same thing. And shepherd Meliboeus, of "Build Soil," knows that he will find himself most satisfactorily in the process of minding his own business—"cutting posts/ Or mending fence." Conversely, the old man of "An Old Man's Winter Night," like the gum-gatherer, has no one but himself, but the old man's situation is informed by a vague but pervasive pathos. The Indian of "The Vanishing Red" and the boy of " 'Out, Out—' " are destroyed—this may be to stretch a point—by their failure to achieve the drumlin woodchuck's adjustment. It may be significant that both deaths are the result of disastrous contact with machinery; one remembers Yvor Winters' comment on "The Egg and the Machine."[31] The speaker of "Misgiving" envisions a failure of his own interest in "the knowledge beyond the bounds of life" as the ultimate defeat; and the Broken One in "The Self-Seeker," crippled by an industrial accident—machinery, again—bleakly confronts a world stripped of value since his injury has incapacitated him from actively pursuing his interest in native orchids. Like marriage, such situations reveal those affirmations and denials, acceptances and refusals, that make life meaningful in the world of Frost's poems.

It is clear, I think, from the poems just discussed that to

[31] Quoted above, p. 115.

Frost ethical significance is a function primarily of anthropocentric man, the man who, by an active effort of the will,
creates or at least selects ("A Drumlin Woodchuck," "The
Gum-Gatherer") his own patterns of meaning in the generally
indifferent world he inhabits. It is only by making such acts
of will that man succeeds in defining himself, whether in success or in failure; only people, once more, can destroy themselves in the manner of "Home Burial." "Every poem,"
writes Frost, "is an epitome of the great predicament; a figure
of the will braving alien entanglements."[32]   Out of his awareness of that predicament, Frost has wrought a conception of
man that attributes to him sympathy, insight, and a capacity
not only to will and to endure but to command respect. Insofar as humanism is an affirmation of man's dignity, Frost is
a humanist, and a worthy one.

And yet surely something vital is missing. And to say
that the missing element is social significance is not to argue
that *Pins and Needles* is greater writing than Frost is capable
of. It is only to say that, ever since Socrates chose death
under Athenian law in preference to life as an honored but
stateless alien, the most enduring assertions of human dignity
that Western civilization has made have faced and in some
fashion come to terms with the fact of man's social nature.
To Plato, the life of individual contemplation might be best,
but his philosophers were also kings. To Aristotle, man was
a political animal, meaning, as H. D. F. Kitto tells us, " 'an
animal whose characteristic it is to live in a city state.' If
you did not do this, you were something less than man at his
best and most characteristic."[33]   To St. Augustine, the City of
God was a natural figure, and Dante's heaven is full of social
imagery. Even Frost's favorite, Thoreau, that adept at making
himself snug in the limitless, wrote approvingly that "to act
collectively is according to the spirit of our institutions,"[34]

[32] Robert Frost, "The Constant Symbol," *Atlantic Monthly,* CLXXVIII
(Oct., 1946), 50.

[33] H. D. F. Kitto, *The Greeks* (Harmondsworth, 1951), p. 11.

[34] Henry David Thoreau, *Walden* (Harmondsworth, 1938), p. 96.

and the remark occurs in a lambaste of Concord society and American village society generally for making second-rate use of its capacity for collective action. In the same passage, Thoreau writes:

let the village . . . not stop short at a pedagogue, a parson, a sexton, a parish library, and three select men, because our pilgrim forefathers got through a cold winter once on a bleak rock with these.[35]

Thoreau's attitude toward the past provides a marked contrast with Frost's preference for pre-industrial New England.[36] Admittedly, such quoting is hitting below the belt; I do not mean to transform Thoreau into a dogmatic collectivist. But it would be difficult to find a comparable passage in Frost's writing;

Keep off each other and keep each other off

comes much more immediately to mind—and, I think, not accidentally.

Now, there is an anomaly here. If I am right in finding in Frost a powerful ethical bias in favor of anthropocentric man, then surely one is justified in asking whether anthropocentric man does not most characteristically express himself in those collective, social designs whose development is a prime characteristic distinguishing man from the lower animals. I have cited "The Tuft of Flowers," "Haec Fabula Docet," and "Triple Bronze"[37] as evidence that Frost does not totally reject man's social nature, and "The Census-Taker," "On a Tree Fallen Across the Road," "Sand Dunes," "Two Tramps in Mud Time," and "The Lost Follower" contain suggestions of the same sort. "Build Soil" even indicates that asociality is really a kind of tactical maneuver undertaken for the good of society:

[35] Thoreau, pp. 95-96.
[36] See above, pp. 117-122.
[37] See above, pp. 113-114, 131.

We're always too much out or too much in.
At present from a cosmical dilation
We're so much out that the odds are against
Our ever getting inside in again.

That is, in an excessively gregarious society, conscientious withdrawal is one means of redeeming the time.[38] It is on this basis that Frost's apologists justify his general insensitivity to collective values—when they do not try to prove that he is really as social as anybody else or that eloquently anarchic individualism needs no defense. Thus G. R. Elliott argues that critics have underemphasized Frost's "representative meaning," which is an affirmation of human brotherhood, and he cites "The Tuft of Flowers" as the speaker's discovery that the societal impulse is the ultimate source of value.[39] And Bernard De Voto declares that

Frost's poetry is a new assertion of eternal things—that, whether indirectly or in fulfillment, life *counts,* is worthy, can be trusted, has dignity. On that infrangible dignity, the worth of the individual's experience, he has based the stubborn singularity that has made him a variegated assortment of enemies in the last quarter

[38] Here again Frost's position is analogous with that of the Southern agrarians. Donald Davidson, for example, writes: "For strategic purposes, at least, I feel [the artist] will ally himself with programs of agrarian restoration. Out of conviction he should do so, since only in an agrarian society does there remain much hope of a balanced life, where the arts are not luxuries to be purchased but belong as a matter of course in the routine of his living. Again, both strategy and conviction will almost inevitably lead him to the sections of America that are provincial, conservative, agrarian, for there only will he find a lingering preference for values not industrial. The very wilderness is his friend, not as a refuge, but as an ally. But he does not need to go into the wilderness. There are American communities throughout the country from the West, even to the fringes of the industrialized East, that are in the industrial sense backward, and are naturally on his side. Negatively to his advantage are the discontent and confusion in the heart of industrialism itself." Donald Davidson, "A Mirror for Artists," in Twelve Southerners, *I'll Take My Stand: The South and the Agrarian Tradition* (New York, 1930), pp. 51-52.

[39] G. R. Elliott, "The Neighborliness of Robert Frost," *Nation,* CIX (Dec. 6, 1919), 713-715.

century, and all his poetic practise as well. It is the only major affirmation that modern American literature has made.[40]

But George Whicher, who reads Frost better than most men, writes, "though deeply attached to neighborhood and nation, he has never been willing to acknowledge any allegiance to the particular age in which he lives,"[41] and again, "there may have been moments when poets did not have to choose between being humanly complete and being contemporary, but our distressed time is not one of them."[42] By choosing human completeness in preference to contemporaneity, we are told, Frost has taken the better alternative.

I suspect that the dilemma Professor Whicher describes is a rigged one, a stacking of the cards in Frost's behalf.[43] For now, it seems to me that tracking down Frost's more or less explicit social affirmations in the body of his work is very like arguing that the Thoreau of "to act collectively is according to the spirit of our institutions" is the real Thoreau—that "Civil Disobedience," with its preference for majorities "of one" and its insistence that "that government is best which governs not at all"[44] is really a kind of *jeu d'esprit*. There is, of course, much more of the antisocial in Thoreau than in Frost; yet even here, Thoreau's position is more solidly grounded than Frost's. However much instinctive antisocial bent may have contributed to "Civil Disobedience," Thoreau makes it very clear that it is governmental *injustice* that legitimizes non-co-operation, that disobedience is a protest against specific evils, instead of—or at least as well as—a positive good in its own right. It is because government does not fulfil those collective desires for which it was established that one has an obligation to disobey; there is an almost Hobbesian

[40] Bernard De Voto, "The Critics and Robert Frost," *Saturday Review of Literature*, XVII (Jan. 1, 1938), 15.

[41] George F. Whicher, "Frost at Seventy," *American Scholar*, XIV (Autumn, 1945), 406.

[42] *Ibid.*, p. 406.

[43] See below, pp. 143, 147-148.

[44] Henry David Thoreau, *Civil Disobedience and A Plea for Captain John Brown* (Chicago, n.d.), p. 1.

logic here. And except for the suggestion in "Build Soil,"
there is little of Thoreau's logic in Frost's poems. The
simple fact is that Frost characteristically does not allow
anthropocentric man the full development of his premises.
Characteristically, "society" means to Frost very much what
it means in Emily Dickinson's "The Soul Selects Her Own
Society"; more often than not, his "divine majority," like Miss
Dickinson's, consists of not more than two souls.

It is impossible to construct a broad, really complete
humanism on such a basis—and perhaps on any basis. But
because Frost deals as movingly and convincingly as he does
with his social atoms, it is important to recognize what he does
not do. What he does not do is to allow us any real conviction that the capacity for pooling intelligence, strength, and
resources for collective purposes is a valid index of human
worth—that man is a social animal, if only among other
things, that he has no real choice but to be a social animal
even if it were really desirable not to be, and that therefore
the collective values he develops are as genuinely human a
phenomenon as the individual insights he achieves. In effect,
Frost denies this, and the denial is deeply implicated in much
of his work. It is something more than a reasonable distrust
of social panaceas, though Frost regularly presents it as such
when he deals with it more or less directly—for example, "A
Case for Jefferson," "The Lost Follower," the "one real re-
former" of "New Hampshire," or this passage:

. . . we may be required by law to throw away patience as we have
been required to surrender gold; since by throwing away patience
and joining the impatient in one last rush on the citadel of evil,
the hope is we may end the need of patience. There will be
nothing left to be patient about. The day of perfection waits on
unanimous social action. Two or three more good national elec-
tions should do the business. It has been similarly urged on us to
give up courage, make cowardice a virtue, and see if that won't
end war, and the need of courage.[45]

[45] *King Jasper*, pp. viii-ix.

Taken at face value, such writing suggests no more than a sound and satirical, if not wholly unprejudiced, conservatism; taken in the context of Frost's writing generally, however, it suggests not so much mere conservatism as an almost instinctive shying away from a whole major area of values.

Such shying away is consistent enough, given Frost's preference for a simplified world, a world quite directly subject to individual will,[46] and he maintains it with remarkable persistence. Even trivial detail in the poems frequently suggests the near-instinctive social balk. It is not enough that the gum-gatherer lives by himself, bringing his wholly natural product to market when he pleases; he goes all the way with his independence and lives in a stolen shack that he has nevertheless built—on the one hand, self-reliant for his necessities; on the other hand, independent even of the law's protection. The census-taker feels a tug at his heart for the society that has vanished from the deserted lumber camp, but the society that moves him is by its very nature, given the scalping of timber land unfortunately still common in back country Vermont, a temporary, transient, unstable, and even destructive thing. In "Two Tramps in Mud Time," a sense of social responsibility tempts the speaker to hand over his satisfying chore to unemployed lumberjacks, who need the work, but the social conflict of interests threatens to destroy the ideally frictionless relationship he has established between vocation and avocation, love and need—in fact, between himself and a nature that is devoid of personal interest in him or of those personal demands on him that society inevitably makes.

How deeply this shying away goes is suggested, I think, in a reminiscence recorded by Ernest Poole:

I remember one still day in October when toward dusk we both stopped and listened. Deep, deep stillness all around. [Frost] said:

"These folks like this. So do I. People say that I hate New York. I don't. I like it, but I get so worked up down there that

[46] See above, pp. 79-84.

I can't sleep nights. I'm made that way. I grew up on a farm and I like it quiet." A cow mooed half a mile away. He smiled. "Even that cow's too much," he said.[47]

The Frost one sees here is a very sympathetic figure. But the interesting thing about that figure is that it is apparently an invention. Born in 1875 in San Francisco, Frost lived there until his father's death in 1885, in which year his mother brought her family east to her father-in-law's home in Lawrence, Massachusetts, already a mill town. (Frost's grandfather was an overseer in a Lawrence mill.) Frost finished high school in Lawrence, and in 1892, at seventeen, entered Dartmouth. Finding college not to his liking, he returned to Lawrence and found work in a cotton mill, in a shoe factory, in his mother's private school, and finally became editor of the weekly Lawrence *Sentinel*. In 1895 he married. In 1897 he entered Harvard and stayed two years. And in 1900, when Frost was twenty-five, his grandfather staked him to a farm in Derry, New Hampshire; five years later, unpaid and apparently unpayable bills induced him to become a schoolteacher at Pinkerton Academy, in Derry.[48] It is not easy to understand how growing up on a farm fits that thirty-year pattern of circumstances except as some kind of myth.

This is not intended as an exercise in debunking. Probably any highly characteristic poet tends to make for himself a role, or even several roles, through which he expresses himself. Oscar Wilde's posing, Emily Dickinson's self-created role as the Nun of Amherst, Whitman's as one of the roughs, or Dylan Thomas' as the wildly Bohemian archromantic are all cases in point. So is the elderly and respectably married Yeats's delighted and masterful representation of himself as a lecherous old goat; and Randall Jarrell aptly "imagines Yeats saying about Frost, as Sarah Bernhardt said about Nijinsky: 'I fear, I greatly fear, that I have just seen the greatest actor

[47] Ernest Poole, "When Frost Was Here," *New Hampshire Troubadour*, XVI (Nov., 1946), 12.

[48] Gorham B. Munson, *Robert Frost: A Study in Sensibility and Good Sense* (New York, 1927), pp. 21-39 *passim*.

in the world.' "[49] I have no doubt that such role-playing is more than a strategic maneuver, that it is in some degree a neurotic symptom, though this is not the occasion for amateur psychoanalytic speculation about Frost's early days. As a strategic maneuver, the fiction of growing up on a farm has the function of providing a credible origin for Frost's characteristic presentation of himself as the independent, thoughtful, sensitively observant New England yeoman. Gorham Munson writes, of the immediate circumstances leading to Frost's application for a position at Pinkerton Academy,

. . . his farming neighbors, probably correctly, did not approve of Frost's methods (he could be caught milking the cows at ten at night in order to sleep later in the morning) and the end of this venture came in 1905 when he drove up to the butcher's to make further purchases on credit. The fattish butcher came brusquely out on the porch of his store, cocked an appraising eye at Frost's horse, and inquired, none too delicately, if anyone had a lien on it.[50]

It is the kind of episode that Frost delights to get into a poem—for example, "New Hampshire"—and the experience of ineffectual farming may provide some of the detail of Brad McLaughlin's methods in "The Star-Splitter." But the episode as such appears nowhere in Frost's poems (though he has evidently been willing to tell it outside of verse), and it is tempting to suppose that the reason for his poetic silence about it is that the episode would tend to undermine his role as the man who has proven by experience that the old New England values of the subsistence farmer are still viable, that one need not come to terms with the industrial present, that highly integrated social structures and collective endeavor are not really necessary—the premises, once more, of the Southern agrarians in *I'll Take My Stand*.[51] What led Frost to assume that role is not a question of literary criticism, but the role is, I think,

[49] Randall Jarrell, *Poetry and the Age* (New York, 1955), p. 30.
[50] Munson, *Robert Frost: A Study* . . . , pp. 38-39.
[51] Cf. above, pp. 64-65.

an essential condition of Frost's poetry; it has contributed to his ability to write convincingly and with conviction.

It has also contributed to his writing incompletely, to the melancholy sense one sometimes has in reading his later books that they are, in Randall Jarrell's words, "the productions of someone who once, and somewhere else, was a great poet."[52] In his later volumes one finds little immediate sense of the tragic implications of Frost's chosen, asocial world, implications that provided a dominant theme in *North of Boston*. That theme never vanishes entirely; *A Witness Tree* has "The Subverted Flower" and "The Discovery of the Madeiras," but there is little such implication in *Steeple Bush*. *Steeple Bush* has instead "One Step Backward Taken":

> Not only sand and gravels
> Were once more on their travels,
> But gulping muddy gallons
> Great boulders off their balance
> Bumped heads together dully
> And started down the gully.
> Whole capes caked off in slices.
> I felt my standpoint shaken
> In the universal crisis.
> But with one step backward taken
> I saved myself from going.
> A world torn loose went by me.
> Then the rain stopped and the blowing
> And the sun came out to dry me.

The poem seems to me to be its own best exegesis; even granting that its central image may be no more than a sand bank in a cloudburst, it is more deadly cold than anything in Yeats's last poems, the utterance of one whom nothing outside his own orbit can touch. Not that it may not be a genuine experience; we have all felt that way at one time or another, and it would

[52] Jarrell, p. 31.

be merely priggish to say either that such feeling is inappropriate to poetry or that it is humanly unworthy. Even if one assumes that the poem is in some fashion about the Second World War (*Steeple Bush* was published in 1947, so the assumption is not unreasonable), one cannot simply write it off, as any number of combat infantrymen can testify. The trouble with "One Step Backward Taken" is not that it says "Thank God it wasn't me" but that it says only "Thank God it wasn't me," in tone as well as in statement. The preference for immedicable woes has been transmuted into a refusal to be touched by external disaster; the preference for "being humanly complete" over "being contemporary,"[53] into a determination not to be contemporary at whatever cost to human completeness.

What has happened, I think, is that Frost's early, instinctive predilection for asocial themes has hardened into something close to a defensive dogma. Like other dogmas, it is capable of providing the substructure for genuinely moving poetry, as it does in "Directive," for example. Like "One Step Backward Taken," "Directive" has to do with wasted energy—the waste of energy involved in the fading out of those patterns anthropocentric man succeeds in developing:

> a house that is no more a house
> Upon a farm that is no more a farm
> And in a town that is no more a town.

The reader is sent into this back country wasteland to experience the emotional ordeal of responding to the life that was once there:

> First there's the children's house of make believe,
> Some shattered dishes underneath a pine,
> The playthings in the playhouse of the children.
> Weep for what little things could make them glad.

[53] Whicher, p. 406; see above, p. 137.

But his real objective is not an understanding of the life that has vanished; for all we know, this might be the house of that Brad McLaughlin who, in "The Star-Splitter," burned down his own house in order to buy a telescope with the insurance money and work for the railroad, and who found it a good bargain on all counts. His real objective is, by drinking at the brook that provided the house with water, to pass through his awareness of lost energy and social waste into a condition of wholeness and invulnerability, a condition in which such waste does not matter.[54] In a way, "Directive" is really a ritual of initiation into the company of those who share Frost's role as the man who knows how little such waste really matters.

And, of course, Frost is right; it doesn't matter. Weeping over abandoned farms is very likely to be a form of sentimentality, and "Directive," far from being a bad poem, is to my mind one of Frost's best. His fundamentally asocial dogma has here served him very well indeed. Certainly "Directive" does not rub one the wrong way to the degree that "One Step Backward Taken" does; it is too skilfully, even too humanely, managed for that. And yet I think the poem is ultimately liable to the same criticism as is "One Step Backward Taken" —not that what it says is untrue but that it is finally not enough; and to indicate what I mean calls for some rather ungraceful maneuvering. Milton's "Lycidas" deals with a theme that, at least formally, is much like that of "Directive." The experience presented in both poems is that of becoming involved in a kind of psychic entrapment that threatens to cripple one; in both poems, the experience is lived through and is followed by a reaffirmation of life and energy:

Tomorrow to fresh woods and pastures new,

and

[54] In my copy of *A Witness Tree*, I find the following gloss to "November," evidently taken down during a talk Frost gave at Breadloaf in 1942: "You wouldn't know that here I was praising waste. You've got to know *how* to waste."

Drink and be whole again beyond confusion.

Neither poem is glib, and neither poem is moralistic, in the offensive sense of the word. "Lycidas" is obviously more elaborately wrought, more formally dense, as it were; but "Directive," with its persistent echoes of the Grail knight's initiatory ordeal[55] and its absorption of detail from *Walden*,[56] is not the work of any "easygoing versifier of all that comes to hand."[57]

The difference I am concerned with here has to do with the kinds of entrapment that the two poems present. In "Directive," it is a matter of losing oneself in sentimentalizing over an abandoned and almost vanished farm. I have said that the real objective of the poem is not an understanding of the life that has passed with the farm's passing, and that is quite as it should be. Without our knowing who these people were, why the farm is no more a farm, such an objective could lead only to a kind of vaguely self-indulgent, pleasantly melancholy brooding, a quite random emotionalism like that of Gray's "Elegy Written in a Country Churchyard."[58] To avoid such entrapment, at least as the final meaning of the poem's experience, is surely an indication of maturity.

And yet the resolution achieved in "Directive," compared with that of "Lycidas," is ultimately an easy one, one not very

---

[55] See Jarrell, p. 48.

[56] See above, pp. 19-20.

[57] R. P. Blackmur, "The Instincts of a Bard," *Nation*, CXLII (June 24, 1936), 818.

[58] Cf. William Empson, *Some Versions of Pastoral* (Norfolk, Conn., n.d.), pp. 4-5. "And yet what is said [in the 'Elegy'] is one of the permanent truths; it is only in degree that any improvement of society could prevent wastage of human powers; the waste even in a fortunate life, the isolation even of a life rich in intimacy, cannot but be felt deeply, and is the central feeling of tragedy. And anything of value must accept this because it must not prostitute itself; its strength is to be prepared to waste itself, if it does not get its opportunity (Empson, p. 5). It seems to me that "Directive" says this even better than the "Elegy," since it contains less of the self-indulgent melancholy that Gray does after all permit himself in arriving at his statement of "one of the permanent truths." And cf. above, p. 144, n. 54.

deeply embedded in the intellectual and social contingencies that mature living, after all, is involved with. The choice "Directive" offers, between sentimental melancholy and the realization that the dead farm does not really touch us personally, is an easy choice.[59] For most of us, sentimental melancholy is an aberration from our ordinary, useful adaptation to the world; we are not seriously tempted really to lose ourselves in it for any length of time. In "Lycidas" the problem goes deeper. Broadly speaking, it is the problem of how one is to maintain belief in an ethically meaningful, purposive world in the face of evidence that suggests nothing so much as a world devoid of such meaning and purpose, a world in which one's intellectual and spiritual leaders have betrayed their trust, cynically and with impunity, while the younger saving remnant die meaninglessly. One need not even share Milton's Christianity to appreciate the problem's depth, a depth that is not only emotional but intellectual and social as well; we are confronted with mutually incompatible theories of reality and, in St. Peter's speech, with an ecclesiastical—i.e., social—organism that is rotten at the core. The poem's resolution includes these elements, as it must, and in so doing it penetrates more deeply than does "Directive" into the complex tissue of psychic maturity. And more than this, the resolution arrived at in "Lycidas" is not merely a resolution of thought and emotion. We are made to feel that, having passed his crisis, the speaker is ready to act:

Tomorrow to fresh woods and pastures new.

To a degree, "Directive" gives the sense of something avoided, "Lycidas" of something mastered; in the latter poem, the speaker has achieved, not only freedom from entrapment, but freedom to act, to achieve objectives.[60] And curiously enough, by leaving us with this sense, Milton's poem provides a more

[59] Cf. above, pp. 16-17, 21.
[60] Cf. above, pp. 87-89.

positive affirmation of Frost's own anthropocentric man than does "Directive." Once more, one is confronted with Frost's implicit feeling that real vitality, real social meaning, is a function of the old New England of subsistence farming, that there is no valid alternative save to cultivate one's integrity, one's devotion to the values that old New England realized. And once more, one is confronted with the essentially incomplete nature of the humanism that Frost has developed.

Gladys Hasty Carroll remarks, of New England writers generally, "To a degree we are all like the rest of New England—a little blind to the exact significance of the present."[61] To insist that a poet be entirely aware of the exact significance of the present would, of course, require him to be God, and no one would attribute divinity even to Milton. But Frost's blindness is not simply to the exact significance of the present; it is also to what are surely inescapable and permanent facts about humanity, about man—that he is a social being, that his present is never the same thing as his past, and that his social ethic must speak to him in terms of those objectives and institutions he has developed, not simply of those he has forgone. Frost's poetry reveals at most an oblique acknowledgment of these facts, offering instead the propositions that minimal social structures are best, that the past lives in the present and renders it meaningful, and that one requires only those values that have stood the test of time. These propositions are not untrue; one can even say that they are as genuine "facts about humanity" as those others I have specified. But without those others, they are incomplete. Professor Whicher, once more, tells us that poets in our time are compelled "to choose between being humanly complete and being contemporary,"[62] and he speaks approvingly of Frost for having "declined to be warped by the pressures of modern living."[63] "Modern living," to Milton, was as shot through with extrava-

[61] Carroll, p. 17.
[62] Whicher, p. 406; see above, p. 137.
[63] Whicher, "Out For Stars: A Meditation on Robert Frost," *Atlantic Monthly*, CLXXI (May, 1943), 67.

gant hope and despair as it has been during the past seventy-five years, and Milton did not decline to be warped by its pressures.   That is one reason why "Lycidas" is a finer poem than "Directive," or *Samson Agonistes* than *A Masque of Reason*.   Oddly enough, one cannot "choose between being humanly complete and being contemporary" without in some measure ceasing to be either; and Frost, as spokesman for certain values to which he attaches a great deal of importance, has not escaped that consequence.   Probably no one does, and Frost has written poems for which no one need apologize. But they are not those poems in which he expresses most clearly his social bias.

5

The human objective

In "On a Tree Fallen Across
the Road," Frost assures us that, in spite of obstacles,

> We will not be put off the final goal
> We have it hidden in us to attain,
> Not though we have to seize earth by the pole
>
> And, tired of aimless circling in one place,
> Steer straight off after something into space.

And yet, as we have seen in Chapter I, Frost is reluctant to
indicate with any sort of finality what that final goal is.
Though unwilling to commit himself to a thorough-going

Lucretianism, he is equally unwilling to commit himself—or at
least to define the terms of such a commitment—to any explicit teleology, to any clear and final statement of why man
is and of what he is supposed to do about it. In this respect,
as in others, Frost's affirmations are more equivocal than his
denials, and the fact has been a source of some difficulty to
his defenders. Sidney Cox writes that, for Frost, "the last
stand must be that of a fighter, not that of an orator sawing
air,"[1] but he does not tell us what we must be prepared to
fight *for*. Peter Viereck, reviewing Frost's *Complete Poems*,
writes that Frost's

cheerfulness is the direct opposite of Mr. Babbitt's or even of Mr.
Pickwick's. It is a Greek cheerfulness. And the apparent blandness of the Greeks was, as Nietzsche showed in his *Birth of
Tragedy*, the result of their having looked so deeply into life's
meaning that they had to protect themselves by cultivating a
deliberately superficial jolliness in order to bear the unbearable.
Frost's benign calm, the comic mask of a whittling rustic, is designed for gazing—without dizziness—into a tragic abyss of desperation.[2]

Bypassing the problem of Aeschylus' superficial jolliness or
the blandness of *The Trojan Women,* we are not told what
Frost sees in the abyss of desperation—only that he demonstrates "the tragic wisdom of those who through the ages have
not only stared into the abyss but have outstared it."[3] The
question raised by "On a Tree Fallen Across the Road" is a
real one. Elizabeth Shepley Sergeant reports of Frost as a
teacher that "he is always bedeviling his students with questions, but never with one—this is his cardinal principle as an
educator—which he can answer himself,"[4] and it may be that
the nature of the

[1] Sidney Cox, *Robert Frost: Original "Ordinary" Man* (New York,
1929), p. 39.
[2] Peter Viereck, "Parnassus Divided," *Atlantic Monthly,* CLXXXIV
(Oct., 1949), 68.
[3] *Ibid.,* p. 68.
[4] Elizabeth Shepley Sergeant, "Robert Frost: A Good Greek Out of
New England," *New Republic,* XLIV (Sept. 30, 1925), 144.

> final goal
> We have it hidden in us to attain

is one of these questions without answers.

Certainly the general drift and the particular emphases of Frost's writing leave little room for final causes in his view of man. Given his view of nature as an impersonal "other,"[5] his sense of a tripartite and all but discontinuous universe,[6] his anti-intellectual bias,[7] his emphasis on getting by or on making one's own patterns of meaning,[8] his tendency to shy away from the major area of broadly social values,[9] and his refusal to commit himself to explicit statements of theory,[10] one may reasonably expect Frost's sense of a human objective, a *raison d'être,* to be pragmatic or intuitive rather than authoritative or reasoned.

> It's knowing what to do with things that counts

say the pragmatic monkeys in "At Woodward's Gardens," and the husband's affirmation in "West-Running Brook"[11] is an intuition, not a received doctrine or a reasoned conclusion. Thinkers and dogmatists do not come off this well, as is clear from "To a Thinker," "The Bear," "The Broken Drought," "A Case for Jefferson," and "The Lesson for Today." Job, in *A Masque of Reason,* learns for the second time that neither rationalism nor orthodoxy is really of much use. Jonah, in *A Masque of Mercy,* learns that intuitions of mercy meet the pragmatic test; they are the only things that work, while reasonable, canonical theories of justice do not. And these two poems occupy a special position in the body of Frost's writing. Reginald L. Cook quotes Frost's comment on *A Masque of Reason:* "All my poetry is a footnote to it."[12] Professor

[5] See above, p. 32.
[6] See above, p. 49.
[7] See above, p. 84.
[8] See above, pp. 49-50, 133-134.
[9] See above, pp. 138-139.
[10] See above, pp. 5-7.
[11] See above, pp. 125-127.
[12] Reginald L. Cook, "Robert Frost's Asides on His Poetry," *American Literature,* XIX (Jan., 1948), 355.

Cook's article was written before the publication of *A Masque of Mercy,* but the two are clearly companion pieces; Frost's remark seems equally applicable to the later poem. And W. G. O'Donnell suggests that "with the publication of the 'Masque of Mercy' . . . [Frost] becomes the only significant American poet whose mind is oriented to a scholastic philosophy."[13] In effect, the two masques are Frost's *summa.*

And yet they do not make any clearly prescriptive statement of what we are here for. Recommending the Sermon on the Mount,

> An irresistible impossibility.
> A lofty beauty no one can live up to
> Yet no one turn from trying to live up to,

A Masque of Mercy condemns us all to equal failure and provides no clear answer to Jonah's question:

> If what you say is true, if winning ranks
> The same with God as losing, how explain
> Our making all this effort mortals make?

Even Keeper, the skeptical rationalist, is made to confess,

> I'm too much afraid of God to claim
> I have been fighting on the angels' side.
> That is for Him and not for me to say.

We cannot even be certain that the objectives we devote ourselves to are the right ones. Recognizing with Job that

> There's no connection man can reason out
> Between his just deserts and what he gets,

---

[13] William G. O'Donnell, "Parable in Poetry," *Virginia Quarterly Review,* XXV (Spring, 1949), 269.

we can only fear with Paul that

> Our sacrifice, the best we have to offer,
> And not our worst nor second best, our best,
> Our very best, our lives laid down like Jonah's,
> Our lives laid down in war and peace, may not
> Be found acceptable in Heaven's sight.

The position here seems close to the Calvinist doctrine of total depravity, but we are not allowed even the cold comfort provided by the complementary doctrine of arbitrary election. All we have is

> the courage in the heart
> To overcome the fear within the soul
> And go ahead to any accomplishment,

a kind of blind capacity for heroism or for getting by, for enduring or for making adjustments, with no certainty that the capacity is at last significant to anything but our own atomic existence.

But if the modified Calvinism of the masques represents Frost's final statement, other and earlier poems indicate, explicitly or by suggestion, that there are objectives sufficiently satisfying for any practical purposes. The most explicit of such statements is the excessively familiar one given in the final stanza of "Two Tramps in Mud Time":

> But yield who will to their separation,
> My object in living is to unite
> My avocation and my vocation
> As my two eyes make one in sight.
> Only where love and need are one,
> And the work is play for mortal stakes,
> Is the deed ever really done
> For Heaven and the future's sakes.

Now, this is clearly capsule philosophy, a kind of fooling around with abstractions that, however seriously intended, is hard to distinguish from a Thought for the Day. But for a number of reasons it demands attention here. First, it probably represents the popular Frost about as completely as any one poem can; second, it is his most unequivocal statement of a human objective; third, it does draw together more of Frost's motifs than may be apparent at first sight; and fourth, it is not a particularly convincing formula for what Frost actually does in a good many of his most successful poems.

Only the last two of these four points call for particular attention here. Recognizing that "play" in line six means gambling rather than gambolling—life is a sort of Russian roulette—one can see the stanza in relation to Frost's fondness for situations in which the problem of choice is reduced to an ultimate either-or,[14] to take the plunge or not to take the plunge. The commitment to a free and whimsical choice in "The Road Not Taken," the desperate resignation of "A Servant to Servants," and the refusal to lament bad luck in "The Self-Seeker" are gambler's gestures, and in the short poem "In Dives' Dive," life is a poker game. Again, the situation in which love and need, desire and necessity, are one recalls Frost's preference for "self-assigned task[s] carried out only at the instant urgency of the worker's own desire,"[15] a preference that, as we have seen, can develop into an essentially blinkered and doctrinaire individualism, a kind of freedom that is achieved by refusing to concern oneself with things that cannot be subdued to one's own individual will— by "Ceasing to Question What Doesn't Concern Us," as Frost puts it in "Too Anxious for Rivers." And once more, it is not easy to unite avocation and vocation, love and need, to achieve an ideally frictionless adjustment, in a world of social obligations and conflicting needs; successful living and social respon-

[14] See above, pp. 16-22.
[15] Sidney Cox, "Robert Frost at Plymouth," *New Hampshire Troubadour*, XVI (Nov., 1946), 20; and see above, pp. 87-89.

sibility are not always and easily compatible. In this respect, it is worth pointing out that the poem's speaker achieves his "object in living" only by a sort of double-dealing with his own sense of what constitutes a "better right." The formula hedges as many problems as it solves; its real function, we suspect, is to assure the speaker that what he wants to do anyway is right.

It is not necessary, of course, to read "Two Tramps in Mud Time" in this admittedly somewhat querulous fashion. Nothing compels us to read it as anything more than an utterance, in character, by a dramatically conceived speaker; nothing compels us to put it into a context of Frost's persistent themes. And, of course, the fact that the doctrine looks a little shaky in this context does not mean either that it is intrinsically bad doctrine or that it is going to look equally shaky in all other contexts. But it seems to me that "Two Tramps in Mud Time," like most of Frost's poems that propose or seem to propose formulas, suffers by comparison with many of his non-formula poems, and in a fairly specific way—by getting the emphasis wrong. I mean—this was the fourth of my four points—that those formulas would give a quite misleading account of what to expect in Frost's poems as a whole. A check of the titles in Frost's *Complete Poems* gives me only seven poems out of more than three hundred that seem clear instances in which love and need really are one, and eight that might be considered such. This is, to be sure, a thoroughly subjective proceeding. But it is difficult to believe that anyone's count would fail to indicate a much greater number of poems in which Frost deals, and often impressively, with people for whom love and need, vocation and avocation, do not very obviously coalesce.[16]

[16] Love and need are one in "In Neglect," "Mowing," "Going for Water," "The Tuft of Flowers," "Putting in the Seed," "Happiness Makes Up in Height for What It Lacks in Length," and "In the Long Night." They may be one in "A Hundred Collars," "The Generations of Men," "In the Home Stretch," "Birches," "The Gum-Gatherer," "West-Running Brook," "A Drumlin Woodchuck," and "The Gift Outright." They are

The same thing is true of other formula poems. "The Tuft of Flowers" concludes:

> 'Men work together,' I told him from the heart,
> 'Whether they work together or apart.'

But surely Frost tells us more about men who work apart even when they work together—the cantankerously independent farm hands in "The Code," Silas in "The Death of the Hired Man," the speaker of "An Empty Threat" (if thinking can be considered working), the mill worker of "A Lone Striker," Meserve in "Snow," or the poet of "The Lost Follower." In "Mowing,"

> The fact is the sweetest dream that labor knows;

even without distorting this into something that it does not mean, how are we to explain it to the woman in "A Servant to Servants," the Broken One in "The Self-Seeker," or the boy in " 'Out, Out—' "? Once more, Frost's formulas, even when they do draw together real motifs of his work, are not the authoritatively final statements they sometimes appear to be. Frost the aphoristic philosopher does not provide a very accurate commentary on Frost the dramatic poet.

Returning, then, to the particular formula offered in "Two Tramps in Mud Time," it seems to me that Frost's most characteristic, and most effective, presentation of its terms is one in which vocation and avocation appear as incompatibles between which one must choose, with a good deal at stake—the gambler's gesture, again—and that real personal tragedy is not so much a matter of choosing wrong or of failing to

---

not one in, for a start, "Love and a Question," "Reluctance," "The Death of the Hired Man," "Home Burial," "A Servant to Servants," "The House-keeper," "The Fear," "The Self-Seeker," "Range-Finding," "The Hill Wife," " 'Out, Out—,' " "The Pauper Witch of Grafton," "Stopping by Woods on a Snowy Evening," "Not to Keep," "The Lovely Shall Be Choosers," and, of course, "Two Tramps in Mud Time."

unite the two as of being denied the chance to choose or of failing to choose, going instead with the drift of things. The real emphasis, that is, is on the act of choice itself rather than on the fortunate or unfortunate consequences of the act. "Every poem is an epitome of the great predicament; a figure of the will braving alien entanglements,"[17] writes Frost, and the comment tells us more about his best poetry than does "Two Tramps in Mud Time." In this respect, "The Trial by Existence," a more elaborate formula poem than those I have cited, is also more accurate. The emphasis is on a heroically simple act of choice—

> And so the choice must be again,
> But the last choice is still the same—

by which, within limits, we determine our own destinies. As Llewellyn Jones observes, the poem is "a recognition that suffering is always in terms of what we are, not an alien something hitting us by chance from without but somehow or other implicit in our very constitutions"[18]—and, one can add, in the choices we have made:

> life has for us on the wrack [*sic*]
> Nothing but what we somehow chose.

Frost has written any number of poems that have such acts of choice as their dynamic center—choices that have been made, choices that will be made or that must be made, choices that have not been made.[19] It is, of course, true that

---

[17] Robert Frost, "The Constant Symbol," *Atlantic Monthly,* CLXXVIII (Oct., 1946), 50.

[18] Llewellyn Jones, "Robert Frost," *American Review,* II (March-April, 1924), 167.

[19] E.g., "The Trial by Existence," "Into My Own," "Love and a Question," "Storm Fear," "Wind and Window Flower," "The Demiurge's Laugh," "The Generations of Men," "The Housekeeper," "The Road Not Taken," "The Exposed Nest," "Snow," "The Star-Splitter," "Stopping by Woods on a Snowy Evening," "The Lockless Door," "The Thatch," "The Lovely Shall

such acts of choice are among the inescapable consequences of conscious life and hence of literature—any literature, from Homer to contemporary magazine fiction; but I think their persistence in Frost's work means more than the obvious fact that Frost is a writer. I think, in fact, that they *are* his theme, not simply a circumstance within which he develops his themes. For Frost, man can very nearly be defined as a choice-making animal; he fulfills himself in the act of choosing, deliberately and, at his best, with a sense of consequences.

It is this capacity for conscious choice that principally distinguishes man from the lower forms of life. "God defend me," wrote Emerson, "from ever looking at man as an animal."[20]   And in "The White-Tailed Hornet," Frost echoes Emerson's sentiment, insisting that it is dismal error to confuse the two orders of being:

> As long on earth
> As our comparisons were stoutly upward
> With gods and angels, we were men at least,
> But little lower than the gods and angels.
> But once comparisons were yielded downward,
> Once we began to see our images
> Reflected in the mud and even dust,
> 'Twas disillusion upon disillusion.
> We were lost piecemeal to the animals,
> Like people thrown out to delay the wolves.

Such confusion is tempting, because the hornet looks as though he were making choices—playing with metaphors, in fact:

Be Choosers," "West-Running Brook," "A Lone Striker," "Provide, Provide," "The Vindictives," "Come In," "The Discovery of the Madeiras," "One Step Backward Taken," "Directive," and *A Masque of Mercy*. The list is not exhaustive.

[20] Ralph Waldo Emerson, *The Heart of Emerson's Journals*, ed. Bliss Perry (New York, 1926), p. 80.

> he might have made me think
> He had been at his poetry, comparing
> Nailhead with fly and fly with huckleberry:
> How like a fly, how very like a fly.

But the appearance is deceptive; the hornet's behavior, far from being avocational, is entirely determined by an entirely fallible instinct, and what looks like choice is merely instinct shooting up a blind alley:

> To err is human, not to, animal.
> Or so we pay the compliment to instinct,
> Only too liberal of our compliment
> That really takes away instead of gives.
> Our worship, humor, conscientiousness
> Went long since to the dogs under the table.
> And served us right for having instituted
> Downward comparisons.

Other animal poems reveal much the same distinction. In "Our Singing Strength" a belated spring snowstorm has driven birds to cluster in the road, the only bare ground left. Victimized by an instinct that determines their behavior and tells them to fly straight away from a pursuer rather than to get around behind him, they can only come

> tamely back in front of me, the Drover,
> To suffer the same driven nightmare over.

In "To a Moth Seen in Winter," for all the wistful attribution of motive to the moth—

> And what I pity in you is something human,
> The old incurable untimeliness,
> Only begetter of all ills that are—

we are aware that the speaker does not choose to make the moth's desperate, instinctive, and deterministic effort to "seek the love of kind in wintertime." In "Departmental," the ants' bureaucracy is admirable only in terms of its instinctively specialized efficiency, and suggests that part at least of the reason for Frost's distaste for complex social institutions is that they departmentalize and thus limit the choices man can make. "A Drumlin Woodchuck," for all his seeming canniness, really owes his success in life to having been

> so *instinctively* thorough [italics added]
> About my crevice and burrow.

Parenthetically, and seen in this context, such poems suggest that Frost may not be altogether content with his own anti-intellectual bias; one remembers "trust my instinct—I'm a bard," from "To a Thinker." What distinction are we to draw between the bardic instinct and the instinct of hornets, birds, and woodchucks? The obvious answer is that "To a Thinker" is at least partly jocular, but as we have seen in Chapter III, jocularity is not the whole answer. I suspect the real point is that Frost has never fully resolved his divided allegiance to prudential man, who gets by, offering minimum resistance to the world that determines him, and to anthropocentric man, who develops values and to that degree determines himself.[21]

Frost's man, then, is essentially a choice-making creature, one that, endowed with something more than a determined and determining set of instincts, possesses the heady but dangerous faculty of making his own choices and thus, to a degree, of consciously selecting his own destiny. Even in "The Road Not Taken," for all that the act of choice is presented as whimsical and unmotivated, the speaker is aware that his choice will have consequences, though he cannot tell what those consequences will be:

[21] See below, pp. 169-170, 184.

> I shall be telling this with a sigh
> Somewhere ages and ages hence:
> Two roads diverged in a wood, and I—
> I took the one less traveled by,
> And that has made all the difference.

And, as in "The Road Not Taken," if the act of choice is real—
if in fact it is to be an act of choice at all—it must be between, or among, alternatives. If the less-traveled road is
chosen, the more-traveled one must be foregone. This is, of
course, elementary logic, if not elementary quibbling. My
point is, once more, that the formula of "Two Tramps in Mud
Time" is not an adequate measure of what Frost actually does
in his more characteristic poems—that it envisages, not a
crucial act of choice, but a situation in which such acts would
be in large part unnecessary. The condition in which love
and need are really one is an Eden condition, a condition in
which we need not choose because the external world is sub-
servient to our will,[22] and as we have seen in Chapter III,[23]
Frost's Eden is an object of ambivalent feeling. If love and
need were really one, there would be no tragic tension, no
figures of the will braving alien entanglements, and no important poems by Frost.

I have said that Frost's most effective presentations of
avocation and vocation, love and need, desire and necessity,
are those in which the terms are treated as incompatibles between which one must choose. The problem is not always
tragic in its implication, and in fact one may be able to work
out a fairly effectively divided life, like Brad McLaughlin, in
"The Star-Splitter," who, having burned down his farm, gets
a job as under-ticket-agent on the Concord railroad to support
himself while devoting his leisure hours to stargazing. In
"Build Soil," shepherd Meliboeus' love for the land does not
easily satisfy his need for money, but on the whole he scrapes

[22] See above, p. 82.
[23] See above, pp. 91-99.

along happily enough. The speaker of "New Hampshire"
solves the same problem by being

> a plain New Hampshire farmer
> With an income in cash of say a thousand
> (From say a publisher in New York City).

"Two Tramps in Mud Time" is cheerful, "A Lone Striker" is
perfectly content to let vocation go hang, at least temporarily,
and in "There Are Roughly Zones," though the couple's desire for home-grown peaches has presumably been frustrated
by the necessary rigors of a Northern winter, they are no more
than mildly and philosophically rueful about it.

In other poems, however, the problem is less easily resolved. The question of "Love and a Question"—

> whether or not a man was asked
> To mar the love of two
> By harboring woe in the bridal house,
> The bridegroom wished he knew—

does not have much to do with vocation and avocation, but
the conflict between one's own love and another's need is not
unlike that of "Two Tramps in Mud Time"; here it remains
suspended in dangerous equilibrium. "A Prayer in Spring"
suggests that, if love is properly managed, need will take care
of itself, or at least be taken care of for us:

> For this is love and nothing else is love,
> The which it is reserved for God above
> To sanctify to what far ends He will,
> And which it only needs that we fulfill.

But the poem's yearning nostalgia suggests that there is more
than a little wishful thinking involved. "Reluctance," again,

declares it treason of the heart to yield to necessity and compromise desire, and the same note is struck, though with more
restraint, in "Stopping by Woods on a Snowy Evening." In
"A Winter Eden," the necessity of maintaining a minimum of
life in a "gaunt luxuriating beast" requires that love be foregone:

> So near to paradise all pairing ends;
> Here loveless birds now flock as winter friends,
> Content with bud inspecting.

And in "Snow," the incompatibility of Meserve's avocation
with his vocation—his irresponsible delight in needlessly buck-
ing blizzards after dark and the responsibility of taking care
of himself in order to keep his family from going on the town—
very nearly destroys the man.

Very few people in Frost's poems actually die of the
choices they have made. Jonah's death, in *A Masque of
Mercy*, is more symbolic than literal; the moth of "To a Moth
Seen in Winter" presumably dies, but through faulty instinct
rather than choice; and in "The Discovery of the Madeiras,"
the lady dies as a consequence less of a choice she has made
than of one she has finally failed to make. But if death is
rare, desolation is not; and if such desolation is to a degree the
inescapable consequence of having to choose, as in "Reluctance"—and perhaps of choosing wrong—Frost's most har-
rowing presentations of it are those in which the crucial act of
choice does not take place, is somehow frustrated or compromised by external circumstances, by bad luck, by habitual
responses, or by failure of integrity. Thus in "The Self-
Seeker," the quest after native orchids is pure avocation:

> 'They never earned me so much as one cent.'

Even though the Broken One has a letter from Burroughs testi-
fying to the quest's significance, there is no question in the

poem either of vocationalizing it or of uniting it in any meaningful way with his job in a sawmill.   Like Brad McLaughlin,
he has divided himself between the two until, crippled by an
unlucky accident in the mill, he is deprived both of that adjustment and of any possibility of choice between its terms.   His
friend Willis, unable wholly to realize how much has been at
issue here, is concerned with a lesser choice—whether the
Broken One should accept five hundred dollars from the company in compensation for his apparently amputated feet or
hold out for more; and Willis' partisanship makes things more
painful by missing the point.   His stakes are not high enough,
not mortal, to echo "Two Tramps in Mud Time" again; the
choice he offers is not one that the whole man can make, and
only emphasizes the point that the Broken One's chance of
choosing to be a whole man has been irretrievably lost.   The
only real choice left him is that between taking his luck quietly
and making a useless fuss about it, and he prefers to abide by
his own principle: " ' What we live by we die by.' "   What we
live by is precisely the capacity to make crucial choices; once
that is gone, once we reach the point of having only petty
choices to make, we are, to all practical intents and purposes,
dead.   It is largely this point, I think, that accounts for the
pathos of such a poem as "An Old Man's Winter Night" or
of such characters as Silas, in "The Death of the Hired Man,"
or the woman in "The Pauper Witch of Grafton."

The circumstances of "A Servant to Servants" are different
from those of "The Self-Seeker," but the emphasis is in a way
similar since the main characters in both poems are faced with
disasters over which they have no control—in the one, a strain
of inherited insanity, in the other, an industrial accident.   In
both poems, the crucial act of choice cannot really be made.
Without feet, the Broken One cannot hunt orchids; without
rest, the woman cannot resist her heredity:

> But it's not medicine—
> Lowe is the only doctor's dared to say so—

It's rest I want—there, I have said it out—
From cooking meals for hungry hired men
And washing dishes after them—from doing
Things over and over that just won't stay done.

And, given her circumstances, rest is as impossible for the woman as new feet are for the man:

By good rights I ought not to have so much
Put on me, but there seems no other way.

There is no other way. Refusing to be querulous, to ask her husband for another change of scene ("I won't ask him—it's not sure enough") or to leave him (in any case, there is no one else to go to), she can only wait, like the Broken One, not raising an outcry over what cannot be helped and not vulgarizing a frightful situation by attaching primary importance to secondary, contingent acts of choice. Both characters, in fact, represent anthropocentric man; if both exhibit a refusal to compromise that approaches the ornery, both exhibit a hard core of personal dignity and integrity, an unwillingness to blur the crucial choices they have made by merely prudential arrangements—the same hard core that one finds in Sophoclean tragedy.[24]

It is frequently the absence of such a core, a prudential willingness to go with the drift of things, that characterizes the victims of what may be called Frost's tragedies of simple demoralization—people who have missed the chance to choose or to abide by their choices not because of external circumstances they cannot control but because of their own habitual responses, failures of nerve, or simple blind spots. "The Housekeeper" presents both hero and victim. Estelle, the common-law wife of fifteen years' standing, makes her choice and leaves, apparently unable at last to continue the compromise between her human dignity and John Hall's unspoken,

[24] Cf. above, p. 21.

unintended affront. He won't marry her, preferring the comfortable but ultimately uncommitted arrangement that has gradually developed;

> Better than married ought to be as good
> As married—that's what he has always said.

But he is wrong. Concerned more for his chickens than for his wife (as far as we know, the Broken One had no human responsibilities save to himself), Hall discovers too late that habitual kindness is no adequate substitute for deliberate commitment. And when Estelle's act of choice forces the issue, he goes to pieces:

> What I think he will do, is let things smash.
> He'll sort of swear the time away. He's awful!
> I never saw a man let family troubles
> Make so much difference in his man's affairs.
> He's just dropped everything. He's like a child,

says Estelle's mother, summing it up,

> All is, he's made up his mind not to stand
> What he has got to stand—

the useless and baffled fuss of the man who has failed to make his own choice. The old woman has the last word:

> Who wants to hear your news, you—dreadful fool!

It would be pointless to quarrel with her characterization.

In "Home Burial" one has only victims, and it is not even clear that there is any question of assigning blame. If the wife had the courage to make a clean break, like Estelle—if the husband had the sensitive, articulate perceptiveness of the husband in "West-Running Brook"—but neither does, and it is in a way no more than bad luck that they find themselves in a situation requiring one or the other. Trapped by their own limitations, they can only drag each other further and further down from any definitive act of choice, either of acceptance or of rejection, demoralizing themselves and one another in the process and destroying whatever potential dignity or integrity they may once have had. A variant form of victimization appears in "The Fear." The woman has made her crucial choice, leaving a husband in order to become common-law wife to another man; but, evidently haunted by guilt, by the fear that she has chosen wrong, she has compromised her commitment and broken her dignity by self-created figures of vengeance that she sees in casual passers-by. And, as we have seen, the stolen lady of "The Discovery of the Madeiras" suffers from a similar failure of nerve, a final inability really to accept her own act of choice.

"Two Tramps in Mud Time" does not prepare one for such poems as these. However tempting its formula may be, the desire to unite seeming incompatibles has very little relevance to the world in which Frost's most powerfully drawn characters reveal their integrity, or their disastrous lack of integrity, in the crucial choices they confront. However pleasant it might be not to have to choose, to be able to travel both roads simultaneously and without self-division or the readiness to commit oneself, nevertheless the wish to have one's cake and also eat it is ultimately a form of treacherous and irresponsible self-indulgence, as in "The Housekeeper," or of paralyzing emotional stalemate, as in "The Discovery of the Madeiras." In this respect, it seems to me that Yvor Winters, in his important—and, within this study, much-cited—article "Robert Frost: or, The Spiritual Drifter as Poet," has greatly overstated part of his case against Frost. Winters writes, of "The Road Not Taken" and "The Sound of the Trees," that Frost

is mistaking whimsical impulse for moral choice, and the blunder obscures his understanding and even leaves his mood uncertain with regard to the value of the whole business. He is vaguely afraid that he may be neither wrong nor right.[25]

Like Emerson, Frost believes that "formative decisions should be made casually and passively."[26]   But Emerson, Winters writes,

> was a Romantic pantheist: he identified God with the universe; he taught that impulse comes directly from God and should be obeyed, that through surrender to impulse we become one with God; he taught that reason is manmade and bungling and should be suppressed. . . . In Frost . . . we find a disciple without Emerson's religious convictions: Frost believes in the rightness of impulse, but does not discuss the pantheistic doctrine which would give authority to impulse. . . .[27]

From this confusion proceed the "ill-natured eccentricity" and "increasing melancholy" of the later poems.[28]   My point is that, however illuminating such commentary may be in a limited context, it is dangerous as the basis for an over-all critical generalization because it does not provide an adequate account of such poems as those just considered, poems in which the act of choice cannot be described as whimsical impulse.

Such incomplete evaluations have been characteristic of the criticism of Frost almost from the appearance of his first volume, partly I think because of his remarkable popularity, not only with critics but also apparently with the reading public;[29] partly because of the ease with which one can select his own Frost from the variety of the *Complete Poems;* partly because of Frost's own tendency to throw out red herrings (his remark about growing up on a farm, for example).[30]   But I think that the overstatement in Winters' article can be seen as the result of an at least partial failure to recognize an important duality—it is one of many—apparent in the body of

[25] Yvor Winters, "Robert Frost: or, The Spiritual Drifter as Poet," *Sewanee Review,* LVI (Autumn, 1948), p. 571.

[26] *Ibid.,* p. 586.   [27] *Ibid.,* p. 567.

[28] *Ibid.,* p. 567.   [29] See below, pp. 189-191.

[30] See above, p. 140.

Frost's writing. Gorham Munson, commenting on the "Speaking of contraries" speech in "West-Running Brook," identifies this particular duality:

There, I say, we have revealed the basic conviction of Mr. Frost about man, and those who are apt in the reading of ideas as well as apt in reading verse will see that the poet's sense of contraries is not far from the humanist's declaration that in man there is a duality of consciousness, a struggle between his impulse to unify himself and his impulse to drift with the stream of life.[31]

The point to be made here is that Frost has never clearly and finally resolved his feeling about that duality. In certain poems, as I have argued, the real man reveals himself by his emphasis on the impulse to unify; in certain poems, as Winters has argued, the real man reveals himself by his emphasis on the impulse to drift. In any given poem, the position is relatively clear, but where does Frost stand? Even in *A Masque of Mercy*, it is not finally clear whether Jonah's death is, in the last analysis, a triumph of something or a defeat of something. "I know what the man wanted of Old King Cole," writes Frost.

He wanted the heart out of his mystery. He was the friend who stands at the end of a poem ready in waiting to catch you by both hands with enthusiasm and drag you off your balance over the last punctuation mark into more than you meant to say. "I understand the poem all right, but please tell me what is behind it?" Such presumption needs to be twinkled at and baffled. The answer must be, "If I had wanted you to know, I should have told you in the poem."[32]

And while Frost's amused irritation is completely understandable, as anyone who has written a poem knows, the question of where Frost stands is still a real question.

It is this unresolved duality that reveals itself in that divided

[31] Gorham B. Munson, "Robert Frost and the Humanistic Temper," *Bookman*, LXXI (July, 1930), 421-422.

[32] Robert Frost, introduction to Edwin Arlington Robinson, *King Jasper* (New York, 1935), p. xii.

allegiance touched on earlier,[33] an allegiance divided between prudential man, on the one hand, and anthropocentric man on the other. It is prudential man who is satisfied with whimsical impulse, who makes his formative decisions casually and passively, who drifts with the stream of life. It is anthropocentric man, or woman, who makes deliberate commitments of himself, who accepts consequences without squirming or recrimination, and who may demonstrate a capacity for heroic action or tragic acceptance. And here, I think, it becomes possible to see what the formula of "Two Tramps in Mud Time" really means. Briefly, it is a formula for prudential man, the man who, concerned primarily with getting by, wants to compromise between incompatibles, to shuffle and blur distinctions, to avoid crucial acts of choice. In Elizabeth Shepley Sergeant's phrase, it expresses "the old New England effort to compromise ideals and facts,"[34] an effort that Emerson brought to full statement:

the perception of real affinities between events (that is to say, of *ideal* affinities, for those only are real), enables the poet thus to make free with the most imposing forms and phenomena of the world, and to assert the predominance of the soul.[35]

Or again, "as the world was plastic and fluid in the hands of God, so it is ever to so much of his attributes as we bring to it."[36] And once more, "mind is the only reality, of which men and all other natures are better or worse reflectors. Nature, literature, history, are only subjective phenomena."[37] To Emerson, the effort to compromise ideals and facts is a proper effort because facts are not really facts, and hence crucial acts of choice are not necessary.

But there is another voice than Emerson's, another "old New England effort," that may be identified as an effort to

---

[33] See above, p. 160.
[34] Sergeant, p. 135.
[35] *The Complete Works of Ralph Waldo Emerson,* ed. Edward Waldo Emerson (Cambridge, Mass., 1904), I, 54.
[36] *Ibid.,* I, 105.
[37] *Ibid.,* I, 333.

comprehend man and the world as tragic. Perry Miller writes that

a strength of Puritanism from the beginning had been its ability to look on life as calamitous, though indeed it frequently therefore ran a danger that, out of contempt for others less tough-minded, it could lend itself to a multiplication of calamities.[38]

One thinks of Hawthorne, of Melville, of Henry Adams and Henry James, as well as of Jonathan Edwards. And one thinks of those characters in Frost's poems who, confronted with calamity, choose to accept it as real rather than to fritter away their capacity for making choices, to compromise their tragic potential by the effort to believe that only ideal affinities are real, that the world is plastic to their diviner attributes, and that they need not really choose. R. W. B. Lewis observes that, in the literature of our time, "the American as Adam has been replaced by the American as Laocoön,"[39] and to Laocoön the snakes were real, by Dr. Johnson's pragmatic test.

They are also real to Frost's anthropocentric man, the man who knows that the universe resists his designs and that, if he shuffles with those designs, they are no longer his. And though it is clear that Frost's allegiance is divided, it is also clear that, to Frost, the prudential John Hall is less admirable than the anthropocentric Estelle; that the gum-gatherer and the drumlin woodchuck have only wistful or whimsical appeal, while the Broken One has tragic dignity. And in the two masques, Jonah and Job, whatever else they may be, are men who ultimately choose to endure the unendurable, to confront the world as they find it, and to render judgment on it rather than compromise their integrity. Both men are right; at least we are sure about Job, who is canonized out of God's own mouth during the course of the poem. And this is curious because, far from providing Job with a coherent understanding of what it was all about, of what ultimate purpose his ordeal really

[38] Perry Miller, *Jonathan Edwards* (New York, 1948), p. 121.
[39] R. W. B. Lewis, *The American Adam: Innocence, Tragedy and Tradition in the Nineteenth Century* (Chicago, 1955), p. 197.

served, of the precise nature of the objective he has achieved, God leaves him not less but more in the dark than he had been previously.   That the experiment established

> once for all the principle
> There's no connection man can reason out
> Between his just deserts and what he gets

(it is God speaking) neither surprises Job nor satisfies him. And if God's arch admission that

> I was just showing off to the Devil, Job,

is surprising, it is no more satisfying.

> I expected more
> Than I could understand and what I get
> Is almost less than I can understand,

says Job, with considerable reason.   Thyatira's practical skepticism seems more convincing:

> Of course, in the abstract high singular
> There isn't any universal reason;
> And no one but a man would think there was.

Job echoes his wife's skepticism, at least briefly:

> The chances are when there's so much pretense
> Of metaphysical profundity
> The obscurity's a fraud to cover nothing.
> I've come to think no so-called hidden value's
> Worth going after.   Get down into things
> It will be found there's no more given there
> Than on the surface.

But this is really the speech of prudential man; it does not
answer Job's real question:

> There's will as motor and there's will as brakes.
> Reason is, I suppose the steering gear.
> The will as brakes can't stop the will as motor
> For very long. We're plainly made to go.
> We're going anyway and may as well
> Have some say as to where we're headed for;
> Just as we will be talking anyway
> And may as well throw in a little sense.
> Let's do so now.

We're plainly made to go. All right; where? and why? God
doesn't say.

And for this chapter's purposes, Job's question is an important one. If the will as brakes—prudential man's reluctance really to commit himself to crucial choices—can't stop
the will as motor—anthropocentric man's active commitment
to such choices—then the will as motor really expresses man,
is man's essence, to a much greater degree than is the will as
brakes. And if this is so, then either there is a reason for it—
a direction to be followed, a potential to be realized, a goal to
be attained—or else "the Whole Goddam Machinery," as
Frost refers to it in "Lucretius Versus the Lake Poets," is
simply an expression of an instinctual determinism and man is
no different in kind from the ants and the white-tailed hornet.
We are back again at the problem of teleology.[40] If it is better
to choose, to engage in active exercise of the will, than to
drift with the stream of instinct or external circumstances, then
why?

I have said that one may reasonably expect Frost's sense
of a human objective to be pragmatic or intuitive rather than
authoritative or reasoned.[41] And Frost's essay "The Figure

[40] See above, p. 40.
[41] See above, p. 151.

a Poem Makes" contains a suggestive proposition in this respect. A good poem, like love, "ends in a clarification of life—not necessarily a great clarification, such as sects and cults are founded on, but in a momentary stay against confusion."[42]   Mere yielding to instinct cannot provide such clarification. The white-tailed hornet obeys his instinct and fails to distinguish between nailheads and huckleberries, huckleberries and flies—or, more important, friends and enemies; he achieves no clarification of life, and the same thing is true when people (John Hall in "The Housekeeper," the husband and wife in "Home Burial") follow lines of least resistance or limit their utterance to instinctive grief or instinctive irritation.   Instinctive behavior may have fortunate consequences, as it does in "A Drumlin Woodchuck," "On a Bird Singing in Its Sleep," or—presumably—"To a Thinker," but it is not clear that life is clarified as a consequence of such behavior—rather that the behavior is the predetermined consequence of a kind of built-in clarification, if that is the word for it, that does its work by very nearly limiting the meaning of "life" to "self-preservation."   And as Job knows, there is more to it than that. It is better to choose than not to choose, to make a deliberate, willed commitment of oneself, because such a commitment at least may lead to clarification.   To extend the principle, a choice is good if it leads to such clarification, bad if it deepens confusion—a thoroughly pragmatic test.   And in either case, one has at least taken the necessary plunge. For Frost, as for Dante and Eliot, it is better to be right than wrong, and better to be wrong than merely neutral or uncommitted, because neutrality affords no clarification; it carries no pragmatic warrant.

And yet this is not final. Pragmatic tests can finally indicate only that something exists, is true, not why it exists or what it is true in terms of. And given Frost's premises, again, it is not easy to see what lies beyond the pragmatic test, what the desired clarification of life will be in terms of; a discon-

[42] *Complete Poems of Robert Frost 1949* (New York, 1949), p. vi.

tinuous other cannot, by any rationally apprehensible means, clarify anything but itself, cannot throw light on the thing that it is other than. Job, once more, has chosen to endure the unendurable: "This is one thing, therefore I said it, He destroyeth the perfect and the wicked."[43] Job has chosen to maintain his human integrity in the teeth of an inhuman cosmos: "Though he slay me, yet will I trust in him: but I will maintain mine own ways before him."[44] And Job's conduct passes the pragmatic test; in the Old Testament, Job has spoken of God "the thing that is right,"[45] and Frost adds canonization. Yet Job's last substantial speech, in Frost's version, expresses not illumination but a kind of polite speculation. "But talk about confusion!" he exclaims:

> Yet I suppose what seems to us confusion
> Is not confusion, but the form of forms,
> The serpent's tail stuck down the serpent's throat,
> Which is the symbol of eternity
> And also of the way all things come round,
> Or of how rays return upon themselves,
> To quote the greatest Western poem yet.
> Though I hold rays deteriorate to nothing,
> First white, then red, then ultra red, then out.

To God's apologetic effort at fuller explanation, Job only responds:

> God, please, enough for now. I'm in no mood
> For more excuses,

and the poem ends with some indecisive whimsy about unidentified "tendencies" and the ontological status of the Devil. Job knows that he has come out all right, and in his final speech we see him "standing dazed with new ideas"; but we

[43] Job ix:22.   [44] Job xiii:15.
[45] Job xlii:7.

are not altogether clear about what those new ideas are, and we are not altogether convinced that Job is either.

The clarification achieved by Jonah, in *A Masque of Mercy,* seems more complete. Like Job, he has had ample evidence of God's unpredictable and incomprehensible operations:

> I've lost my faith in God to carry out
> The threats He makes against the city evil.
> I can't trust God to be unmerciful.

Confronted with certain facts that admit of only one interpretation, Jonah too insists on maintaining his own ways:

> God comes on me to doom a city for Him.
> But oh, no, not for Jonah.   I refuse
> To be the bearer of an empty threat.

And he adds, in response to Jesse Bel's thrust:

> There's not the least lack of the love of God
> In what I say. Don't be so silly, woman.
> His very weakness for mankind's endearing.
> I love and fear Him. Yes, but I fear for Him.
> I don't see how it can be to His interest
> This modern tendency I find in Him
> To take the punishment out of all failure
> To be strong, careful, thrifty, diligent,
> Everything we once thought we had to be.

Jonah chooses to risk divine displeasure rather than participate in God's absurd program of *lèse majesté*.   And if we can believe Paul, who claims authority to release Jonah from his persistently undersold mission of preaching destruction to wicked cities, Jonah too is justified.   (Paul may be remotely akin to Aeschylus' Apollo, who was authorized to release

Orestes from another impossible situation; as Christian psychiatrist, he also seems related to Eliot's Sir Henry Harcourt-Reilly, though if there is a question of influence, it is from Frost to Eliot rather than the other way round, since *A Masque of Mercy* was published two years before the first production of *The Cocktail Party*.)

But *A Masque of Mercy,* unlike *A Masque of Reason,* has the look at least of a final pronouncement. In fact, one gets the rather startling sense that Frost has dropped his mask and is talking doctrine, albeit with a certain roguishness. It is possible to wish that Keeper would not talk about "Moby Dick/ By Rockwell Kent," about "Bohning up on Thomism," or about his diabolical stokers Jeffers and O'Neill; that Jesse Bel—a name that ought to finish any poet—would skip the chance of warning Jonah not to get himself laughed at by the *New Yorker;* that Paul might resist the opportunity of saying that Alexander Greeced the world, or of being snide about Yeats (he learned the trick from Job's wife in *A Masque of Reason*), particularly when his point is not particularly different from Yeats's.[46] But the poem *is* doctrinal, and in the final scene the characters have by and large quit being clever. In their last speeches, Keeper and Paul reach agreement about fundamentals:

KEEPER: Courage is of the heart by derivation,
       And great it is. But fear is of the soul.
       And I'm afraid. . . .

      .   .   .   .   .

PAUL: The fear that you're afraid with is the fear
       Of God's decision lastly on your deeds.
       That is the Fear of God whereof 'tis written.
KEEPER: But not the fear of punishment for sin
       (I have to sin to prove it isn't that).
       I'm no more governed by the fear of Hell
       Than by the fear of the asylum, jail, or poorhouse,

[46] See below, pp. 205–206.

The basic three the state is founded on.
But I'm too much afraid of God to claim
I have been fighting on the angels' side.
That is for Him and not for me to say.
For me to say it would be irreligious.
(Sometimes I think you are too sure you have been.)
And I can see that the uncertainty
In which we act is a severity,
A cruelty, amounting to injustice
That nothing but God's mercy can assuage.
I can see that, if that is what you mean.
Give me a hand up, if we are agreed.

PAUL: Yes, there you have it at the root of things.
We have to stay afraid deep in our souls
Our sacrifice, the best we have to offer,
And not our worst nor second best, our best,
Our very best, our lives laid down like Jonah's,
Our lives laid down in war and peace, may not
Be found acceptable in Heaven's sight.
And that they may be is the only prayer
Worth praying.   May my sacrifice
Be found acceptable in Heaven's sight.

KEEPER: Let the lost millions pray it in the dark!
My failure is no different from Jonah's.
We both have lacked the courage in the heart
To overcome the fear within the soul
And go ahead to any accomplishment.
Courage is what it takes and takes the more of
Because the deeper fear is so eternal.
And if I say we lift him from the floor
And lay him where you ordered him to lie
Before the cross, it is from fellow feeling,
As if I asked for one more chance myself
To learn to say (*He moves to Jonah's feet*)
Nothing can make injustice just but mercy.

My point is that such conclusions as these cannot be reached pragmatically. Pragmatic methods alone cannot establish theories of either cosmic justice or cosmic mercy, though they may prepare one to accept such theories on intuitional grounds. That is what happens to Jonah in *A Masque of Mercy*—and it is after all Jonah's play; the others only talk, while Jonah dies. And the crucial point in the play is not Jonah's death; by then he has made his commitment:

> I think I may have got God wrong entirely.

The crucial point is that at which Jonah, egged on by Paul's exegesis on the Sermon on the Mount and by his own recollection of *The Pilgrim's Progress,* says:

> You ask if I see yonder shining gate,
> And I reply I almost think I do.

The moment is one of a crucial intuition that alters the course and the meaning of Jonah's life.

> Yes, Pilgrim now instead of runaway,
> Your fugitive escape become a quest,

says Paul; and Jonah:

> I want to run
> Toward what you make me see beyond the world.

The intuition provides him with that "clarification of life" that Job does not clearly receive, a sense of a final goal, of a purpose that is not man's in its origin but that man can make his, thus bridging the discontinuity between divine and human, legitimizing the "limitless trait" that leads anthropocentric man to pursue his own designs, and providing an alternative to prudential man's efforts at adjusting himself to an imper-

sonal nature. Briefly, there is more in the universe than meets
the pragmatic eye. Frost, writes Sidney Cox,

frankly calls himself superstitious; by which he means that he
accepts no explanation of mystery. He is religious. One memo-
rable night, in 1916, he rejected my convenient disposal of God
as the summation of Most High Things, and of religion as care
for things spiritual. God, he said, is that which a man is sure
cares, and will save him, no matter how many times or how completely he has failed. We have talked of religion repeatedly since
then, and he has never recanted. . . .[47]

Now, *A Masque of Mercy* is Frost's last substantial poem
to date, and the fact that he has given it final position in the
volume entitled *Complete Poems* (there were two earlier volumes entitled *Collected Poems*) strongly suggests that he
thinks of it as a final statement, in terms of doctrine if not
necessarily of chronology. And it would be convenient to
leave things as they stand; but it is not really clear that one
can. Even the God that Frost defined for Sidney Cox is less
ultimate than He seems at first sight. God is not categorically
"that which cares"; He is "that which a man is sure cares."
The habit of equivocation, of the covered hand—and it is
surely more than a habit—is apparent even here, revealing
itself in the conclusion of *A Masque of Mercy,* a conclusion
that, if less ambiguous than that of *A Masque of Reason,* is
still ambiguous. Has Jonah's death, after all, brought him to
that shining gate Paul made him see beyond the world? We
have to fear, once more, that even

> Our very best, our lives laid down like Jonah's,
> . . . may not
> Be found acceptable in Heaven's sight.

And if this is true, if our very best—which after all is the best
there is—may not be enough, then Job's skepticism about
metaphysical profundities seems thoroughly warranted. If a

[47] Cox, . . . *Original "Ordinary" Man,* pp. 40-41.

given cause does not produce a particular effect, then what is
the ontological status of the alleged effect and of the intuition
by which we perceive it? Is the shining gate really there, the
real final cause of all our effort, or is it a will-o'-the-wisp, a
self-engendered projection of man's emotional need for a *raison
d'être,* for the assurance that something does care? Is it, in
fact, no more than an "as if," an intuited snark but a pragmatic
boojum?

Frost never really resolves this ambiguity. We are never
clearly and unambiguously certain whether intuitions like
Jonah's genuinely imply the existence of something beyond
nature, the "other," that is positively relevant to man's condition, or whether they are "as ifs," *made* values, like Plato's
noble lie. But the weight of the evidence, I think, suggests
the "as if"—suggests at least that Frost prefers to accept the
"as if" and to shy away from the alternative possibility. There
are few poems indeed that can be read as clear indications of
belief in a divinity that shapes our ends or for that matter is
concerned with our ends. The most clearly theistic of the
poems, apart from the masques, are "A Prayer in Spring,"
"The Trial by Existence," "I Will Sing You One-O," and "Too
Anxious for Rivers." But in the latter two poems, God's
function is almost exclusively that of an Aristotelian prime
mover. "The Trial by Existence" is obviously a made myth
rather than a statement of literal belief, and "A Prayer in
Spring" has a degree of wistfulness about it that suggests less
a belief than a will to believe. And against these one can set
a number of poems that at least invite, and sometimes strongly,
the "as if" reading. There is "All Revelation," in which, as
we have seen,[48] the last line's perfect ambiguity suggests that
our sense of a meaningful universe is the product of solipsism.
There is "Two Look at Two," in which, as we have also seen,[49]
the intuited sense of kinship with the earth is presented by an
explicitly "as if" metaphor. There is "For Once, Then, Some-

---

[48] See above, pp. 48-49.
[49] See above, pp. 31, 45.

thing," in which the speaker remains uncertain whether the unidentified whiteness at the bottom of the well is or is not really more important, more real, than his own godlike reflection at the surface—whether, in fact, there is anything more final than his own equally uncertain image looking back at him.   There is "The Black Cottage," in which the minister's whimsy about truth and belief can be slanted in either of two directions:

> For, dear me, why abandon a belief
> Merely because it ceases to be true.
> Cling to it long enough, and not a doubt
> It will turn true again, for so it goes.
> Most of the change we think we see in life
> Is due to truths being in and out of favor.
> As I sit here, and oftentimes, I wish
> I could be monarch of a desert land
> I could devote and dedicate forever
> To the truths we keep coming back and back to.

The lines may mean that truth is fixed and eternal and hence will keep bobbing up again and again in spite of fashionable error; or they may equally well mean that any belief works as well as any other, is as good as if it were true, and that consequently there is nothing to be gained by abandoning one's own beliefs in favor of someone else's.   "A Star in a Stone-Boat" sounds as though the speaker is pursuing an ordained quest, fulfilling a divinely ordained purpose, in his hunt after a misplaced meteorite:

> It went for building stone, and I, as though
> Commanded in a dream, forever go
> To right the wrong that this should have been so.

The quest has religious overtones:

Some may know what they seek in school and church,
And why they seek it there; for what I search
I must go measuring stone walls, perch on perch.

But the final stanza, instead of revealing a clarification of life
or a shining gate, executes a strategic shift to a kind of self-
deprecatory understatement:

Such as it is, it promises the prize
Of the one world complete in any size
That I am like to compass, fool or wise,

a conclusion that Job could share.

The two masques do not really provide a resolution of this
ambiguous suspension. And the cryptic, oracular conclusion
to the introduction Frost wrote for Edwin Arlington Robinson's *King Jasper,* though it antedates the masques by more
than ten years, is extremely suggestive here:

Not for me to search [Robinson's] sadness to its source! He knew
how to forbid encroachment. And there is solid satisfaction in
a sadness that is not just a fishing for ministration and consola-
tion. Give us immedicable woes—woes that nothing can be done
for—woes flat and final. And then to play. The play's the thing.
Play's the thing. All virtue in "as if."
                     As if the last of days
               Were fading and all wars were done.
               As if they were. As if, as if![50]

One thinks of the emphasis on make-believe in "Directive,"
of Frost's persistent sense of life as gambling, of the frequency
with which his people make formative choices whimsically,
committing themselves to a kind of pure risk by which they
make their destinies—Yvor Winters' objection. One thinks
of the shining gate that Jonah almost thinks he sees. And
one thinks of the value-confirming "clarification of life," a
clarification that is "not necessarily a great clarification, such

[50] Frost, *King Jasper,* p. xv.

as sects and cults are founded on, but . . . a momentary stay against confusion."[51] Such statements and such emphases strongly suggest that to Frost even our best intuitions, our most nearly total commitments of ourselves, are probably no more than "as ifs."

And if this is so, it becomes possible to see why Frost's allegiance has been persistently divided between anthropocentric man and prudential man. If the designs anthropocentric man makes for himself are finally unverifiable hypotheses, momentary stays against confusion that are valuable only in the pragmatic sense that they *are* such stays, then it is finally impossible to say that he is better than his prudential counterpart whose willingness to drift, to get by, to dig in, serves the same purpose, and with less fuss. It becomes impossible, on any but idiosyncratic grounds, to judge between the man who says "Good fences make good neighbors" and the man who says "What we live by we die by," between the man who dies in pursuit of something he almost thinks he sees or the woman who confronts madness with Stoic integrity and the woman who dies of emotional indecision on a tropical island. The drumlin woodchuck and the husband of "West-Running Brook" pass the same test—they have got by. I have said that Frost's habit of equivocation is more than a habit; it is, in fact, the product of a basic philosophical indecision, an unwillingness or an inability to make that crucial act of choice by which anthropocentric man fulfils himself. Ultimately, Yvor Winters is right, though the root of the matter is not so much a matter of ethical confusion as it is a matter of ontological indecisiveness.

It would clearly be Procrustean to maintain either that such indecisiveness is deplorable in itself or that it has prevented Frost from writing excellent poems. As Thomas Henry Huxley pointed out three quarters of a century ago, a refusal to dogmatize on the basis of insufficient evidence is deplorable only to the fanatic; and the fact that Frost has written good

[51] Frost, *Complete Poems*, p. vi.

poems proves that the refusal is not incompatible with good poetry. And yet I think the refusal does more than leave in doubt that

> final goal
> We have it hidden in us to attain

mentioned in "On a Tree Fallen Across the Road." R. P. Blackmur, writing about Yeats, says:

. . . his early poems are fleeting, some of them beautiful and some that sicken, as you read them, to their own extinction. But as he acquired for himself a discipline, however unacceptable to the bulk of his readers, his poetry obtained an access to reality. So it is with most of our serious poets. It is almost the mark of the poet of genuine merit in our time—the poet who writes serious works with an intellectual aspect which are nonetheless poetry—that he performs his work in the light of an insight, a group of ideas, and a faith, with the discipline that flows from them, which taken together form a view of life most readers cannot share, and which, furthermore, most readers feel as repugnant, or sterile, or simply inconsequential.[52]

What Blackmur writes is certainly true of Yeats; the poetry Hopkins wrote before he had accepted the Jesuit discipline is frequently callow and derivative; the Anglo-Catholic Eliot of "Ash Wednesday" is more impressive than the other Eliot of "The Hippopotamus." Auden's Marxian-Freudian-Grod-deckian-Christian syncretism, Wallace Stevens' aesthetic ideal-ism, and, as Blackmur notes, Hardy's fatalism provide similar accesses to reality. And in Hart Crane, whose poetry seems to have arisen principally from random moments of ecstasy, one can see a particularly compelling instance of an obviously talented poet who failed to achieve such discipline and whose work remains largely a matter of brilliant patches.

Frost's incompleteness is not like Crane's—patchy, often inflated, and sometimes out of control altogether. Rather it

[52] R. P. Blackmur, *Form and Value in Modern Poetry* (Garden City, 1957), p. 35.

reveals itself in his tendencies toward the arch or the snide or the oracular, in his role as—Louise Bogan's phrase—"the inspired purveyor of timeless and granitic wisdom,"[53] in his persistent refusal to be pinned down, in his suspended judgments and his refusals to judge. In Frost's poems there are not only no villains but very few people whom one is clearly asked to condemn; by the same standard, there are very few people to whom one is seriously tempted to attribute a capacity for human greatness—no Schweitzers, no Gandhis, no Tolstois. Yeats had a galaxy of such heroes—Parnell, John Synge, Lady Gregory, her son Robert, Hugh Lane, John O'Leary, the men and women of the Easter rising; Eliot has his Becket and his Celia Coplestone; even Crane had Whitman. Frost gives us few people who *matter* as much as these do. We are moved, as Frost is moved, by the Broken One, by the couple in "West-Running Brook," by the witch of Grafton, or by Jonah, but neither we nor Frost are committed to any of these as Yeats, addressing the ghost of Parnell in "To a Shade," was committed to Hugh Lane:

> A man
> Of your own passionate serving kind who had brought
> In his full hands what, had they only known,
> Had given their children's children loftier thought,
> Sweeter emotion, working in their veins
> Like gentle blood . . . .[54]

And in none of Frost's poems do we find that gust of energy devoted to a passionately held conviction or even prejudice that Yeats was capable of.

David Daiches writes, of A. E. Housman:

Housman denied himself so much . . . because he could find no valid reason why what he liked was worth doing, because he could

---

[53] Louise Bogan, *Achievement in American Poetry, 1900-1950* (Chicago, 1951), p. 51.
[54] *The Collected Poems of W. B. Yeats* (New York, 1951), p. 108.

find no real basis on which to ground his life and work; and, being sensitive, afraid to do what he could not justify, he took the stoic view and saw himself living to endure rather than to enjoy. . . . Honest idealist as he was (though how he would have hated being called that!) he was reluctant to engage in any activity whose value could not be attested in his own eyes by some valid standard. He could find no such standard. The only real belief he held was that in his own integrity: his basic emotion was pride.[55]

Frost's poems exhibit little if any of the latent hysteria characteristic of Housman's, and while Housman denies, Frost only refuses to commit himself. But even allowing for these substantial differences, Daiches' comment is relevant to both poets. Like Housman, Frost has found "no real basis on which to ground his life and work," no "valid standard" beyond one's sense of his own integrity, manifest in one's ability to endure or to get by. More capable than Housman of genuine pity for those who lack that ability (there is something theatrical and melodramatic even about Housman's pity) Frost exhibits a more complex basic emotion, one involving both pity and humility. But pride is one of its components—pride in one's getting by, in one's independence, in one's ability to take it, in one's bardic wisdom. At their best, once more, Frost's people possess a hard core of personal integrity that enables them to confront reality without wincing. But the reality they confront has no settled nature; they have no "access" to it, to echo Blackmur, because their creator is not sure what it is, what may emerge from the will's braving of alien entanglements. Conceiving of man as a choice-making animal, Frost has ultimately been unwilling or unable to choose his own conviction about the world he inhabits, and the result is that he offers nothing larger than isolated individuals in a world they seldom attempt to understand.

My failure is no different from Jonah's.
We both have lacked the courage in the heart

[55] David Daiches, *Poetry and the Modern World: A Study of Poetry in England between 1900 and 1939* (Chicago, 1940), pp. 20-21.

To overcome the fear within the soul
And go ahead to any accomplishment,

says Keeper, at the end of *A Masque of Mercy*. It would be foolish to accuse Frost of a lack of courage in any but a highly impersonal and metaphysical sense; in such a sense, however, Keeper's confession might well be Frost's.

A momentary stay against confusion

Among contemporary poets, Robert Frost's position is probably unique. On the one hand, he has been praised by such diverse critics as Ezra Pound, George Whicher, Amy Lowell, Randall Jarrell, Granville Hicks, Yvor Winters, and Robert P. Tristram Coffin; he has been elected to honorary membership in the International P. E. N. Club and his poems have been required reading at the Sorbonne;[1] by early 1957, he had received twenty-four honorary degrees—one each from Michigan, Vermont, Wes-

[1] Gorham B. Munson, *Robert Frost: A Study in Sensibility and Good Sense* (New York, 1927), p. 72.

leyan, St. Lawrence, Yale, Middlebury, Bowdoin, New Hampshire, Columbia, Williams, Dartmouth, Bates, Pennsylvania, Harvard, Colorado, Princeton, Marlboro, Colgate, Massachusetts, Durham, California, Duke, and two from Amherst, plus appointment as Phi Beta Kappa poet by Tufts, William and Mary, Harvard (twice), and Columbia;[2] later in 1957, he received honorary degrees from both Oxford and Cambridge, "the first American poet to be so honored since James Russell Lowell and Henry Wadsworth Longfellow."[3] He has received the Pulitzer Prize for poetry four times—for *New Hampshire,* for the 1930 *Collected Poems,* for *A Further Range,* and for *A Witness Tree.*

On the other hand, Frost's popularity is not limited to critics, universities, and prize committees. Reviewing *North of Boston* in 1914, Ezra Pound wrote:

. . . but why, IF there are serious people in America, desiring literature of America, literature accepting present conditions, rendering American life with sober fidelity—why, in heaven's name, is this book of New England eclogues given us under a foreign imprint?[4]

Nobody answered, but Frost's reception since his return to America in 1915 suggests that the reading public has made up for the initial publication-in-exile. *North of Boston,* the first of his books to appear in America, was published in January, 1915, a small edition of 150 copies made up from sheets imported from England. In March, 1915, the first American printing—1300 copies—appeared, and the book went through six printings that year and six more before the end of 1922.[5] Gorham Munson estimates a total of 20,000 copies.[6] *A Further Range,* Frost's third Pulitzer Prize book, was selected in

[2] *Who's Who in America* (Chicago, 1957), XXIX, 908.

[3] "Oxford and Cambridge to Honor Frost," *Christian Science Monitor,* XLIX (April 25, 1957), 2.

[4] Ezra Pound, "Modern Georgics," *Poetry: A Magazine of Verse,* V (Dec., 1914), 129.

[5] Wesleyan University Library, *Robert Frost: A Chronological Survey* (Middletown, Conn., 1936), p. 26.

[6] Munson, p. 70.

1936 for distribution by the Book-of-the-Month Club—
50,000 copies over and above the trade edition.[7] My copy of
The Pocket Book of Robert Frost's Poems, an expanded version of *Come In,* indicates a publishing history of three editions and eight printings through September, 1946, and the
1949 *Complete Poems* is in its fifth printing. An anonymous
writer in *Time* reported that "in the United States his books
have sold about 375,000 copies in all editions"[8] as of 1950.
And in 1922, before he had received his first Pulitzer Prize, he
was appointed by the Women's Clubs of Vermont as Poet
Laureate of that state.[9] Pound evidently was not impressed;
in 1918 he wrote to Edgar Jepson, "Frost sinks of his own
weight."[10] But from 1915 on, Frost has been successfully
demonstrating what Randall Jarrell calls, perhaps with more
irritation than justice, his "daemonic gift of always getting on
the buttered side of both God and Mammon."[11]

It took forty years for that gift to begin making itself apparent. Born in 1875, Frost had begun writing verse in his
teens, and a scattering of these early poems were published,
the first in 1892.[12] But *A Boy's Will,* his first book, was not
published until 1913, in London, and there were still two
years to go before the American edition of *North of Boston*
made him a part of the literary scene in this country. Frost's
was a late start, but it was a good one. The early reviews were
at worst kind, and at best enthusiastic.[13] By 1915 he had
achieved anthology status,[14] and shortly thereafter he was
being given substantial attention in critical studies of twen-

[7] Wesleyan, p. 51.
[8] "Pawky Poet," *Time,* LVI (Oct. 9, 1950), 76.
[9] Munson, p. 72.
[10] *The Letters of Ezra Pound: 1907-1941,* ed. D. D. Paige (New York,
1950), p. 135.
[11] Randall Jarrell, *Poetry and the Age* (New York, 1955), p. 35.
[12] Munson, pp. 29-30, 58.
[13] Gorham Munson has reprinted a selection from the earliest reviews
of *A Boy's Will* and *North of Boston:* see Munson, pp. 117-124.
[14] In W. S. B. Braithwaite's *Anthology of Magazine Verse* for 1915;
Wesleyan, p. 27.

tieth-century American writing—by Amy Lowell in 1917,[15] by Louis Untermeyer[16] and Waldo Frank[17] in 1919. True, Miss Lowell found him to be Theocritus rather than Homer;[18] but as Untermeyer compared him with Whitman,[19] so Miss Lowell compared him with Burns, with Synge, and with Mistral, concluding that "it is perhaps not too much to say that he is the equal of these poets, and will so rank in future generations."[20]

This tradition of high praise has, of course, continued, in books and articles. In 1925, John Freeman wrote, ". . . there is heard from his first book to his latest a man's voice affirming and accepting, rather than an intellectual eunuch's questioning and despairing."[21] In 1939, Granville Hicks declared that

'Collected Poems' shows and shows clearly that Frost has written as fine poetry as any living American and that the proportion of first-rate poetry to the whole is greater than that in the work of any other contemporary.[22]

(Hicks's evaluation was subsequently described by Robert S. Newdick, another admirer of Frost, as "the absurd strawman representation" of a "straining thesis critic.")[23] In 1936, Robert Hillyer wrote to Frost,

> in cloistered minds like yours
> The classic wisdom of the past endures.[24]

[15] Amy Lowell, *Tendencies in Modern American Poetry* (New York, 1917), pp. 79-136.

[16] Louis Untermeyer, *The New Era in American Poetry* (New York, 1919), pp. 15-39.

[17] Waldo Frank, *Our America* (New York, 1919), pp. 175-179.

[18] Lowell, p. 135.   [19] Untermeyer, p. 39.

[20] Lowell, p. 136.

[21] John Freeman, "Robert Frost," *London Mercury*, XII (Dec., 1925), 177.

[22] Granville Hicks, "The World of Robert Frost," *New Republic*, LXV (Dec. 3, 1930), 77.

[23] Robert S. Newdick, "Robert Frost Speaks Out," *Sewanee Review*, XLV (April-June, 1937), 240.

[24] Robert Hillyer, "A Letter to Robert Frost," *Atlantic Monthly*, CLVIII (Aug., 1936), 161.

In 1938, Robert P. Tristram Coffin named Frost

the real radical among modern poets. Men like E. E. Cummings
and T. S. Eliot are the pseudo-radicals. The pseudo-ones get the
most space in the papers and with the critics. They are radicals
who leave out capitals and punctuation marks, or, as in the case of
James Joyce and T. S. Eliot, in their most typical books, *Ulysses*
and *The Waste Land,* they pursue the novelty of grafting healthy
tissue onto dead.[25]

In that same year, Bernard De Voto belligerently asserted
that, when you really look at the poetry Frost has written,

unless your nerves are sealed with wax, you immediately and
overwhelmingly perceive that this is the work of an individual and
integrated poet, a poet who is like no one else, a major poet—not
only in regard to this age but in regard to our whole literature, a
great American poet.[26]

Ten years later, in an essay largely devoted to a sharp attack
on Frost as a "spiritual drifter," Yvor Winters declared in his
opening sentence that "Robert Frost is one of the most talented
poets of our time."[27]   And in 1949 Sidney Cox wrote that *A
Masque of Mercy* "at last takes its place with Euripides'
Alcestis and Shakespeare's *King Lear.*"[28]   In quantitative
terms, at least, the weight of critical opinion has been very
much in Frost's favor.

But in two respects this critical consensus is less conclusive than it seems.   In the first place, a good deal of the more
insistent enthusiasm for Frost has the atmosphere of a cult
about it.   When Sidney Cox writes of *A Masque of Mercy*
that

whether implicit or explicit in his expression, Robert Frost now

[25] Robert P. Tristram Coffin, *New Poetry of New England: Frost and
Robinson* (Baltimore, 1938), p. 71.
[26] Bernard De Voto, "The Critics and Robert Frost," *Saturday Review
of Literature,* XVII (Jan. 1, 1938), 14.
[27] Yvor Winters, "Robert Frost: or, The Spiritual Drifter as Poet,"
Sewanee Review, LVI (Autumn, 1948), 564.
[28] Sidney Cox, "Robert Frost and Poetic Fashion," *American Scholar,*
XVIII (Winter, 1948-1949), 86.

and always thinks astronomic circles round other writers who have weathered the same wars, panics, booms and unemphatic seasons,[29]

one suspects that the statement is less a proposition to be tested than an assertion that the king can do no wrong. When Robert P. Tristram Coffin tells us that Frost

has great friends at his elbow: the seasons, frost and rain, night and day, and others, too. Not the great aristocratic friends in books, preaching perfection, but the great commoners who teach a man how to get along: gladness, compassion, fear, grief,

and something rather alarmingly designated as " 'he-ness,' to bring out the 'she-ness' in a mate,"[30] it seems clear that we are being invited to share an ecstasy rather than to understand a poet. Robert S. Newdick's immoderate condemnation of Granville Hicks is immoderate; it sounds suspiciously like an anathematizing gesture, an accusation of heresy. Hicks doesn't admire Frost enough, or admires him for the wrong reasons. And the frequency with which other poets, named or nameless, are castigated for Frost's benefit—John Freeman's "intellectual eunuch," Coffin's version of Cummings, Joyce, and Eliot, the "other writers" round whom Cox's Frost "thinks astronomic circles"—suggests not merely an illuminating critical contrast but the denunciation of false gods. As Malcolm Cowley has written:

. . . if . . . I still say that there is a case against [Frost] and room for a dissenting opinion, perhaps I chiefly mean that there is a case against the zealous admirers who are not content to take the poet for what he is, but insist on using him as a sort of banner for their own moral or political crusades . . . as an excuse for berating and belittling other poets, who have supposedly fallen into the sins of pessimism, obscurity, obscenity, and yielding to foreign influences; we even hear of their treachery to the American dream. Frost, on the other hand, is depicted as loyal, autochthonous and almost aboriginal.[31]

Such indiscriminate enthusiasm has, I believe, done Frost's

[29] Cox, p. 80.   [30] Coffin, p. 53.
[31] Cowley, p. 312.

critical reputation a disservice, tending to lump first-rate and
fifth-rate poems together and producing a climate of opinion
not very favorable to the making of critical reservations, reservations that some of Frost's admirers are more than willing to
make about poets whose work is markedly different from
Frost's.

But such reservations have also been made about Frost,
and it is their persistent presence as a kind of undercurrent in
the tradition of high praise for Frost's poetry that constitutes
the second respect in which the majority report must be qualified.   In his 1913 review of *A Boy's Will,* Ezra Pound ad-
mitted that "Mr. Frost's book is a little raw, and has in it a
number of infelicities."[32]   Four years later, Amy Lowell imposed a more complex qualification on her praise:

Mr. Frost's work is undoubtedly more finished in its kind than the
work of any other living American poet, but this very finish pre-
cludes growth.   In some other poets we feel potentialities, in Mr.
Frost we find achievement.[33]

And Gorham Munson, whose *Robert Frost: A Study in Sensibility and Good Sense* was the first book-length discussion of
the poet, concludes:

There are certain all-important questions which only the greatest
literature raises and attempts to answer, and these questions it is
not appropriate to ask of every poet.   Frost makes no pretense of
great inclusiveness and great profundities.   The canniness of good
sense forbids such rash over-reachings of one's self.[34]

In their contexts, such qualified judgments mean simply that
Frost is not in the absolute first rank of poets; they provide a
wholesome counterirritant to the loud cries of the cultists.

They also provide early evidence of a critical note that
was to be sounded more persistently and developed more
articulately from about 1930 on.   That note has not been

[32] Ezra Pound, "A Boy's Will," *Poetry: A Magazine of Verse,* II (May,
1913), 72.
[33] Lowell, p. 135.
[34] Munson, p. 114.

exactly—at least not simply—one of disparagement, an effort to prove that Frost is not a good poet. Rather it has represented, broadly speaking, an attempt to determine why he is not a better poet. As early as 1924 T. K. Whipple had written, "Mr. Frost's poetry, in sum, is a poetry of exclusions, of limitations, not of area only and of subject matter, but chiefly of temperament."[35] And in 1928, reviewing Munson's book, Robert Penn Warren pointed out a degree of incoherence, the lack of a controlling concept, in Frost's attitude toward nature.[36] In subsequent years such revaluations were attempted with a good deal of frequency—by Granville Hicks in 1930,[37] by Frederic I. Carpenter in 1932[38] (this article provoked a counterblast from Robert Hillyer),[39] by R. P. Blackmur in 1936,[40] by Merrill Moore in 1937,[41] by Malcolm Cowley in 1944,[42] by Randall Jarrell in 1947[43] (Cowley and Jarrell were singled out for high scorn by Sidney Cox in 1949[44]—the same article that equated *A Masque of Mercy* with *King Lear*), by William G. O'Donnell[45] and by Yvor Winters[46] in 1948, by Louise Bogan in 1951.[47] These articles have not led to any

[35] T. K. Whipple, "Robert Frost," *Literary Review* (March 22, 1924), p. 606.

[36] Robert Penn Warren, "Hawthorne, Anderson and Frost," *New Republic,* LIV (May 16, 1928), 400.

[37] Hicks, pp. 77-78.

[38] Frederic I. Carpenter, "The Collected Poems of Robert Frost," *New England Quarterly,* V (Jan., 1932), 159-160.

[39] Robert Hillyer, "Robert Frost 'Lacks Power,'" *New England Quarterly,* V (April, 1932), 402-404.

[40] R. P. Blackmur, "The Instincts of a Bard," *Nation,* CXLII (June 24, 1936), 817-819.

[41] Merrill Moore, "Poetic Agrarianism: Old Style," *Sewanee Review,* XLV (Oct.-Dec., 1937), 507-509.

[42] Cowley, pp. 312-313; also "The Case Against Mr. Frost: II," *New Republic,* CXI (Sept. 18, 1944), 345-347.

[43] Randall Jarrell, "The Other Robert Frost," *Nation,* CLXV (Nov. 29, 1947), 588-592.

[44] Cox, pp. 78-86.

[45] William G. O'Donnell, "Robert Frost and New England: A Revaluation," *Yale Review,* XXXVII (Summer, 1948), 698-712.

[46] Winters, pp. 564-596.

[47] Louise Bogan, *Achievement in American Poetry, 1900-1950* (Chicago, 1951), pp. 47-51.

perceptible moderation of tone on the part of Frost's unquali-
fied and unreconstructed admirers. In the 1950 edition of
Modern American Poetry, Louis Untermeyer still found that
Frost's poetry,

with its genius for suggestive understatement, establishes Frost
among the first of contemporary writers and places him with the
very best of American poets past or present. It is not the technique nor even the thought, but the essence which finally convinces; the reader is fortified by Frost's serenity, strengthened by
his strength.[48]

But meanwhile Randall Jarrell had written, with a kind of sad
energy:

. . . the man who called himself "the author/ Of several books
against the world in general"; who said that he had learned from
Marlowe's Mephistopheles to say his prayers, "Why this is Hell,
nor am I out of it"; who said to Henry Hudson, drowned or frozen
somewhere in Hudson's Bay: "You and I and the Great Auk";
who could be annoyed at a hornet for not recognizing him as "the
exception I like to think I am in everything"; who in poems like
"A Servant to Servants," "Home Burial," and "The Witch of
Coös" had a final identifying knowledge of the deprived and dispossessed, the insulted and injured, that one matches in modern
poetry only in Hardy—this poet is now, most of the time, an elder
statesman like Baruch or Smuts, full of complacent wisdom and
cast-iron whimsy.[49]

In the same article, Jarrell accused Frost "of not only allowing, but taking a hard pleasure in encouraging, fools and
pedants to adore him as their own image magnified," adding
that such tendencies have "helped to keep us from seeing
Frost for what he really is."[50] Oddly enough—it must have
seemed very odd to some—the essay in which the last two
quoted phrases appeared was written with the purpose of
showing how unusually good Frost's best poems really are.

Odd as it may seem, however, the oddity is no accident,

[48] Louis Untermeyer, ed., *Modern American Poetry* (New York, 1950),
p. 181.
[49] Jarrell, *Poetry and the Age,* p. 30.
[50] *Ibid.,* p. 35.

nor is it a mere critical affectation. Rather it is Jarrell's device for coping with something that anyone who is seriously concerned with evaluating Frost's poetry as a whole has to cope with sooner or later—the blunt facts that Frost's best is very good indeed and that his worst is very nearly unforgivable, not in the sense that it is bad verse but in the sense that it is arch verse, or complacent verse, or cute verse, the verse of a man who chuckles quietly to himself at being told he is a character, because *he* knew all the time that he was a character. It would not have been easy to predict such unevenness on the strength of his first books, though Amy Lowell's sense that potentialities were lacking in those books may have been prophetic (nearly so, anyway; on the strength of the early books it would also have been difficult to predict such poems as "The Subverted Flower," "The Discovery of the Madeiras," or "Directive").

But with the wisdom of hindsight, recognizing that the man who wrote "Home Burial" and "The Pauper Witch of Grafton" is the same man who wrote "Triple Bronze," "One Step Backward Taken," and "A Wish to Comply," one can detect a series of danger signals from as far back as *Mountain Interval* (1916). *A Boy's Will* and *North of Boston* can be left out of account here, *A Boy's Will* because of its derivative, unformed, first-bookish quality, *North of Boston* because its quite solidly dramatic frame compels the intrusively editorial "I"—the "I" of the bardic wisdom—to keep its distance. But *Mountain Interval* opens with "The Road Not Taken" and closes with "The Sound of the Trees," and both these crucially placed poems present moments in which crucial acts of choice are made in an entirely whimsical manner. "The Bonfire" celebrates and recommends irresponsibility. "The Gum-Gatherer" presents a nostalgic picture of a man who has succeeded in freeing himself from all responsibility to others. "An Encounter" demonstrates arch jocularity at the expense of civilization. And "The Exposed Nest," with its apparent questioning of the value and even the reality of humanitarian impulses, foreshadows the later callousness of "One Step Backward Taken." In the title poem of *New Hampshire* (1923), one finds deliberate cultivation of a kind of professional New England wisdom, the utterance of a twentieth-century Sam Slick of Slickville. In *West-Running Brook* (1928), "The Bear" and "The Egg and the Machine" indicate developing anti-intellectualism and sympathy for motiveless hatred of complex machinery. "The Rose Family," "The Door in the Dark," and "The Armful" suggest satisfaction with the merely trivial. And the book's title poem is Frost's last explicitly dramatic poem except for "Build Soil" and the two masques, which are something else again. Even in "West-Running Brook," the effect is not that of the fine dramatic poems in *North of Boston.* There the emphasis was on the moving presentation of character; here it is on the presentation—also moving, I think—of a character's philosophy. The dramatist is turning into the editorialist, and that process is completed in *A Further Range* (1936), in such poems as "A Lone Striker," "Two Tramps in Mud Time," "The White-Tailed Hornet," "A Drumlin Woodchuck," "A Roadside Stand," "At Woodward's Gardens," and "Build Soil." Not that these poems have no redeeming features; most of them do. But all of them, involve, not the at least potentially tragic acceptance of "The Self-Seeker" or "West-Running Brook," but certain canny or defensive denials; one is much more aware of what Frost dislikes than of what he values. Frost had, to be sure, passed sixty at the time *A Further Range* was published—but one remembers Yeats at seventy.

A Witness Tree (1942) shows a surprising degree of recovery from hardening mannerisms; it includes "The Gift Outright," "The Most of It," "All Revelation," and the quite unpredictable "The Subverted Flower" and "The Discovery of the Madeiras." The latter two poems are as powerful in their way as anything in *North of Boston,* and their way is something new in Frost's poetry. Their novelty lies partly, I think, in their independence of a specifically New England locale, partly in their exploitation of a motif of guilt (there are few guilt-ridden characters in *North of Boston;* even in "The Fear," where such a motif does appear, Frost does not give it the exploitation in depth that these later poems manifest), partly in their presentation of unconscious dynamics.[51] These characteristics do not, of course, necessarily make "The Subverted Flower" and "The Discovery of the Madeiras" better poems than "The Self-Seeker" or "West-Running Brook," but they make the poems different at least in degree, and they do suggest reserves of power that Frost has very seldom capitalized on.

But 1945 saw the publication of *A Masque of Reason,* and it is hard not to sympathize with Randall Jarrell's judgment of it as

a frivolous, trivial, and bewilderingly corny affair, full of jokes inexplicable except as the contemptuous patter of an old magician certain that *he* can get away with anything in the world. . . . Besides, Frost has long ago divorced reason for common sense, and is basking complacently in his bargain; consequently, when common sense has God justify His ways to Job by saying, "I was just showing off to Satan," the performance has the bleak wisdom of Calvin Coolidge telling you what life comes to at 2½ % .[52]

Jarrell's irritation is excessive; *A Masque of Reason* is in its way a serious poem. But its seriousness, tangled up with such devices as God's prefabricated plywood throne or Satan's unfortunate involvement with a "tendency," too frequently confuses wit with cuteness, and labored cuteness at that. *A Masque of Reason* was followed two years later by *Steeple Bush.* And in *Steeple Bush,* "Directive," which demonstrates some of the depth of "The Discovery of the Madeiras,"[53] appears in company with a poem entitled "An Importer," which begins,

[51] Cf. above, pp. 107-109.
[52] Jarrell, *Poetry and the Age,* p. 32.
[53] See above, pp. 143-145.

> Mrs. Someone's been to Asia.
> What she brought back would amaze ye,

and concludes,

> Teach those Asians mass production?
> Teach your grandmother egg suction.

Steeple Bush contains substantially more poems comparable with "An Importer" than with "Directive." There is "Beyond Words":

> That row of icicles along the gutter
> Feels like my armory of hate;
> And you, you . . . you, you utter . . .
> You wait!

There is "Etherealizing," in which Frost rebuts anyone who wants to argue that we would be better if we would go on evolving into ultimate "blobs of brain." There is "A Wish to Comply," which means, if it means anything much, that the proper attitude for the layman to take toward nuclear physics is an obliging but skeptical jocularity. To anyone who admires *North of Boston*—except for members of the cult; Louis Untermeyer found *Steeple Bush* "particularly salted with wit and peppered with satire"[54]—*Steeple Bush* is a painful book, a little treasury of the trivial, with Frost finally become his own Boswell. That he was still capable of such a poem as "Directive" makes the rest of the book that much more distressing. *A Masque of Mercy* also appeared in 1947, and, in spite of its sometimes trying whimsy, is sufficiently compelling to indicate that "Directive" was not just a lucky accident.

This brief chronological survey has, of course, been a loaded one; there is perfectly competent work in all Frost's

[54] Untermeyer, *Modern American Poetry*, p. 182.

If there were not, the vulnerable work would not mat-
could dismiss Frost as simply a second- or third-rate
o had the luck to produce one good book, or as a poet
who got started too late and then ran dry. But such dismissal
will not do. No third-rate poet or dried-up poet, no matter
how lucky, could produce a sequence like "Stars" (from *A
Boy's Will*), "A Servant to Servants" (from *North of Boston*),
"Snow" (from *Mountain Interval*), "An Empty Threat" (from
New Hampshire), "Acquainted With the Night" (from *West-
Running Brook*), "Neither Out Far Nor In Deep" (from *A
Further Range*), "The Most of It" (from *A Witness Tree*),
and "Directive" (from *Steeple Bush*), a sequence that extends
over a period of at least thirty-four years, with Frost in his
seventies at its close. The important question is not whether
Frost is a good and important poet, but rather why a good
and important poet should, with increasing persistence, take
refuge in the arch, the cute, the complacent, the trivial, gradually abandoning areas of proven strength (the dramatic poems
of *North of Boston, Mountain Interval,* and *New Hampshire*),
and not really following up promising new departures ("The
Subverted Flower," "The Discovery of the Madeiras," "Directive"). As Louise Bogan has said:

Frost's later work never completely realized the tragic power that
North of Boston promised. In *West-Running Brook* (1928) he
began to play with the role of self-conscious homespun philosopher. He began to give reasons for his innate, countryman's
conservatism, and not only reasons, but arguments which were
half apologies. His own native shrewdness began to get the upper
hand. . . . he reinforced his stoicism, which in itself had a certain
dignity, with an active insistence upon burrowing under and
digging safely in. We see in this attitude the ancient conservatism
of the man who depends upon the earth for his living;[55] but Frost's
later work seems to base its skepticism less upon intelligent common sense than upon unthinking timidity. The appeal Frost made

[55] Frost's self-created role, again; his dependence upon the earth for his
living lasted only five years, more than fifty years ago. See above p. 140.

to large numbers of people began to be attached to a series of refusals rather than to a set of affirmations.[56]

And the question to be answered is, Why?

Obviously, no answer to such a question can be more than tentative. Lionel Trilling has written of Wordsworth:

. . . given the fact of the great power, the desire to explain its relative deterioration will no doubt always be irresistible. But we must be aware, in any attempt to make this explanation, that an account of why Wordsworth ceased to write great poetry must at the same time be an account of how he once did write great poetry. And this latter account, in our present state of knowledge, we cannot begin to furnish.[57]

Now, Frost's importance is not comparable to Wordsworth's; Wordsworth, after all, with Milton, Spenser, Chaucer, is one of the handful of poets who have not simply worked within a tradition but have been instrumental in shaping and giving direction to their tradition, and it would be rash indeed to attribute such weight to Frost, at least in our time. Even the cultists do not deny that Eliot has been the more powerfully influential poet; they merely deplore the fact and appeal to the judgment of history. But Trilling's warning is as applicable to Frost as it is to Wordsworth. The problem of why Frost has written unsatisfactory poems is inextricably involved with the problem of how he has written excellent poems; and if the latter problem were soluble, there would be no occasion for speculative criticism.

Insofar as art is important, however, the problem of unsatisfactory art is also important, however speculative and provisional one's examination of the problem may be. And I think that the most rewarding approach to that problem with respect to Frost is by way of comparison between Frost and some of his principal contemporaries. In a number of ways, Yeats is a particularly useful figure here. Both men have

[56] Bogan, pp. 49-50.
[57] Lionel Trilling, *The Liberal Imagination: Essays on Literature and Society* (New York, 1950), p. 153.

written a substantial quantity of poetry; Yeats's *Collected Poems* (most of the plays omitted) runs to over four hundred pages, Frost's *Complete Poems* (including the masques) to over six hundred. Both men began writing in the eighties or nineties of the last century, and their earliest work exhibits a comparable degree of vague, nostalgic yearning. Both were in their seventies at the time their most recent books were published, and both had been writing and publishing quite steadily from the time of their first books. (Yeats, of course, died in 1939; Frost continues to write. *Complete Poems* contains three poems evidently completed since the publication of *Steeple Bush* and *A Masque of Mercy,* and his privately printed Christmas poems keep appearing.) To a degree, they exhibit similar crotchets and prejudices. Both are fond of making cryptically oracular pronouncements—compare Yeats's "Lapis Lazuli" with Frost's concluding remarks on Robinson.[58] Both are scornful toward efforts at social reform—compare Yeats's "On a House Shaken by the Land Agitation" with Frost's "A Roadside Stand," or Yeats's treatment of Constance Markievicz in "Easter 1916" with Frost's "To a Thinker" or "The Lost Follower." Both profess a distrust of excessive intellection—compare Yeats's

> I would be ignorant as the dawn,

from "The Dawn," or

> An intellectual hatred is the worst,
> So let her think opinions are accursed,

from "A Prayer for My Daughter," with Frost's "The Bear" or with Thyatira's skepticism in *A Masque of Reason.* Both create more or less eccentric roles for themselves—Frost as the canny Yankee, Yeats as the fisherman of "The Tower,"

[58] Quoted above, p. 183.

as the wild old wicked man of *Last Poems,* as one of "the indomitable Irishry" of "Under Ben Bulben."[59]

As a matter of fact, Yeats has evidently been a curiously attractive figure to Frost. As we have seen in Chapter I,[60] Frost produced two of Yeats's plays at Pinkerton Academy in 1910. And in the two masques, Frost indicates that Yeats is on his mind. In *A Masque of Reason,* Thyatira, preparing to take a group snapshot of God, Job, and Satan, says:

> There, that's just the right arrangement.
> Now someone can light up the Burning Bush
> And turn the gold enameled artificial birds on.
> I recognize them. Greek artificers
> Devised them for Alexius Comnenus.
> They won't show in the picture.

But "Sailing to Byzantium" does. And in *A Masque of Mercy,* Paul explains Keeper and Bel to Jonah:

> Don't you be made feel small by all this posing.
> Both of them caught it from Bel's favorite poet
> Who in his favorite pose as poet thinker
> (His was the doctrine of the Seven Poses)
> Once charged the Nazarene with having brought
> A darkness out of Asia that had crossed
> Old Attic grace and Spartan discipline
> With violence. The Greeks were hardly strangers
> To the idea of violence. It flourished
> Persisting from old Chaos in their myth
> To embroil the very gods about their spheres
> Of influence. It's been a commonplace
> Ever since Alexander Greeced the world.
> 'Twere nothing new if that were all Christ brought.

[59] *The Collected Poems of W. B. Yeats* (New York, 1951), pp. 144, 187, 343.
[60] See above, p. 42, n. 63.

Christ came to introduce a break with logic
That made all other outrage seem as child's play:
The Mercy on the Sin against the Sermon.

No other contemporary poet gets such sustained attention from
Frost, even though Edward Thomas and Ridgely Torrence
have poems addressed to them.   To be sure, he is being snide
at Yeats's expense, yet it is not easy to see why Yeats should
have been so singled out.   In *A Masque of Reason* the allu-
sion is irrelevant, dragged in, and in *A Masque of Mercy,*
though a connection is made, it is not clear what the quarrel
is about.   Paul conveniently forgets, in his closing lines, that
it was precisely

In pity for man's darkening thought

that Yeats's Christ came in "Two Songs from a Play," and he
says nothing about the arrogant idealism with which Yeats's
poem closes, an idealism that would surely have been anath-
ema to the historical Paul:

Whatever flames upon the night
Man's own resinous heart has fed.[61]

The whole situation strongly suggests, to one reader at least,
a reluctant but powerful attraction toward Yeats's poetry and
perhaps toward Yeats's general position as well.[62]

[61] Yeats, pp. 210, 211.
[62] To carry this matter further, in Yeats's *Collected Poems,* "Two Songs
from a Play" is followed immediately by "Fragments":
"Locke sank into a swoon;
The Garden died;
God took the spinning-jenny
Out of his side." (Yeats, p. 211.)
The author of "The Egg and the Machine" would hardly quarrel with the
sentiment here expressed.
"Where got I that truth?
Out of a medium's mouth,
Out of nothing it came,
Out of the forest loam,

It would be possible to explain this situation simply as one craftsman's interest in another sufficiently like himself to make attraction possible but sufficiently different to prevent that attraction from ever approaching identification, to make possible an amused irritation at this other one's foibles. And perhaps that is the most that can safely be suggested. But at the risk of abandoning safety, I think something more fundamental is involved—at least that Yeats's particular achievement illuminates to a degree Frost's relative incompleteness. As we have seen in Chapter V,[63] Frost is unable or unwilling to indicate what the reality is that his characters confront, and the result is a degree of inconclusiveness; we are never quite sure what Jonah's death means, whether his commitment of himself implies an apprehension of reality or a self-destructive surrender to an impulsive whim—or whether surrender to whim *is* a means of apprehending reality.

Now, precisely one of the things that *A Vision* provided Yeats was an elaborately articulated theory of reality and a means of apprehending it—twenty-six such means, in fact; Frost was too moderate in attributing only seven poses to Yeats. And those poems that are now almost universally

---

> Out of dark night where lay
> The crowns of Nineveh." (Yeats, p. 211.)

Or, as Frost would put it, "trust my instinct—I'm a bard." Also, Jonah's conduct toward the end of *A Masque of Mercy* has an at least formal resemblance to the conduct of Yeats's antithetical man in pursuit of his Mask. The "irresistible impossibility" that Paul compels Jonah to see and follow—

> "Yes, Pilgrim now instead of runaway,
> Your fugitive escape become a quest"—

sets up remote echoes of Yeats's man of the second quarter who, in "The Phases of the Moon,"

> "follows whatever whim's most difficult
> Among whims not impossible." (Yeats, p. 161.)

Keeper, be it noted, simply turns away from that irresistible impossibility; but it is Jonah who is saved—presumably—at the end and Keeper who confesses his lack of courage, concerned more with finding himself than with finding an image. And the myth Frost constructs in "The Trial by Existence," like Yeats's myth in *A Vision,* involves a doctrine of successive reincarnations, though Frost's poem, included in *A Boy's Will,* antedates the privately printed version of *A Vision* by at least twelve years.

[63] See above, pp. 186-188.

accepted as Yeats's finest were written after the theory had been worked out. That theory is more or less incredible; in R. P. Blackmur's temperate phrasing, it presents "a view of life most readers cannot share, and which, furthermore, most readers feel as repugnant, or sterile, or simply inconsequential."[64]   But its incredibility does not matter much except in ultimate terms. For one thing, incredibility of one sort or another is a common characteristic of statements about the nature of reality. Yeats's spheres and gyres are intrinsically neither more nor less difficult to believe in than the Christian doctrine of the Incarnation; and, as Alfred North Whitehead has written of "the characteristic scientific philosophy which closed the seventeenth century,"

it has held its own as the guiding principle of scientific studies ever since. It is still reigning. Every university in the world organizes itself in accordance with it. No alternative system of organizing the pursuit of scientific truth has been suggested. It is not only reigning, but it is without a rival.

And yet—it is quite unbelievable.[65]

And for another thing, while such incredibility may be disadvantageous as the basis for a totally adequate philosophy, it is not necessarily disadvantageous as the basis for a poet's strategy, especially when the poet translates his private, eccentric symbols into more generally accessible ones. We lose nothing by knowing that the "widening gyre"[66] of "The Second Coming" is explained in a good deal of detail in *A Vision,* but the sense of accelerating and disruptive centrifugal forces wrenching a culture apart is conveyed clearly enough without such knowledge. At its best, the system described in *A Vision* served to give shape and precision to Yeats's thinking and to the images he made. Of his own belief in that system, Yeats wrote:

[64] R. P. Blackmur, *Form and Value in Modern Poetry* (Garden City, 1957), p. 35.
[65] Alfred North Whitehead, *Science and the Modern World* (New York, 1948), p. 56.
[66] Yeats, p. 184.

. . . some will ask whether I believe in the actual existence of my circuits of sun and moon. . . . To such a question I can but answer that if sometimes, overwhelmed by miracle as all men must be when in the midst of it, I have taken such periods literally, my reason has soon recovered; and now that the system stands out clearly in my imagination I regard them as stylistic arrangements of experience comparable to the cubes in the drawing of Wyndham Lewis and the ovoids in the sculpture of Brancusi. They have helped me to hold in a single thought reality and justice.[67]

This admission is a curiously complicated thing. On the one hand, it means that to Yeats the "truth" of *A Vision* is really on a par with Frost's "as ifs";[68] it is a "momentary stay against confusion,"[69] a useful hypothesis that enables one to get by, "to hold in a single thought reality and justice," even though reality and justice may not strictly speaking belong in the same thought. On the other hand, it means that Yeats has done vastly more with his "as ifs" than has Frost, that he has compelled them to take their places in an elaborate closed system. Frost wrote, "The play's the thing. Play's the thing. All virtue in 'as if!' "[70] And yet, of all contemporary poets, it is not Frost but Yeats who has most completely and seriously acted on that premise, who has compelled his "momentary stay against confusion" to take on the status and the elaboration of a "clarification of life."[71] Frost tells us, of his own experience of writing poems,

the impressions most useful to my purpose have always been those I was unaware of and so made no note of at the time when taken, and the conclusion is come to that like giants we are always hurling experience ahead of us to pave the future with against the day when we may want to strike a line of purpose across it for somewhere.[72]

[67] Quoted by Louis MacNeice, *The Poetry of W. B. Yeats* (New York, 1941), p. 129.
[68] See above, pp. 180-184.
[69] *Complete Poems of Robert Frost 1949* (New York, 1949), p. vi.
[70] Robert Frost, introduction to Edwin Arlington Robinson, *King Jasper* (New York, 1935), p. xv; see above, p. 183.
[71] Frost, *Complete Poems*, p. vi.
[72] *Ibid.*, p. vii.

Precisely. But Yeats took extraordinary pains to see to it that the future would be paved in the direction he wished to take. Frost has by and large trusted his luck. Poets and scholars, he writes,

differ most importantly in the way their knowledge is come by. Scholars get theirs with conscientious thoroughness along projected lines of logic; poets theirs cavalierly and as it happens in and out of books. They stick to nothing deliberately, but let what will stick to them like burrs where they walk in the fields.[73]

Poetry, that is, is a chancy thing, a matter of the right man and the right burr crossing orbits at the right moment. And, of course, it is. But even the most casual collector of burrs may find it valuable to systematize his collection.

Yeats achieved such a systematization in the crazy symbolic machinery of *A Vision*. In 1928, three years after the first edition of *A Vision*, Yeats published *The Tower*—first *A Vision*, then such poems as "Sailing to Byzantium," "The Tower," "Nineteen Hundred and Nineteen," "Two Songs from a Play," "Leda and the Swan," and "Among School Children." In 1928 Yeats was sixty-three. But in 1939, at sixty-four, Frost published the essay "The Figure a Poem Makes" as preface to his second *Collected Poems*. In that essay, Frost maintained that the poet is essentially an accidental collector of impressions and of knowledge; that the making of a poem is largely a matter of trusting to luck; that a poem's logic is "backward, in retrospect, after the act";[74] and that the reality a poet touches is chaos, "the vast chaos of all I have lived through."[75] From his contacts with that reality the poet may produce, if he is lucky, "a clarification of life—not necessarily a great clarification, such as sects and cults are founded on, but . . . a momentary stay against confusion."[76] And the implication is, I think, that whatever order a poem may express is a fortuitous thing—verbal rather than substantial, something to be enjoyed and admired for its originality, to derive com-

[73] *Ibid.*, pp. vii-viii.   [74] *Ibid.*, p. vii.
[75] *Ibid.*, p. vii.   [76] *Ibid.*, p. vi.

fort from, but not really to be trusted, not really real. The work is play, but not really for mortal stakes. Yeats committed himself to his laborious play, developed a coherent if absurd theory of reality, and wrote great poems. Frost has not made that mortal commitment; we can never really accept or reject his vision of reality, because it is never quite clear, never quite coherent, never quite there. Once more, the meaning of Jonah's death, of Job's revelation, slips away from us.

Yet these cryptic events are the central events of the poems in which they occur; they exemplify that "clarification of life" that Frost tells us poetry should provide. And we are compelled to conclude that in Frost's terms life cannot really be clarified, cannot be subjected to the order-engendering discipline Yeats achieved; we are compelled to conclude that our momentary stays against confusion are not really stays, that death is merely baffling, and that all ends in jocular snapshot-taking. There is a sense in which, compared with Yeats, Frost is not really serious about his poetry and the convictions it embodies, and that unseriousness is not simply a matter of habitual irony and whimsical jocularity; rather it is a matter of refusing to recognize certain kinds of difficulty[77]—the difficulty of sticking to things deliberately rather than collecting them like burrs, the difficulty of making "stylistic arrangements of experience" out of one's perceptions of order, the difficulty of holding reality and justice in a single thought. As we have seen,[78] "Directive" deals with psychic entrapment; but we have also seen that the entrapment in "Directive," compared with that in "Lycidas," is not really difficult to avoid. Common sense confronts sentimentality and wins, and though we applaud the outcome, we recognize that Milton's sense of the difficult and of man's capacity for dealing with the difficult is more compelling than Frost's. Both Milton and Yeats were tempted to conceive of life and reality as chaos, and the fact that neither surrendered to chaos is not unrelated to the se-

[77] Cf. below, p. 221.
[78] See above, pp. 144–147.

riousness with which, confronting emotional and intellectual difficulty, they clarified life and demonstrated man's capacity for arranging his experience.

Frost, of course, does not really conceive of life as chaos either; in however rudimentary a sense, any poem is an assertion of order and meaning. Yet the later Frost is more aware of human limitations than of human potentiality; he is more aware of how little man can do than of how much he can do in his confrontation of difficulty. And the result is a degree of narrowness, of incompleteness, even of falsification, in that vision of man and the world that Frost offers us in his more recent books. Keeper's failure, once more,[79] that failure of

> the courage in the heart
> To overcome the fear within the soul
> And go ahead to any accomplishment,

is also Frost's; and that failure helps to explain, perhaps Frost's irritated awareness of Yeats in the masques, and almost certainly the degree to which Frost's later work exploits, in Louise Bogan's phrase, "a series of refusals rather than . . . a set of affirmations."[80] It has interfered with the clarity of his convictions; we are not sure what precisely is the nature of the wholeness achieved in "Directive," of the insight Jonah manages in *A Masque of Mercy*. It has compromised those convictions' seriousness; Frost's Mrs. Someone, of "An Importer," his Harrison, of "A Case for Jefferson," or the theorizers of "Etherealizing" are straw men compared with Yeats's Black and Tans in "Nineteen Hundred and Nineteen," or the sisters in "In Memory of Eva Gore-Booth and Con Markievicz." It has limited Frost's originality, the originality he prized in "The Figure a Poem Makes"; even at a purely literal level, it is more original to make good poetry out of absurd doctrine than out

[79] See above, pp. 187-188.
[80] Bogan, p. 50.

of isolated insights, to achieve a stylistic arrangement of experience than to let what will stick to one like burrs to trousers.

As Frost suffers by comparison with Yeats, so does he suffer by comparison with Eliot, and for broadly similar reasons. Like Yeats's cycles of sun and moon, Eliot's Anglo-Catholicism provides him with a hierarchy of values, a theory of reality, and a set of meaningful symbols—in brief, with a myth—that enables him to make large-scale, coherent, consistent propositions about man and the world he lives in. We need not agree with those propositions; we may be convinced that Celia Coplestone is dreadfully wrong in taking the road to martyrdom, or that Edward and Lavinia Chamberlayne are simply victims of hocus-pocus. But we are convinced that beneath or behind Eliot's writing there is a deliberate, sustained, and difficult effort, intellectual or emotional or whatever, to comprehend "the vast chaos of all [we] have lived through,"[81] rendering that chaos deeply relevant to man's condition. "Theme alone," writes Frost, "can steady us down."[82] But Frost rarely convinces us that for him the need for theme operates in a context larger than that of the single poem, that there is any real necessity for themes of wider extension than those provided by luck, by bent, by the bardic instinct. Again, we may detect a sense in which Frost is not really serious about his convictions, a sense in which he is finally unwilling really to follow his thought to a sustaining conclusion. He leaves himself outs—the drumlin woodchuck's "strategic retreat"— and the result is that the tragic potential of *North of Boston* is never realized or even repeated in the later books. Eliot accepts the purposive universe of traditional Christianity, and in that acceptance finds his themes—salvation and damnation, purgatorial and infernal suffering, making perfect the will, accepting the past and thereby altering its meaning. His conclusions are sometimes not unlike Frost's. Like the woman in "The Discovery of the Madeiras," Prufrock cannot really

[81] Frost, *Complete Poems,* p. vii.
[82] *Ibid.,* p. vi.

bring himself to act, to commit himself to his own insight, and
both are lost.   Like the speaker of "Directive," the speaker of
"Burnt Norton" knows that the past, though real, is past, that
one may not merely surrender to the past save at the cost of
aimless self-indulgence.   Like Jonah or the speaker of "The
Road Not Taken," Julia Shuttlethwaite knows that

> Everyone makes a choice, of one kind or another,
> And then must take the consequences.[83]

Harcourt-Reilly's lesson to Edward Chamberlayne—

> Let me free your mind from one impediment:
> You must try to detach yourself from what you
>   still feel
> As your responsibility—[84]

is the lesson mastered by the speaker of "The Thatch,"[85] that
surrender to sentimental feelings of guilt and pity is self-
destruction.   While Keeper learns of his own failure of the
courage to "go ahead to any accomplishment," Peter Quilpe
is told by Lavinia that

> You've only just begun.
> I mean, this only brings you to the point
> At which you *must* begin.[86]

And as we have seen, Eliot's Harcourt-Reilly and Frost's Paul
are curiously like each other.[87]
      But such incidental similarity does not really mean much.
At least, its meaning is sharply limited by the absence in Frost
of anything comparable to Eliot's sustained theme of sin and
redemption, and to the use Eliot makes of that theme, that

---

[83] Thomas Stearns Eliot, *The Cocktail Party* (New York, 1950), p. 187.
[84] *Ibid.*, p. 185.   [85] See above, pp. 100, 106-107.
[86] Eliot, p. 178.   [87] See above, p. 177.

conviction, as a statement of the human condition and a measure of human worth. I have said that Frost gives us neither
heroes nor villains.[88] More important, at least in comparing
him with Eliot, he gives us neither good people nor evil people,
neither saints nor sinners. His people are attractive or admirable, pitiable or unpleasant or even contemptible, and to
Frost such qualities are evidently sufficient. But Celia Coplestone, like the speaker of "Ash Wednesday," has both a sense
of sin and a capacity for sainthood; possessing these characteristics, she is a much more complex image of man than are
Frost's people, perhaps excepting Jonah. Whatever her merits
as an effectively drawn dramatic character, she is in the tradition of Spenser's nameless protagonist, of Milton's Samson, and
of Browning's Caponsacchi—ethically and teleologically meaningful figures, who choose, not the necessary or the expedient
or the admirable, but the best. Again, as with Yeats, one
need not accept Eliot's values or his doctrine in order to recognize that they enable him to deal with man in a larger, tra-
ditionally richer, more broadly meaningful context than Frost
permits himself. There is no "best" in Frost, only the more or
less rewarding. The word appears, to be sure; in Paul's last
speech, it appears very emphatically:

> Our sacrifice, the best we have to offer,
> And not our worst nor second best, our best,
> Our very best, our lives laid down like Jonah's,
> Our lives laid down in war and peace. . . .

But its meaning floats away from one, refusing to attach itself
to anything more graspable than a willingness to die in pursuit of—something, a shining gate we almost think we see,
but that may not really be there. Eliot's world, his sense of
the valuable and the real, may offend one. It may strike one
as hieratic, or prim, or unhealthy, or simply repellent; but at
least, like Yeats's, it is *there*, a determining and informing

[88] See above, p. 186.

feature of his thought, contributing to his major poems a degree of solidity and commitment that Frost never really achieves.

There is little to be gained, I think, from pursuing such comparisons further, and it is quite true that the comparisons have been, in a way, both irrelevant to poetry and unfair to Frost. On the one hand, poetry is not necessarily required to provide us with a fully developed sense of man's potentialities and of the world he inhabits. We do not demand a consistent philosophy of Shakespeare, nor do we ask that

> Western wind, when will thou blow?
> The small rain down can rain!—
> Christ, if my love were in my arms
> And I in my bed again!

convince us of its moral and intellectual adequacy as a guide to life. The same thing is true of Frost's "Home Burial" or "The Fear," of "Moon Compasses" or "Devotion" or "The Pasture." Yet Shakespeare at least assures us that man is capable of tragic stature. And *A Masque of Mercy* is not precisely either a play or a pure lyric; like Pope's "An Essay on Man," though less didactic, it is a suasive poem, as are many of Frost's later poems, especially. Frost's role[89] involves the advocacy of certain convictions about man and the world. There is a vatic element in his poetry, as there is in Eliot's; that element is a proper object of critical concern, and, as I have indicated in the preface, my concern is not primarily with aesthetics but with convictions.

On the other hand, the comparisons have been narrowly *ad hoc;* the critical questions they involve, though broad and important, are not the only important critical questions, even within the limits of my approach. One may legitimately wish that Eliot had more of the early Frost's sympathetic respect for humanity. Eliot writes of hollow men, men with no sus-

[89] See above, pp. 140-142.

taining religious belief, and though he knows they are hollow, he does not always know that they may really be men, capable of dignity and stature and joy; Frost does, as he has demonstrated in "The Self-Seeker," "The Lovely Shall Be Choosers," "The Pauper Witch of Grafton," "West-Running Brook," and "Two Look at Two." As Stephen Spender has written:

> Eliot seems to think, quite rightly, that what makes people living is their beliefs. But to him it seems impossible to accept any belief that is not a religious belief; one either rejects all belief . . . or else one accepts a religious belief in salvation and damnation.[90]

Even in *A Masque of Mercy,* Frost's sense of human worth is less rigorously exclusive than Eliot's. And if Frost's attitude toward New England is anachronistic and hence of limited value, Yeats's attitude toward the Ireland of "Hard-riding country gentlemen"[91] does not escape the same limitation.

And yet I think such comparisons are legitimate, as long as one recognizes that they do not tell all about anything. One of the tests any significant poet must submit to is that of comparison with his contemporaries. And that comparison may legitimately be concerned with more than craftsmanship and verse technique. Yeats, Eliot, Auden, Stevens—men whose bare talent for writing verse, if there is such a thing, may well be no greater than Frost's—have done more than Frost has done; and that "more" has been persistently involved with those difficult questions of the ultimately real and valuable that Frost has persistently ducked. Twenty-five years ago, Frederic I. Carpenter wrote:

> . . . the fault of Mr. Frost lies merely in this—that he is a poet, only. His criticism of life is merely poetic. He has not the cosmic imagination which creates its own world. . . .[92]

"Cosmic" and "creates" may be the wrong words for Eliot

[90] Stephen Spender, *The Destructive Element* (London, 1935), pp. 146-147.
[91] Yeats, p. 343.
[92] Carpenter, pp. 159-160.

and Auden, but the point is a sound one. Frost's world is fragmentary and meaningless—fragmentary *because* meaningless, except as an alien entanglement that our wills must confront. It is, once more, "the vast chaos of all I have lived through,"[93] within which a poem may exist but only as "a momentary stay against confusion."[94]   One thinks of Oscar Wilde's impressions, of the Imagists' reverential fragments, and if the conjunction of Frost and Wilde is startling, that is partly because Frost has been less consistent than Wilde in abiding by his professed principles; the shining gate may be there, after all; the sphere of art and the sphere of morality, or of metaphysics, may not be absolutely distinct and separate. But Frost will not commit himself.   And without such commitment, Frost offers us no tragic acceptance—only the drumlin woodchuck's canny adjustment.

It would be absurd to blame Frost for not being something that he is not, a man with a wholly coherent message.   (The two masques look as though they have such a message, but, as we have seen, the message is more equivocal than it looks.) Yet Frost's apparent inability to find or invent a myth that would permit the development of sustained and sustaining themes, themes with a tragic potential, has had, I think, two unfortunate consequences for his art.   On the one hand, there is the thinning out of his later writings, after *North of Boston*—the scattering of effects, the accelerating tendency to editorialize, to play the Yankee character, to destroy straw men, to be querulous or cranky or arch—the gestures of one who is not sure where he stands and who finds it increasingly difficult to make adequate compensation for that fundamental uncertainty.   On the other hand, and complementary to that uncertainty, there is the tendency to value Frost as the author of certain good poems rather than as one who offers a body of work, an embodied vision of man.   That latter point is surely a requisite, though it is not the only requisite, for a poet

[93] Frost, *Complete Poems,* p. vii.
[94] *Ibid.,* p. vi.

to whom one can confidently attribute the highest status as a
recorder of enduring human values. Frost never gives one
the clear sense of having mastered, even wrongly, any large-
scale aggregation of human phenomena; his clarifications of
life are seldom more than momentary stays against confusion.
They rarely have the authority of Yeats's

> Whatever flames upon the night
> Man's own resinous heart has fed,[95]

of Eliot's

> The hint half guessed, the gift half understood, is
>   Incarnation.
> Here the impossible union
> Of spheres of existence is actual,[96]

of Auden's

> We must love one another or die,[97]

of Stevens'

> The prologues are over. It is question, now,
> Of final belief. So, say that final belief
> Must be in a fiction. It is time to choose.[98]

Set Frost's

> You ask if I see yonder shining gate
> And I reply I almost think I do

[95] Yeats, p. 211.

[96] Eliot, *Four Quartets* (New York, 1934), p. 27.

[97] Wystan Hugh Auden, "September 1, 1939," in *New Poems 1940,* ed.
Oscar Williams (New York, 1941), p. 28. The stanza containing this line
does not appear in the version of the poem printed in Auden's *Collected
Poetry.*

[98] *The Collected Poems of Wallace Stevens* (New York, 1954), p. 250.

against such statements as these, and the uncertainty of Frost's affirmations, his fundamental indecisiveness, is clear.

What, then, is Frost's importance?—for his importance is real. I think there are two answers. In the first place, Frost is important because he has demonstrated, by his performance in *North of Boston* and in a substantial scattering of poems since then, how much a poet can accomplish by a sympathetic identification with officially unimportant people, by absorption in a locale, by the ability to hear and retain and reconstruct the sound of speech, and by fidelity to a limited concept of experience. (Ezra Pound wrote of *North of Boston:* "Mr. Frost's people are distinctly real. Their speech is real; he has known them. I don't want much to meet them, but I know that they exist, and what is more, that they exist as he has portrayed them.")[99] Such characteristics alone cannot produce major poetry, although they may define a point from which major poetry starts. In this respect, Frost stands— and I think will continue to stand—as proof that poetry of less than absolute first rank need not mean incompetent poetry, or derivative poetry, or trivial poetry, or merely slick poetry. That demonstration, if obvious, cannot be made too often, and Frost has made it very well indeed.

And in the second place, Frost is important as a kind of American culture hero, as an index of certain persistent American characteristics. Discussing V. L. Parrington, Lionel Trilling has aptly characterized this aspect of Frost. Parrington's "best virtue was real and important . . . . He knew what so many literary historians do not know, that emotions and ideas are the sparks that fly when the mind meets difficulties."[100] Like Parrington, and like the perhaps mythical representative American, Frost "admires will in the degree that he suspects mind."[101] Like Parrington, Frost "still stands at the center of American thought about American culture because . . . he expresses the chronic American

[99] Pound, "Modern Georgics," p. 129.
[100] Trilling, p. 4.   [101] *Ibid.,* p. 5.

belief that there exists an opposition between reality and mind and that one must enlist oneself in the party of reality."[102]   It does not of course follow that Frost is really a kind of New England Babbitt; and even if he were, it is worth remembering that Babbitt is ultimately an object, not of hatred nor even of contempt, but of love, and that Christopher Newman is in many respects Babbitt's brother.   Frost is more articulate than any Babbitt, more self-aware, more sensitive to those whose organizations and circumstances are different from his own. Above all, he is more intelligent, more aware, in Denis Brogan's words, that "man does not live by bread alone, even pre-sliced bread, and [that] the material optimism bred by American experience has not been accompanied by an equally incontestable spiritual self-confidence."[103]   Like Brogan, Frost knows that "life in Gopher Prairie, in Zenith, in New York, even in Paris, [is] hard to live."[104]

And yet, like Trilling's Parrington, Frost has "after all but a limited sense of what constitutes a difficulty."[105]   Distrusting intelligence, emphasizing will, he offers us a world in which those difficulties that cannot be resolved by an exercise of the will simply cannot be resolved, and had better be left alone.   And in this respect, Frost's limitation is a limitation of the American literary tradition; in this respect, criticism of Frost is criticism of that tradition.   Richard Chase writes:

. . . one of the peculiarities of American literature is that on the whole it has been aware of only one philosophical question— namely, necessity vs. free will.   This is a considerable limitation, to be accounted for by the Calvinist heritage and our American social disposition—which has so sharply set the individual off against society, and by failing to provide those mediating ideas and agencies natural to an aristocratic order, has produced a habit of mind favorable to the philosophical preoccupation of which I speak.[106]

[102] *Ibid.,* p. 10.
[103] Denis W. Brogan, *The American Character* (New York, 1944), p. 65.
[104] *Ibid.,* p. 73.   [105] Trilling, p. 4.
[106] Richard Chase, *Walt Whitman Reconsidered* (New York, 1955), pp. 103-104.

The one difficulty that Frost really recognizes is that of main-taining the will in a world of largely alien necessity. Salvation, happiness, as Jonah learns, is a matter of devoting all one's energies, all one's will, to the pursuit of

> An irresistible impossibility.
> A lofty beauty no one can live up to
> Yet no one turn from trying to live up to.

Jonah's conversion, in 1947, brings one back to the myth of "The Trial by Existence," of 1913. In both poems, what really matters is not the exercise of intelligence; what matters is the joyfully, arduously willed acceptance of a world we never made, a world we can neither alter nor understand. It is Frost's strength that, within the narrow and comfortless limits that world provides, he has not gone merely sour, has not betrayed himself into gestures of despair. It is Frost's weakness that he has never transcended that world, has never found or developed a more variously meaningful discipline within which his own very considerable intelligence can move, enabling him to realize a coherent vision of man. "All I would keep for myself," writes Frost, "is the freedom of my material—the condition of body and mind now and then to summons aptly from the vast chaos of all I have lived through."[107] And that is not enough—aptness alone is not enough—for consistently major art. It is his too frequent satisfaction with the merely apt—ultimately it may be only his too frequent satisfaction with the merely apt—that has kept Frost from an unequivocal greatness.

And yet aptness is important. When all else has been said, one of the final tests of a poet's excellence is his sense of what is relevant to his purpose, of what does or does not apply to a given situation in a given poem. In this respect, as in others, Frost's work is uneven. And yet in his best poems, his touch is sure. In "The Death of the Hired Man," "Home

[107] Frost, *Complete Poems,* p. vii.

Burial," "A Servant to Servants," or "The Fear," there is
nothing that does not belong, nothing that needs to be added.
In such poems, the last lines are reliable touchstones. "Home
Burial" concludes with one final exchange between husband
and wife; the wife speaks first:

> '*You*—oh, you think the talk is all. I must go—
> Somewhere out of this house. How can I make you—'

> 'If—you—do!' She was opening the door wider.
> 'Where do you mean to go? First tell me that.
> I'll follow and bring you back by force. I *will!*—'

In a sense, the whole poem is there, epitomized in the door
that is neither open nor shut. The wife cannot really leave;
the husband cannot make her really stay. The talk *is* all, in
the sense that neither husband nor wife is capable of conclusive action, of liberating either himself or the other. Not
quite capable of tragic self-realization, they have only will,
with no object for it to work on but one another: " 'How can
I make you—' "; " 'I'll follow and bring you back by force' ";
and the unshut, unopen door. This, at least, is the aptness of
great poetry.

List of works cited

Anderson, Sherwood. *Winesburg, Ohio*. New York, 1946.

Auden, Wystan Hugh. *The Collected Poetry of W. H. Auden*. New York, 1945.

Baxter, Sylvester. "New England's New Poet," *American Review of Reviews*, LI (April, 1915), 432-434.

Blackmur, Richard P. *Form and Value in Modern Poetry*. New York, 1957.

————. "The Instincts of a Bard," *Nation*, CXLII (June 24, 1936), 817-819.

Blitzstein, Marc. *Pins and Needles*. [Apparently not published.]

Bodkin, Maud. *Archetypal Patterns in Poetry: Psychological Studies of Imagination*. London, 1934.

Bogan, Louise. *Achievement in American Poetry, 1900-1950*. Chicago, 1951.

Bowra, C. M. "Robert Frost," *Adelphi*, XXVII (November, 1950), 46-64.

Boynton, Percy H. "Robert Frost," *English Journal,* XI (October, 1922), 455-462.

Brogan, Denis W. *The American Character.* New York, 1944.

Brooks, Cleanth. *Modern Poetry and the Tradition.* Chapel Hill, N. C., 1939.

Bush, Douglas. *English Literature in the Earlier Seventeenth Century 1600-1660.* Oxford, 1945.

Carpenter, Frederic I. "The Collected Poems of Robert Frost," *New England Quarterly,* V (January, 1932), 159-160.

Carroll, Gladys Hasty. "New England Sees It Through," *Saturday Review of Literature,* XIII (November 9, 1935), 3-4, 14, 17.

Carus, Titus Lucretius (Lucretius). *Of the Nature of Things,* trans. William Ellery Leonard. London, 1947.

Chase, Richard. *Walt Whitman Reconsidered.* New York, 1955.

Coffin, Robert P. Tristram. *New Poetry of New England: Frost and Robinson.* Baltimore, 1938.

Conrad, Joseph. *Heart of Darkness and The Secret Sharer.* New York, 1950.

Cook, Reginald L. "Robert Frost's Asides on His Poetry," *American Literature,* XIX (January, 1948), 351-359.

Cornford, F. M., ed. *Greek Religious Thought from Homer to the Age of Alexander.* London, 1923.

Cowley, Malcolm. "The Case Against Mr. Frost: II," *New Republic,* CXI (September 18, 1944), 345-347.

———. "Frost: A Dissenting Opinion," *New Republic,* CXI (September 11, 1944), 312-313.

Cox, Sidney. "Robert Frost and Poetic Fashion," *American Scholar,* XVIII (Winter, 1948-1949), 78-86.

———. "Robert Frost at Plymouth," *New Hampshire Troubadour,* XVI (November, 1946), 18-22.

———. *Robert Frost: Original "Ordinary" Man.* New York, 1929.

Cummings, Edward Estlin. *Collected Poems.* New York, 1938.

Daiches, David. *Poetry and the Modern World: A Study of Poetry in England between 1900 and 1939.* Chicago, 1940.

Davidson, Donald. "A Mirror for Artists"; *see* Twelve Southerners.

De Voto, Bernard. "The Critics and Robert Frost," *Saturday Review of Literature,* XVII (January 1, 1938), 3-4, 14-15.

Eliot, Thomas Stearns. *The Cocktail Party.* New York, 1950.

————. *Four Quartets.* New York, 1943.

Elliott, G. R. "The Neighborliness of Robert Frost," *Nation,* CIX (December 6, 1919), 713-715.

Emerson, Ralph Waldo. *The Complete Works of Ralph Waldo Emerson,* ed. Edward Waldo Emerson. 12 vols. Cambridge, Mass., 1904.

————. *The Heart of Emerson's Journals,* ed. Bliss Perry. New York, 1926.

Empson, William. *Some Versions of Pastoral.* Norfolk, Conn., n.d.

Frank, Waldo. *Our America.* New York, 1919.

Frankfort, Henri, Mrs. Henri Frankfort, John A. Wilson, and Thorkild Jacobsen. *Before Philosophy: The Intellectual Adventure of Ancient Man.* Harmondsworth, Middlesex, England, 1949.

Freeman, John. "Robert Frost," *London Mercury,* XIII (December, 1925), 176-187.

Freeman, Mary E. Wilkins. *A Humble Romance and Other Stories.* New York, 1915.

————. *A New England Nun and Other Stories.* New York, 1920.

Freud, Sigmund. *A General Introduction to Psychoanalysis,* trans. Joan Riviere. Garden City, 1943.

Frost, Robert. *A Boy's Will.* New York, 1915.

————. *Collected Poems of Robert Frost 1939.* New York, 1941.

————. *Complete Poems of Robert Frost 1949.* New York, 1949.

————. "The Constant Symbol," *Atlantic Monthly,* CLXXVIII (October, 1946), 50-52.

————. Introduction to Edwin Arlington Robinson, *King Jasper.* New York, 1935.

————. *The Pocket Book of Robert Frost's Poems,* ed. Louis Untermeyer. New York, 1946.

————. *Steeple Bush.* New York, 1947.

————. "Stephen Burroughs," in *Cupid and Lion.* New York, n.d. [ca. 1924], pp. 11-14.

Hardy, Thomas. *Collected Poems of Thomas Hardy.* New York, 1928.

Hesiod; *see* Cornford.

Hicks, Granville. "The World of Robert Frost," *New Republic,* LXV (December 3, 1930), 77-78.

Hillyer, Robert. "A Letter to Robert Frost," *Atlantic Monthly,* CLVIII (August, 1936), 158-163.

––––––. "Robert Frost 'Lacks Power,' " *New England Quarterly,* V (April, 1932), 402-404.

Howells, William Dean. *My Literary Passions: Criticism and Fiction.* New York, 1910.

Jacobsen, Thorkild; *see* Frankfort *et al.*

Jarrell, Randall. "The Other Robert Frost," *Nation,* CLXV (November 29, 1947), 588-592.

––––––. *Poetry and the Age.* New York, 1955.

Jewett, Sarah Orne. *The Country of the Pointed Firs.* Boston, 1927.

Jones, Llewellyn. "Robert Frost," *American Review,* II (March-April, 1924), 165-171.

Jung, Carl Gustav, and Caroly Kerényi. *Essays on a Science of Mythology: The Myth of the Divine Child and the Mysteries of Eleusis.* Bollingen Series XXII. New York, 1949.

Kazin, Alfred. *On Native Grounds: An Interpretation of Modern American Prose Literature.* New York, 1942.

Keats, John. *The Selected Letters of John Keats,* ed. Lionel Trilling. Garden City, 1956.

Kitto, H. D. F. *The Greeks.* Harmondsworth, Middlesex, England, 1951.

Krutch, Joseph Wood. *Henry David Thoreau.* New York, 1948.

Lewis, R. W. B. *The American Adam: Innocence, Tragedy and Tradition in the Nineteenth Century.* Chicago, 1955.

Lowell, Amy. *Tendencies in Modern American Poetry.* New York, 1917.

Lucretius; *see* Carus, Titus Lucretius.

MacNeice, Louis. *The Poetry of W. B. Yeats.* New York, 1941.

Malinowski, Bronislaw. *Magic, Science and Religion and Other Essays.* Garden City, 1954.

Miller, Perry. *Jonathan Edwards.* New York, 1948.

Moore, Merrill. "Poetic Agrarianism: Old Style," *Sewanee Review,* XLV (October-December, 1937), 507-509.

Morse, Stearns. "The Wholeness of Robert Frost," *Virginia Quarterly Review,* XIX (Summer, 1943), 412-416.

Munson, Gorham B. "Robert Frost," *Saturday Review of Literature,* I (March 28, 1925), 625-626.

––––––. *Robert Frost: A Study in Sensibility and Good Sense.* New York, 1927.

————. "Robert Frost and the Humanistic Temper," *Bookman,* LXXI (July, 1930), 419-422.

Newdick, Robert S. "Robert Frost and the Dramatic," *New England Quarterly,* X (June, 1937), 262-269.

————. "Robert Frost Speaks Out," *Sewanee Review,* XLV (April-June, 1937), 239-241.

O'Donnell, William G. "Parable in Poetry," *Virginia Quarterly Review,* XXV (Spring, 1949), 269-282.

————. "Robert Frost and New England: A Revaluation," *Yale Review,* XXXVII (Summer, 1948), 698-712

"Oxford and Cambridge to Honor Frost," *Christian Science Monitor,* XLIX (April 25, 1957), 2.

"Pawky Poet," *Time,* LVI (October 9, 1950), 76-82

Pierson, George Wilson. "The Moving American," *Yale Review,* XLIV (September, 1954), 99-112.

————. "The Obstinate Concept of New England: A Study in Denudation," *New England Quarterly,* XXVIII (March, 1955), 3-17.

Poole, Ernest. "When Frost Was Here," *New Hampshire Troubadour,* XVI (November, 1946), 10-13.

Pound, Ezra. "A Boy's Will," *Poetry: A Magazine of Verse,* II (May, 1913), 72-74.

————. *The Letters of Ezra Pound: 1907-1941,* ed. D. D. Paige. New York, 1950.

————. "Modern Georgics," *Poetry: A Magazine of Verse,* V (December, 1914), 127-130.

Richards, Grant. *Housman 1897-1936.* New York, 1942.

Robinson, Edwin Arlington; *see* Frost, Robert.

Rourke, Constance. *American Humor: A Study of the National Character.* Garden City, 1953.

Sergeant, Elizabeth Shepley. "Robert Frost: A Good Greek Out of New England," *New Republic,* XLIV (September 30, 1925), 144-148.

Shaw, George Bernard. *Man and Superman.* New York, 1912.

Spender, Stephen. *The Destructive Element.* London, 1935.

Spenser, Edmund. *The Complete Poetical Works of Edmund Spenser,* ed. R. E. Neil Dodge. Boston, 1908.

Stevens, Wallace. *The Collected Poems of Wallace Stevens.* New York, 1954.

Stowe, Harriet Beecher. *Oldtown Folks and Sam Lawson's Oldtown Fireside Stories.* Cambridge, Mass., 1896.

Swift, Jonathan. *Gulliver's Travels.* New York, 1948.

Thompson, Lawrance. *Fire and Ice: The Art and Thought of Robert Frost.* New York, 1942.

Thoreau, Henry David. *Civil Disobedience and A Plea for Captain John Brown.* Chicago, n.d.

————. *Walden, or Life in the Woods.* Harmondsworth, Middlesex, England, 1938.

Tindall, William Yorke. *Forces in Modern British Literature 1885-1946.* New York, 1947.

Trilling, Lionel. *The Liberal Imagination: Essays on Literature and Society.* New York, 1950.

————. *Matthew Arnold.* New York, 1955.

Troy, William. "The Altar of Henry James," in *The Question of Henry James,* ed. F. W. Dupee. New York, 1945, pp. 267-272.

Twelve Southerners. *I'll Take My Stand: The South and the Agrarian Tradition.* New York, 1930.

Untermeyer, Louis, ed. *Modern American Poetry: Mid-Century Edition.* New York, 1950.

Untermeyer, Louis. *The New Era in American Poetry.* New York, 1919.

Viereck, Peter. "Parnassus Divided," *Atlantic Monthly,* CLXXXIV (October, 1949), 67-70.

Warren, Robert Penn. "Hawthorne, Anderson and Frost," *New Republic,* LIV (May 16, 1928), 399-401.

Wesleyan University Library. *Robert Frost: A Chronological Survey.* Middletown, Conn., 1936.

Whicher, George F. "Frost at Seventy," *American Scholar,* XIV (Autumn, 1945), 405-414.

————. "Out for Stars: A Meditation on Robert Frost," *Atlantic Monthly,* CLXXI (May, 1943), 64-67.

Whipple, T. K. "Robert Frost," *Literary Review* (22 March, 1924), pp. 605-606.

Whitehead, Alfred North. *Science and the Modern World.* New York, 1948.

Willey, Basil. *The Seventeenth Century Background: Studies in the Thought of the Age in Relation to Poetry and Religion.* London, 1949.

Williams, Oscar, ed. *New Poems: 1940.* New York, 1941.

Wilson, John A.; *see* Frankfort *et al.*

Winters, Yvor. "Robert Frost: or, The Spiritual Drifter as Poet,"
    Sewanee Review, LVI (Autumn, 1948), 564-596.
Wordsworth, William. *The Poetical Works of Willam Wordsworth,*
    ed. Thomas Hutchinson. London, 1906.
Yeats, William Butler. *The Collected Poems of W. B. Yeats.*
    New York, 1951.

Index

Abercrombie, Lascelles, 28
"Acquainted with the Night," 38-40, 49, 92, 202
Adams, Henry, 171
Addison, Joseph, 53
Aeschylus, 150, 176
"After Apple-Picking," 92
"Afterflakes," 58
"The Aim Was Song," 22, 43
"All Revelation," 29-30, 46, 48, 54, 64, 67, 101, 181, 199
Anderson, Sherwood, 45
Aristotle, 21, 127, 134
"The Armful," 199
Arnold, Matthew, 15, 54
    "The Buried Life," 54 n.
    "Growing Old," 54 n.
"Asking for Roses," 81
"At Woodward's Gardens," 22, 54, 86, 151, 199
Auden, Wystan Hugh, 83, 84, 94, 110, 111, 185, 217, 218, 219
    "Mundus et Infans," 83

Augustine, St., 134
"The Ax-Helve," 10, 43, 76

Baxter, Sylvester, 28
"The Bear," 46, 61, 62, 64, 86, 105, 151, 199, 204
"The Bearer of Evil Tidings," 56
Bergson, Henri, 25 n.
"Beyond Words," 201
"Birches," 54, 155 n.
"The Birthplace," 24
"The Black Cottage," 9, 79, 86, 123, 182
Blackmur, Richard P., 55, 87, 145 n., 185, 187, 196, 208
Blake, William, 58, 70
        "The Ancient of Days," 58
Blitzstein, Marc, 110 n.
        Pins and Needles, 110, 123, 134
"Blueberries," 9, 62, 93, 123
Bodkin, Maud, 72, 73, 74, 82
"Boeotian," 6, 85 n.
Bogan, Louise, 39, 60, 122, 186, 196, 202, 212
"The Bonfire," 86, 198
"A Boundless Moment," 31
Bowra, C. M., 28 n.
Boynton, Percy, 85
A Boy's Will, 28, 36 n., 37, 43, 50, 75, 77, 78, 80, 85, 86 n., 91, 115, 191, 195, 198, 202
Braithwaite, W. S. B., 191 n.
"Bravado," 96
Brogan, Denis, 221
"The Broken Drought," 50, 151
"A Brook in the City," 7, 11, 13
Brooke, Rupert, 28
Brooks, Cleanth, 54, 55
Browning, Robert, 95, 215
        "Childe Roland to the Dark Tower Came," 95
        The Ring and the Book, 127
"Brown's Descent," 10, 59
Bryant, William Cullen, 5, 27
"Build Soil," 9, 50, 87, 111 n., 114, 115, 133, 135, 138, 161, 199
Burns, Robert, 59, 192
Burroughs, Stephen, 61, 62, 120
"Bursting Rapture," 26
Bush, Douglas, 52 n.
Bushnell, Horace, 71

"Canis Major," 55
Carpenter, Frederic I., 196, 217
Carroll, Gladys Hasty, 121, 147
"A Case for Jefferson," 115, 138, 151, 212
"The Census-Taker," 23, 54, 135
Chase, Richard, 47 n., 221

Chaucer, Geoffrey, 203
Coffin, Robert P. Tristram, 85, 107, 119, 189, 193, 194
"The Code," 8, 54, 113, 114, 156
Coleridge, Samuel Taylor, 30, 73
    "The Rime of the Ancient Mariner," 73, 106
Collected Poems of Robert Frost, 180, 190, 192, 210
"Come In," 92, 94, 95, 96, 158 n.
Come In, 107, 191
Complete Poems of Robert Frost, 4 n., 28, 36 n., 113, 150, 155, 168, 180,
        191, 204, 209 n., 213 n., 218 n., 222 n.
Conrad, Joseph, 34, 93, 97, 105 n.
    Chance, 34
    Heart of Darkness, 34, 99, 105 n.
"The Constant Symbol," 134 n., 157 n.
Cook, Reginald L., 151, 152
"The Courage to Be New," 50
"The Cow in Apple Time," 46
Cowley, Malcolm, 28, 194, 196
Cox, Sidney, 84, 87, 108, 115, 150, 154 n., 180, 193, 194, 196
Crane, Hart, 185, 186
Crane, Stephen, 33
Cummings, E. E., 26, 193, 194

Daiches, David, 186, 187
Dante, 36, 53, 54, 67, 134, 174
    Paradiso, 53
Davidson, Donald, 136 n.
Davies, W. H., 5
Death of a Salesman (Arthur Miller), 62
Death of the Heart, The (Elizabeth Bowen), 71
"The Death of the Hired Man," 92, 123, 156, 156 n., 164, 222
"The Demiurge's Laugh," 28, 46, 85, 157 n.
"Departmental," 111, 160
"Desert Places," 67, 97
"Design," 38, 40, 75, 99, 99 n.
"Devotion," 22, 66, 216
De Voto, Bernard, 136, 193
Dickinson, Emily, 23, 138, 140
    "The Soul Selects Her Own Society," 138
"Directive," 4, 18-20, 22, 24, 26, 37, 40, 43, 75, 95, 101, 120, 121, 143-147,
        148, 158 n., 183, 198, 200, 201, 202, 211, 212, 214,
"The Discovery of the Madeiras," 75, 79, 100, 102-103, 106, 108, 124, 129,
        130-132, 142, 158 n., 163, 167, 198, 199, 200, 202, 213
Donne, John, 51, 52, 57, 63, 68, 70, 71, 73, 78
    "The First Anniversary," 52, 70
    "The Flea," 52
    "A Valediction: Forbidding Mourning," 57
"The Door in the Dark," 58, 199
Dostoievsky, Feodor, 33
Dowson, Ernest, 91

Drayton, Michael, 69
    "To the Virginian Voyage," 69-70
"A Dream Pang," 77, 78
Dreiser, Theodore, 33
"A Drumlin Woodchuck," 36, 50, 111, 114, 115, 124, 133, 134, 155 n., 160, 174, 199
"Dust in the Eyes," 98
"Dust of Snow," 97

Edwards, Jonathan, 32, 171
    "Sinners in the Hand of an Angry God," 32
"The Egg and the Machine," 115, 133, 199, 206 n.
Eliot, T. S., 67, 107, 108, 174, 177, 185, 186, 193, 194, 203, 213-216, 217, 219
    Ash Wednesday, 185, 215
    "Burnt Norton," 214
    The Cocktail Party, 177, 214 n.
    The Family Reunion, 108
    "The Hippopotamus," 185
    "The Love Song of J. Alfred Prufrock," 64
    Murder in the Cathedral, 108
    The Waste Land, 113, 193
Elliott, G. R., 136
Emerson, Ralph Waldo, 5, 6, 9, 21, 25, 27, 30 n., 32, 37, 40, 47 n., 52, 54, 117, 119, 158, 168, 170
Empson, William, 145 n.
"An Empty Threat," 21, 22, 23, 24, 46, 66, 95, 96, 98, 156, 202
"An Encounter," 198
Epicurus, 35
"Etherealizing," 201, 212
Euripides, 108, 193
    Alcestis, 193
    Electra, 108
    The Trojan Women, 150
"Evil Tendencies Cancel," 60
"The Exposed Nest," 11, 157 n., 198

"The Fear," 16, 18, 78, 92, 99, 124, 129, 156 n., 167, 200, 216, 223
Fearing, Kenneth, 110
"The Figure a Poem Makes," 88, 173-174, 210, 212
Fitzgerald, F. Scott, 71
Fletcher, Phineas, 51, 52
    The Purple Island, 52
"The Flood," 63
"Flower Gathering," 75, 77, 78
"For Once, Then, Something," 38, 99 n., 181-182
Frank, Waldo, 192
Freeman, John, 27, 29, 31, 192, 194
Freeman, Mary Wilkins, 117, 118
Freud, Sigmund, 47, 65, 108
Frost, Robert: as nature poet, 3-5; his distrust of theory, 6-7; on going against nature, 7-9; his multiple sense of nature, 11-13, 49-50;

nature as simplifier, 13-22; imagery from *Walden*, 19-20, 43 n.; nature as impersonal, 24-26; and Wordsworth, 27-32, 57-59; nature as "other," 32-37; and Calvinism, 32, 153; and Naturalism, 33-34; and Lucretius, 35-37; imagery from Hardy, 37 n.; his ambiguous attitude toward nature, 37-40; nature as purposive, 41-45; nature as vehicle for revelation, 45-49; his cosmology, 49-50; his limited use of metaphor, 54-55; his intellectual skepticism, 55-57; as moralist, 59-62; his use of symbols, 63-67; and southern agrarianism, 64-65, 136 n., 141; archetypal patterns in, 72-75; Eden motifs, 75-78; idyllic love poems, 78-79; poems of innocence, 79-90; innocence and plastic environment, 79-82; innocence as infantile, 82-84; anti-intellectualism, 84-87; his limited sense of freedom, 87-90; poems of melancholy, 90-93; ambivalence, 93-105; his images of stars and snow, 96-99; nightmarish poems, 99-105; ambivalence as alternative to anti-intellectualism, 105-107; his handling of unconscious motifs, 107-109; his attitude toward social values, 110-113; his distrust of collective action, 114-117; his attitude toward New England, 117-122; childless married couples as his real social unit, 123-124; marriage as source of values, 125-133; his discounting of man's social nature, 134-139; his role as New England yeoman, 139-142; his callousness, 142-143; compared with Milton, 144-148; his sense of a final cause, 149-153; his formula poems, 153-156; his emphasis on the act of choice, 156-163; his animal poems, 158-160; his poems of frustrated choice, 163-168; his dual attraction to whim and conscious choice, 168-170; his sense of choice as fulfilment, 170-171, 176-177; his pragmatism, 173-175; his intuitionism, 179-181; his "as ifs," 181-184; his philosophical indecisiveness and its effects, 184-188; his critical reputation, 189-197; his unevenness, 197-203; compared with Yeats, 203-213; compared with Eliot, 213-216; relative unfairness of such comparisons, 216-217; his fundamental uncertainty, 217-220; his importance, 220-223

A Further Range, 86, 111, 112, 190, 199, 202

"The Generations of Men," 120, 123, 155 n., 157 n.
Genesis, 68, 72, 73, 82
"Ghost House," 24, 81, 91
Gibson, W. W., 28
"The Gift Outright," 9, 64-66, 67, 121, 155 n., 199
"Going for Water," 78, 124 n., 155 n.
"Good-by and Keep Cold," 59, 63, 97
Gray, Thomas, 145, 145 n.
"The Gum-Gatherer," 50, 133, 134, 155 n., 198

"Haec Fabula Docet," 113, 135
"Hannibal," 50
"Happiness Makes Up in Height for What It Lacks in Length," 46, 124 n., 155 n.
Hardy, Thomas, 5, 6, 27, 34, 37-38 n., 97, 185, 197
    The Dynasts, 6, 27
    "In Time of 'The Breaking of Nations,' " 38 n.
    The Return of the Native, 34

Hawthorne, Nathaniel, 71, 171
Hemingway, Ernest, 47 n.
Hesiod, 69 n., 72, 82
    Works and Days, 68
Hicks, Granville, 189, 192, 194, 196
"The Hill Wife," 18, 56, 78, 119, 156 n.
Hillyer, Robert, 192, 196
Holmes, Oliver Wendell, 71
"Home Burial," 16, 24, 78, 82, 92, 99, 106, 112, 119, 122, 123, 124, 129-
        130, 134, 156 n., 166, 174, 197, 198, 216, 222-223
Homer, 192
    Odyssey, 59
Hopkins, Gerard Manley, 185
The House at Pooh Corner (A. A. Milne), 71
"The Housekeeper," 78, 117, 118, 124, 156 n., 157 n., 165, 167, 174
Housman, A. E., 23, 111, 186, 187
Howells, William Dean, 33, 34
"A Hundred Collars," 8, 86, 92, 155 n.
Huxley, Thomas Henry, 184
"Hyla Brook," 36, 50, 54

"I Will Sing You One-O," 29, 30, 46, 48, 50, 59, 96, 97, 181
I'll Take My Stand (Twelve Southerners), 64, 136 n., 141
"An Importer," 200, 201, 212
"In a Vale," 27, 28, 81, 84, 87
"In Dives' Dive," 154
"In Equal Sacrifice," 50
"In Hardwood Groves," 24, 59
"In Neglect," 78, 124 n., 155 n.
"In the Home Stretch," 124, 127-129, 155 n.
"In the Long Night," 75, 95, 133, 155 n.
"In Time of Cloudburst," 10, 24, 111
"Into My Own," 4, 80, 91, 92, 94, 95, 157 n.
"Iris by Night," 12, 29, 31, 95
"It Bids Pretty Fair," 26

Jacobsen, Thorkild, 69 n.
James, Henry, 71, 171
Jarrell, Randall, 19 n., 47, 99 n., 140, 142, 189, 191, 196, 197, 198, 200
Jeffers, Robinson, 5, 6, 23
Jepson, Edgar, 191
Jewett, Sarah Orne, 117, 118
Jones, Llewellyn, 157
Job, 175 n.
Jonson, Ben, 64
Joyce, James, 59, 67, 97, 107, 108, 193, 194
    "The Dead," 97
    Finnegans Wake, 63, 108
    Ulysses, 59, 193
Jung, C. G., 72, 74, 77 n., 82

Kazin, Alfred, 34 n.
Keats, John, 6, 7, 23, 27, 40 n., 70, 73
    "The Eve of St. Agnes," 70
    Letters, 7, 40 n.
    "Ode on a Grecian Urn," 70
    "Ode to a Nightingale," 7, 70
Kilmer, Joyce, 64
King Jasper, introduction, 6, 61, 116 n., 117 n., 138 n., 169 n., 183, 209 n.
"The Kitchen Chimney," 59, 61
Kitto, H. D. F., 134
Krutch, Joseph Wood, 32 n.

"The Last Mowing," 22, 24, 26
"A Late Walk," 81, 92
"A Leaf Treader," 21, 98
"The Lesson for Today," 43, 151
Lewis, R. W. B., 71, 171
Li'l Abner (Al Capp), 71
"The Line-Gang," 11
"A Line-Storm Song," 66, 78, 101, 124 n.
"The Lockless Door," 157 n.
"A Lone Striker," 10, 111, 114, 115, 122, 156, 158 n., 162, 199
Longfellow, Henry Wadsworth, 33, 190
"A Loose Mountain," 63
"The Lost Follower," 50, 116, 135, 138, 156, 204
Lost Horizon (James Hilton), 71
"Lost in Heaven," 96
"Love and a Question," 78, 79, 156 n., 157 n., 162
"The Lovely Shall Be Choosers," 100, 102, 108, 117, 118, 124, 129, 156 n.,
    157-158 n., 217
Lowell, Amy, 189, 192, 195, 198
Lowell, James Russell, 190
Lowes, John Livingston, 73
Lucretius, 5, 35, 37, 41, 44
    De Rerum Natura, 5, 35
"Lucretius Versus the Lake Poets," 35, 173

MacLeish, Archibald, 111
MacNeice, Louis, 67 n., 209 n.
Malinowski, Bronislaw, 69 n., 72 n.
Mann, Thomas, 97
Markievicz, Constance, 204
Marlowe, Christopher, 197
Marvell, Andrew, 63, 70
    "To His Coy Mistress," 70
A Masque of Mercy, 25, 107, 151, 152, 158 n., 163, 169, 176-181, 188, 193,
    196, 201, 204, 205, 206, 207 n., 212, 216, 217
A Masque of Reason, 43, 107, 116, 129, 148, 151, 171-176, 177, 180, 200,
    205, 206
"The Master Speed," 25 n.
Mather, Cotton, 117

Melville, Herman, 47 n., 71, 171
    Moby-Dick, 59, 99 n.
"Mending Wall," 8, 54, 92
Miller, Perry, 32, 171
Milton, John, 69, 71, 73, 78, 93, 144-148, 203, 211, 215
    "Lycidas," 144, 145, 146, 148, 211
    Paradise Lost, 69, 76, 79
    Samson Agonïstes, 148
"Misgiving," 133
Mistral, Frederic, 192
"Moon Compasses," 58, 216
Moore, Merrill, 122, 196
Morse, Stearns, 34
"The Most of It," 31, 45, 84, 92, 199, 202
Mountain Interval, 28, 78, 86, 119, 198, 202
"Mowing," 36, 50, 54, 75, 77, 81, 88, 155 n., 156
Munson, Gorham B., 33 n., 118, 119, 140 n., 141, 169, 189 n., 190, 191 n.,
        195, 196
"My Butterfly," 46, 91
"My November Guest," 27, 28, 91

"A Nature Note," 5
"The Need of Being Versed in Country Things," 18, 20, 26, 54
"Neither Out Far Nor In Deep," 46-48, 49, 86, 202
"Never Again Would Birds' Song Be the Same," 31, 76
"New Hampshire," 14-16, 33, 35, 76, 80, 138, 141
New Hampshire, 50, 75, 78, 92, 119, 162, 190, 199, 202
Newdick, Robert S., 42, 192, 194
Norris, Frank, 33, 130
North of Boston, 28, 34, 50, 78, 86, 92, 119, 122, 123, 142, 190, 191, 198,
        199, 200, 201, 202, 213, 218, 220
"Nothing Gold Can Stay," 76
"Not to Keep," 156 n.
"November," 144 n.

Odets, Clifford, 110
O'Donnell, William G., 36 n., 91, 119, 121, 152, 196
"An Old Man's Winter Night," 117, 133, 164
"On a Bird Singing in Its Sleep," 174
"On a Tree Fallen Across the Road," 12, 26, 135, 149, 150, 185
"On Looking Up by Chance at the Constellations," 62, 96
"On Making Certain Anything Has Happened," 96
"On Taking from the Top to Broaden the Base," 59
"Once by the Pacific," 26
"One Step Backward Taken," 50, 142-143, 144, 158 n., 198, 199
"The Onset," 98, 99 n.
"Our Hold on the Planet," 24, 26
"Our Singing Strength," 98, 159
" 'Out, Out—,' " 22, 24, 99, 133, 156, 156 n.
"The Oven Bird," 36, 59

"Pan With Us," 27-28
Parrington, V. L., 220, 221
"The Pasture," 5, 75, 79, 80, 89, 216
"A Patch of Old Snow," 22
"Paul's Wife," 76, 78, 124 n.
"The Pauper Witch of Grafton," 46, 98, 100, 101-102, 119, 156 n., 164, 198, 217
"Pea Brush," 24
"The Peaceful Shepherd," 75, 79
Physiologus, 51, 53, 67
Pierson, George W., 120, 121
The Pilgrim's Progress (John Bunyan), 179
"Place for a Third," 118
"The Planners," 26
Plato, 41, 67, 71, 134, 181
The Plumed Serpent (D. H. Lawrence), 71
The Pocket Book of Robert Frost's Poems, 107, 191
Poole, Ernest, 139
Pope, Alexander, 216
Pound, Ezra, 67, 116, 189, 190, 191, 195, 220
    "Homage to Sextus Propertius," 116
"A Prayer in Spring," 21, 75, 77, 162, 181
"Provide, Provide," 158 n.
"Putting in the Seed," 22, 24, 155 n.

"The Rabbit Hunter," 22
"Range-Finding," 8, 156 n.
"Reluctance," 10, 21, 37, 40, 41, 43, 46, 75, 77, 82, 127, 156 n., 162, 163
"Revelation," 54, 78
Rice, Elmer, 110
"Riders," 50
"The Road Not Taken," 17, 18, 21, 56, 86, 154, 157 n., 160, 161, 167, 198, 214
"A Roadside Stand," 111, 114, 115, 122, 199, 204
Robinson Crusoe (Daniel Defoe), 33, 70, 88
Robinson, Edwin Arlington, 6, 61, 183, 204
    "Miniver Cheevy," 59
"The Rose Family," 199
Rourke, Constance, 127 n.

"Sand Dunes," 135
"The Secret Sits," 46, 49
"The Self-Seeker," 92, 99, 117, 133, 154, 156, 156 n., 163, 164, 199, 200, 217
Sergeant, Elizabeth Shepley, 40, 150, 170
"A Servant to Servants," 17, 21, 23, 25, 43, 78, 86, 92, 99, 112, 117, 119, 123, 124, 129, 154, 156, 156 n., 164, 197, 202, 223
Shakespeare, William, 127, 193, 216
    As You Like It, 11
    Hamlet, 62
    King Lear, 193, 196

Shaw, George Bernard, 25, 27
    Back to Methuselah, 71
    Man and Superman, 25, 127
Shelley, Percy Bysshe, 27
"The Silken Tent," 54
"Sitting by a Bush in Broad Sunlight," 25, 54
Sitwell, Edith, 111
"Snow," 21, 93, 129, 156, 157 n., 163, 202
Socrates, 134
"The Soldier," 50
"Something for Hope," 24, 26, 50, 60, 61
Sophocles, 21
"The Sound of the Trees," 56, 167, 198
Spender, Stephen, 217
Spenser, Edmund, 6, 7, 36, 51, 52, 53, 54, 57, 67, 203, 215
    The Faerie Queene, 6, 57
"The Spoils of the Dead," 28
"A Star in a Stone-Boat," 8-9, 11, 13, 54, 55, 182
"Stars," 22, 92, 96, 202
"The Star-Splitter," 62-63, 93, 96, 107, 141, 144, 157 n., 161
Steeple Bush, 37, 43, 75, 113, 142, 143, 200, 201, 202, 204
"Stephen Burroughs," 61 n., 120 n.
Stevens, Wallace, 54, 185, 217, 219
"Stopping by Woods on a Snowy Evening," 22, 44, 92, 94, 95, 96, 97, 156 n.,
    157, 163
"Storm Fear," 17, 18, 21, 78, 98, 157 n.
Stowe, Harriet Beecher, 117
"The Strong Are Saying Nothing," 37, 39, 40
"The Subverted Flower," 78, 100, 102, 103-106, 118, 139, 142, 198, 199,
    200, 202
Swift, Jonathan, 25, 27, 63
    Gulliver's Travels, 25 n.
    "A Modest Proposal," 63
Symons, Arthur, 91
Synge, John Millington, 192

"The Telephone," 87
Tennyson, Alfred Lord, 24
"The Thatch," 100-101, 103, 106-107, 157 n., 214
Theocritus, 192
"There Are Roughly Zones," 8, 46 n., 54, 62 n., 98, 162
Thomas, Dylan, 140
Thomas, Edward, 28, 95, 206
Thompson, Lawrance, 25 n., 33, 37 n., 56, 60, 70
Thoreau, Henry David, 5, 6, 16, 18, 19, 20, 27, 32, 33, 34, 43 n., 70, 99,
    117, 134, 135, 137, 138
    "Civil Disobedience," 137
    Walden, 19, 20, 33, 43 n., 70, 88, 145
"The Times Table," 24
Tindall, William York, 111 n.
"To a Moth Seen in Winter," 8, 12, 46, 50, 159, 163
"To a Thinker," 6, 87, 89, 105, 151, 160, 174, 204

"To E. T.," 50
"To Earthward," 29, 30, 46
"To the Right Person," 114
"Too Anxious for Rivers," 35, 45, 154, 181
Torrence, Ridgely, 206
Traherne, Thomas, 70
"The Trial by Existence," 28, 41-43, 44, 82, 85, 157, 157 n., 181, 207 n.,
      222
Trilling, Lionel, 203, 220, 221
"Triple Bronze," 90, 114, 131, 135, 198
Troy, William, 71
"The Tuft of Flowers," 54, 113, 135, 136, 155 n., 156
"Two Look at Two," 12, 29, 31, 41, 45, 46, 50, 55, 124, 181, 217
"Two Tramps in Mud Time," 44, 54, 63, 88, 135, 153-155, 156, 156 n., 157,
      161, 162, 164, 167, 170, 199

"Unharvested," 76
Untermeyer, Louis, 33 n., 107, 192, 197, 201

"The Vanishing Red," 99, 100, 114, 133
"The Vantage Point," 36, 81
Vaughan, Henry, 70
Viereck, Peter, 150
"The Vindictives," 54, 115, 158 n.

"Waiting," 78, 91
Warren, Robert Penn, 36 n., 196
"West-Running Brook," 16, 25 n., 44, 124, 125-127, 128, 129, 130, 151,
      155 n., 158 n., 166, 169, 184, 186, 199, 200, 217
West-Running Brook, 75, 86, 92, 199, 202
Whicher, George, 96 n., 137, 143 n., 147, 189
Whipple, T. K., 96 n., 113, 196
"The White-Tailed Hornet," 86, 105, 158-159, 199
Whitehead, Alfred North, 52, 53 n., 59, 208
Whitman, Walt, 23, 47 n., 71, 140, 186, 192
Whittier, John Greenleaf, 27
"Why Wait for Science?" 26
Wilde, Oscar, 71, 77, 91, 140, 218
      "The Harlot's House," 71
      "Impression du Matin," 71
      The Picture of Dorian Gray, 71
Willey, Basil, 27, 28 n., 30, 40 n.
Wilson, John A., 69 n.
"Wind and Window Flower," 78, 98, 157 n.
"A Winter Eden," 75, 76, 98, 163
Winters, Yvor, 56, 86, 115, 132, 133, 167, 168, 169, 183, 184, 189, 193, 196
"A Wish to Comply," 198, 201
"The Witch of Coös," 16, 117, 120, 197
A Witness Tree, 43, 78, 85, 92, 142, 144 n., 190, 199, 202
Wordsworth, William, 5, 7, 11, 27, 28, 29, 30, 31, 36, 47 n., 52, 53, 57, 58,
      59, 62, 70, 203
      "Lines, Composed a Few Miles above Tintern Abbey," 6, 28, 30

"Ode: Intimations of Immortality from Recollections of Early Childhood," 47 n.
"Preface to the Edition of 1814," 58 n.
The Prelude, 6, 59

Yeats, William Butler, 27, 41, 42n., 67, 91, 130, 140, 142, 177, 185, 186, 203-213, 215, 217, 219
"Among School Children," 210
Cathleen ni Houlihan, 42 n.
Collected Poems, 204, 206 n.
"The Dawn," 204
"Easter 1916," 204
"Fragments," 206 n.
"In Memory of Eva Gore-Booth and Con Markievicz," 212
The Land of Heart's Desire, 42 n.
"Lapis Lazuli," 204
Last Poems, 205
"Leda and the Swan," 210
"Nineteen Hundred and Nineteen," 210, 212
"On a House Shaken by the Land Agitation," 204
"The Phases of the Moon," 207 n.
"A Prayer for My Daughter," 204
"Sailing to Byzantium," 205, 210
"The Second Coming," 208
"To a Shade," 186
"The Tower," 204, 210
The Tower, 210
"Two Songs from a Play," 206, 206 n., 210
"Under Ben Bulben," 205
A Vision, 27, 67, 207, 207 n., 208, 209, 210
"The Wanderings of Oisin," 42
"A Young Birch," 5